ART DECO

AN ILLUSTRATED GUIDE TO THE
DECORATIVE STYLE 1920–40

ART DECO

AN ILLUSTRATED GUIDE TO THE DECORATIVE STYLE 1920–40

THE WELLFLEET PRESS

WELLFLEET

A QUINTET BOOK

Published by Wellfleet Press
110 Enterprise Avenue
Secaucus, New Jersey

Copyright © 1989 Quintet Publishing Limited

ISBN 1-55521-571-8

This book was designed and produced by
Quintet Publishing Limited
6 Blundell Street
London N7 9BH

Creative Director: Peter Bridgewater
Art Director: Ian Hunt
Designer: Annie Moss
Artwork: Danny McBride
Project Editor: Mike Darton
Editor: Belinda Giles

Typeset in Great Britain by
Central Southern Typesetters, Eastbourne
Manufactured in Hong Kong by
Regent Publishing Services Limited
Printed in Hong Kong by
Leefung-Asco Printers Limited

The material in this book previously
appeared in *A Guide to Art Deco Style,*
Art Deco Source Book, and *The Encyclopedia*
of Art Deco.

CONTENTS

 The description 'art deco' means different things to different people – but in a very specific way. To purists, for instance, it implies opulent Parisian furnishings. To students of Modernism, on the other hand, it suggests minimalism in design. To romantics in general the term recalls glittering Manhattan skyscrapers. And to aficionados of industrial art it evokes memories of bakelite radios.

The school of luxuriant French design which reached its peak at the 1925 Paris World's Fair – the *Exposition Internationale des Arts Décoratifs et Industriels Modernes*, whence the term Art Deco is derived – is generally considered pure, high-style Art Déco (with an accent on the 'e'). Over the years, however, the output of other schools and countries of the so-called Machine Age has come to be covered by the catch-all term, which, incidentally, did not begin to be used until the 1960s.

Thus, the parameters of Art Deco (generally without the accent), or *Le Style 25* as others call it, have expanded to include an extensive array of modern western architecture, design, decoration, graphics, motifs, products and even fine art dating from approximately 1915 to 1940, with the 1939–40 World's Fair in New York acting as an endpoint of sorts. Some non-French Art Deco works relate directly to Parisian design – the furniture of the German Bruno Paul or the jewellery of the American firm Black, Starr & Frost, for instance. Many other designers throughout Europe and the United States paid vestigial homage to the French style, among them the creators of the spectacular American and English motion picture palaces, the Russian-born Serge Chermayeff and the Briton Clarice Cliff with her jazzy, brightly hued pottery. Still others such as the Bauhaus school or the Scandinavian glassmakers created their own distinctive styles, blazing new, seemingly antithetical trails to those forged by the majority of the French.

So, far from being a school of design characterized only by geometric forms, lavishly decorated surfaces, stylized flowers, lithe female and animal figures, vivid colours and the like, as so many think of it, Art Deco is a multifaceted style for all seasons, and for all tastes.

The seeds of Art Deco were sown well before the 1925 Paris Exposition, indeed as early as the last years of the 19th and the first years of the 20th centuries, when Art Nouveau still reigned supreme. This nature-inspired, essentially curvi-linear and asymmetrical style experienced its zenith at the 1900 *Exposition Universelle*, which also took place in Paris, but the style's decline began soon afterwards, hastened in part by the rise of industrialization.

Sparks of modernism were set off in Vienna, where the architect-designers Otto Wagner (1841–1918), Josef Hoffmann (1870–1956) and Koloman Moser (1868–1918) started a trend towards rectilinearity which was to be adopted, either consciously or not, at first by French and German and later by American designers. Some of the Austrians' furniture, glass and flatware designs, even those as early as 1902, are quite modern-looking. In the same way, the Glaswegian Charles Rennie Mackintosh (1868–1928), who was much admired by the Viennese, created furniture, interiors and buildings which reflected an understated, proto-modern sensibility with their light colours, subtle curves and stark lines. They were a world apart from the uninhibited, undulating designs of his French contemporaries. Two Mackintosh clocks, for instance, both dating from

BELOW The 17in (42cm) high René Lalique sculpture, is called *Oiseau de Feu (Firebird)*. The square base of this stunning c.1925 design could be fitted for electricity to illuminate the top. The feathery hybrid creature occupying the demilune of moulded glass was probably inspired by Stravinsky's *Firebird*, to which the Ballets Russes danced in Paris.

1917, are blatantly modern, rectilinear and architectonic. They even make use of erinoid, an early synthetic made from resin or protein plastic.

Even before Mackintosh, British designers were creating mass-produced pieces with startlingly modern looks. The silver and electroplated tableware of one of the most accomplished, Christopher Dresser (1834–1904) – his pitchers, candlesticks, tureens and tea services were designed in the 1880s – is displayed today in such esteemed and decidedly contemporary collections as that of the Museum of Modern Art in New York.

But the French designers whose works have come to exemplify Art Deco – Emile-Jacques Ruhlmann, Jean Dunand, Armand-Albert Rateau, Süe et Mare, René Lalique *et al* – were influenced less by their immediate European predecessors than by earlier periods, and even by far-off, exotic places, *if* they can be said to have been dependent on outside factors at all.

To trace the sources of Art Deco is indeed a difficult exercise. Since the style had so many often unrelated and even contradictory manifestations, its inspiration can only have been both manifold and diverse. Best known among the influences are African tribal art, Central American (Aztec and Mayan) architecture and Pharaonic Egyptian art, this last due in large part to the discovery of Tutankhamen's tomb in 1922. Influential as well were the bold designs and bright colours of the Ballets Russes, the glazes and lacquerwork of the Far East and the imagery and metalwork of classical Greece and Rome. French furniture forms of the Louis XV and Louis XVI periods also contributed and even contemporaneous fine arts such as Fauvism, Constructivism and Cubism played a part, mostly in terms of colours and shapes, especially as applied to textiles.

The exponents of the streamlined school of the Art Deco period were primarily from the United States, where industrial designers such as Raymond Loewy, Walter Dorwin Teague and Walter von Nessen helped to define modern culture with their tableware, hardware, household appliances, automobiles and aircraft. Though blatantly antithetical to the Gallic school, the work of these talented Americans shaped the future in a positive, exciting way, not at all grounded in a romantic, ornamented past.

The Art Deco period is renowned for its contributions in other disciplines as well as in architecture, furniture and industrial design. These include textiles and carpets, fashion, bookbinding, graphics (embracing posters, typography and advertising) and two entirely new fields in their time, lighting and cinema. Glass, ceramics, silver and other metalwork, jewellery, painting and sculpture were also treated in entirely decidedly Art Deco ways.

What of the Art Deco style today? The great *objets*, of course, which were produced at the height of the period's creativity are prized possessions in museums and private collections; and many of the finest buildings are being conscientiously conserved by caring enthusiasts and civic officials. Even mass-produced baubles and bric-a-brac are now sought after and saved.

Some of the world's top designers and craftsmen are now producing furniture and architecture with Art Deco-style embellishments, and many great pieces of the 1920s have been revived in excellent contemporary reproductions. The Cristal Lalique glass firm still makes several pieces created by René Lalique in the 1920s and 1930s, and Clarice Cliff's colourful 'Bizarre' ware is being manufactured again and sold in the china departments of exclusive stores.

Art Deco typefaces, graphics and colour combinations often appear in advertisements, and many stores and restaurants give prominence to Art Deco-style fittings, furniture and menu designs. Contemporary films are frequently set in the 1920s and 1930s, with stunning period interiors and costumes, and interest in the original films themselves has intensified, with video cassettes readily available and revivals often taking place in 1930s picture palaces.

Despite the implicit diversity of theme, interest in Art Deco is not waning. The subject and the artefacts attributed to it are likely to remain a source of fascination for decades to come.

ABOVE The Eastern-Columbia building in Los Angeles (Claud Beelman, architect), is sheathed in glazed aquamarine and gold terracotta tiles, with recessed copper spandrels. The stepped structure was built in the 1930s as a retail centre.

WHAT IS ART DECO?

 It is not always easy to define the main characteristics of Art Deco, because the style drew on such a host of diverse and often conflicting influences. Many of these came from the avant-garde painting styles of the early years of the century, so that elements from Cubism, Russian Constructivism and Italian Futurism – abstraction, distortion and simplification – are all evident in the Art Deco decorative arts vernacular. But this was not all: examination of the style's standard repertoire of motifs – such as stylized flower clusters, young maidens, geometry and the ubiquitous *biche* (doe) – reveals influences from the world of high fashion, from Egyptology, the Orient, African tribalism and Diaghilev's Ballets Russes. From 1925 the growing impact of the machine can be discerned in repeating or overlapping images, or later, in the 1930s, by streamlined forms derived from the principles of aerodynamics. All this resulted in a highly complex amalgam of artistic influences, defying description by one single phrase, although the term 'Art Deco', derived from the *Exposition des Arts Décoratifs et Industriels Modernes*, held in Paris in 1925, remains the most appropriate one.

One of the most important aspects of the Exposition was the impact of pavilions on the four major Paris department stores. Each of these stores had realized that quality and price could be supplemented by good design, and each had its own design studios. The recognition that a retail outlet could profit by employing designers provided a boost to the whole industry. Even specialist producers of glass, porcelain and ironwork at the luxury end of the market had to maintain exceptionally high standards in order to compete.

The style evolved in France, notably in Paris, where it manifested itself emotionally, with exuberance, colour and playfulness. Elsewhere in Europe, and later in the United States, it was given a more intellectual interpretation based on theories of functionalism and economy, and this element of design is known today as Modernism, to distinguish it from the high-style French variant, which is sometimes referred to as high Art Deco. Both, however, are aspects of a 20th-century preoccupation with contemporary sources and inspiration, unlike the pre-war styles which were largely the product of period revivalism.

RIGHT Emerson, the American firm, produced this radio in the 1930s. The bright red bakelite body is typical of American radios of the time, which were cheerier and more colourful than their British counterparts. The development of more compact electronic components allowed smaller radio bodies (which were also small enough to be moulded from plastic).

RIGHT The two condiment sets were made for Woolworth's by Streetly Manufacturing, the biggest plastic-moulding company in Britain in the 1930s. Streetly was the first British firm to produce light-coloured, lightweight plastics ideal for domestic use.

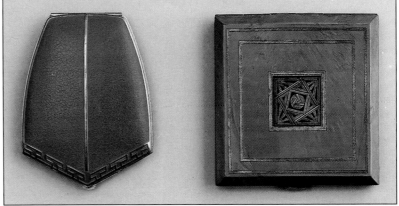

The style followed on immediately from Art Nouveau at the end of the 19th century. The latter had mostly relied on floral motifs to pattern and ornament its buildings and other artefacts, whereas Art Deco was thoroughly modern in turning away from the winding, sinuous qualities of Art Nouveau, looking instead to those of abstract design and colour for colour's sake; and when turning to nature for inspiration, it preferred to portray animals, or the beauties of the female form.

Where Art Nouveau had been heavy, complex and crowded, Art Deco was clean and pure. The lines in Art Deco did not swirl around like the centre of a whirlpool; if they curved, they were gradual and sweeping, following a fine arc; if they were straight, they were straight as a ruler. After Art Nouveau, with its intricate, heavily-worked floral patterns and intertwining vines, and Empire and Consulate furniture, the coming of Art Deco and the pure, no-nonsense simplicity of everyday objects must have filled their users with a sense of relief and clean,

uncluttered well-being. If Art Deco design was bold, bright and innocent, the reality of the age was far more sinister, far less comfortable and secure. Art Deco could be light-hearted on one level and deadly serious and practical on another. As the style in a time of unprecedented change, it was fluid enough to reflect that change.

Although World War I has generally been taken as the dividing line between the Art Nouveau and the Art Deco epochs, in fact that latter was conceived in the transitional pre-war years, and like its predecessors, it was an evolving style that neither began nor ended at any precise moment. Many items now accepted as pure Art Deco – such as furniture and *objets d'art* by Emile-Jacques Ruhlmann, Paul Iribe, Clément Rousseau and Paul Follot – were designed either before or during the oubreak of hostilities, and thus the movement cannot be rigidly defined within the decade 1920–1930. Had it not been for the four-year hiatus created by World War I, in fact, the Art Deco style would probably have run its full and natural course by 1920.

Just as the Art Deco style had replaced Art Nouveau in France, so did Art Deco in turn yield to Modernism in the mid-1920s, its demise beginning at its very moment of triumph, the International Exposition. The movement's first tenet, that form must follow function, remained unchallenged by any later schools of design, but its second, relating to decoration and craftsmanship, proved its undoing. By 1926 the loosely-knit band of French Modernists – Francis Jourdain, Pierre Chareau, Le Corbusier, Robert Mallet-Stevens and René Herbst – had become increasingly outspoken in their criticism of the Art Deco designers who catered to select clients

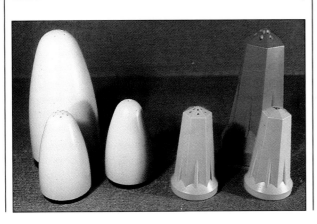

The powder compacts (**ABOVE**), are two examples of the many thousands which were mass-produced in the United States and Europe during the Art Deco period. On the left is a handsome yellow-metal and red-leather-like compact by Elgin American; the plastic square on the right is probably French.

Olivetti's MP1 typewriter (**ABOVE LEFT**) was designed by Aldo Magnelli in 1932. The firm's founder, Camillo Olivetti, who designed its first typewriter in 1913, stated that a typewriter should be 'serious and elegant'; MP1 is both, and compact as well.

by creating elaborately crafted *pièces uniques*, or limited editions. The Modernists argued that the new age required nothing less than excellent design for everyone, and that quality and mass-production were not mutually exclusive. The future of the decorative arts, they believed, did not rest with the wealthy few and should not be formed by their aesthetic preferences alone; an object's greatest beauty lay in its perfect adaptation to its usage. Each age must create a decorative style in its own image to meet its specific needs, and in the late 1920s this aim was best realized by industry's newest means of production, the machine. Existing concepts of beauty, based on the artisan and his handtools, thus needed to be redefined to meet the dictates of the new machine age.

Modernism made rapid progress in the late 1920s, although most designers took a stance somewhat short of the severe functionalism espoused by its most ardent adherents – even if logic called for the immediate elimination of all ornamentation, mankind was not psychologically prepared for such an abrupt dislocation in lifestyle. Most designers therefore opted for a middle ground, creating machine-made items that retained an element of decoration – which, ironically, had often to be hand-finished.

Outside France, functionalism had a longer history, having dominated decorative-arts ideology since the end of the Victorian era. In Munich, the

formation of the Deutscher Werkbund in 1907 carried forward the logic and geometry at the heart of the Vienna Secession and Glasgow movements some years earlier. In contrast to both the French Art Nouveau repertoire of flowers and maidens and Germany's own lingering Jugendstil, the Werkbund placed emphasis on functional designs which could be mass-produced. A reconciliation between art and industry, updated to accommodate the technological advances of the new century, was implemented, with ornament given only secondary status. These ideals were realized more fully with the formation of the Bauhaus in Germany, which in turn inspired the Modernist strain that took root in American decorative arts in the late 1920s. After World War I many Euro-pean and Scandinavian designers followed the German example by creating Bauhaus-inspired furnishings and objects. Indeed, examination of contemporary European art reviews shows that ornament was sparingly applied outside France, and although a certain amount was tolerated, the high-style embellishments of Paris between 1910 and 1925 were viewed as a Gallic eccentricity which should not be permitted outside French borders. The high style's only real success abroad was in American architecture, where it was adopted to enhance America's new buildings, particularly skyscrapers and movie palaces. The United States lacked a modern style of its own in the early 1920s, so its architects looked to Paris for inspiration and leadership in art as they always had in the past.

Art Deco was modern because it used aspects of machine design as inspiration, the wings of an aeroplane, the bow of a yacht, the porthole of the cabin window of the new ocean liners, the cogs and wheels of a sewing machine or a motorcar engine. It was even more modern because it accelerated the adoption of new materials such as plastic, bakelite and chrome.

The mixing of all these influences made Art Deco the style it is. In the hands of genius, the objects transcended their sources. In the hands of competent designers, or plagiarists, they might become drab or garish, but they were, nevertheless, truly Art Deco.

Art Deco survives today as the last truly sumptuous style, a highly fertile chapter in the history of the applied arts.

ARCHITECTURE

Art Deco was very much a case of reinterpreting old ideas in a new way. Since the middle of the 19th century, there had been great concern about the alienating effect of the Industrial Revolution. Although welcomed by many, it posed the very immediate problem of how to retain the medieval sense of pride in craftsmanship. Many forward-thinking people were genuinely worried that industrialization would culminate in a situation in which workers would be totally divorced from the creative process, and would ultimately become the tools of the machinery that had been meant to serve them. The concern was genuine. The reality became worse. In a city such as Manchester where the average life expectancy of factory workers had been reduced to 13 years by the early 1860s, there was a real need to curb the more

BELOW On America's West Coast, many sparkling-white Art Deco structures were built along palm-lined streets. The Los Angeles edifice, below, massive and temple-like, is awash with Art Deco elements: floral capitals, neo-classical urns, stepped sections, and simple lines and circles.

extreme aspects of the industrial process. It was not very surprising that Britain, the country that had industrialized first, was also the first country to attempt to re-establish an equilibrium between the individual and his workplace.

Following the teachings of Thomas Carlyle, Pugin and Ruskin, William Morris attempted to find some answers. Morris was the founder of the Arts and Crafts Movement; and his follower CR Ashbee attempted to reintroduce a sense of humanity to the workplace. In the face of accelerating industrialization it was a brave attempt to make time stand still.

The most important legacy of the Arts and Crafts Movement for Art Deco was the concept of collaboration between craftsmen. The heroic example of the Renaissance Man who could turn his hand to anything had been replaced by specialization in particular trades and crafts. At the turn of the century, there were two men who singlehandedly proved themselves exceptions to the rule. The American Frank Lloyd Wright, and Josef Hoffman, an Austrian, were geniuses, giants in the history of architecture and design. Both proved to be invaluable examples and forerunners of the Art Deco style. Frank Lloyd Wright's massive project for the Midway Gardens in Chicago, contemporary with the zenith of the Art Deco style, and his 1912 designs for the Avery Coonley Playhouse in Chicago, Illinois, are well ahead of their time. Hoffmann's Palais Stoclet in Belgium shows a similar attention to detail while still maintaining a sense of the whole.

The introduction of new materials brought new problems, and the search for a new style demanded a new approach to the large commission or project. What was needed was co-operation between all the mastercraftsmen. The example of Modernism which stressed a need to reappraise all given ideas promoted an atmosphere in which interchange between different disciplines was encouraged and promoted. Why bother to learn to weld, inlay wood, work with lacquer, bend chrome, blow glass, mould plastics, cast bakelite, when all you needed to do was seek out the relevant craftsman? Art Deco was revolutionary in that it promoted the concept of the designer. The designer could be at worst a dilettante or mediocre amateur, at best a brilliant innovator and promoter of the possibilities created by other people's expertise.

Although Art Deco is best known to us through its smaller objects, such as posters, textiles and ceramics, it is the large commissions which display the full possibilities of the style. The 1925 Paris Exposition, the magnificent French ocean liner, the *Normandie*, the glass entrance to the Strand Palace Hotel, now in the Victoria and Albert Museum, London, the preserved splendours of the ballroom in London's Park Lane Hotel, and New York's Radio City Music Hall, the stylized elegance of the Hoover factory in England, marooned on the A40 London to Oxford road or, more spectacularly, the dizzying, skyscraping summit of the Chrysler building are just some examples of Art Deco at its most ambitious and successful.

THE 1925 **I**NTERNATIONAL **E**XPOSITION

The most distinctive and cohesive examples of French Art Deco architecture were designed for an intended lifespan of six months only, at the 1925 International Exposition. The show's short duration, and the fact that the entire site would be razed by a demolition crew on its closure, invited experimentation with radical architectural forms and untried materials. Stone and brick yielded to laminates and plastics. The Exposition's charter, in fact, made radicalism a prerequisite: 'Works admitted to the Exposition must show new inspiration and real originality. They must be executed and presented by artisans, artists, manufacturers, who have created the models, and by

ABOVE Henry Hohauser (architect): Century Hotel, 140 Ocean Drive, Miami Beach. Most of the residential hotels on Miami Beach, such as this one, have recently been restored.

RIGHT Josef Hoffmann's masterpiece of 1905–11, the Palais Stoclet in Brussels, Belgium. Described as Art Nouveau or the shrine of the Vienna Secession, it is a singular example of Hoffmann's ingenuity and unique standing as the transitional figure between Art Nouveau and Art Deco. With the exception of the friezes in the dining hall by Klimt, the Palais Stoclet was a singlehanded *tour de force*.

editors, whose work belongs to modern decorative and industrial art. Reproductions, imitations, and counterfeits of ancient styles will be strictly prohibited.'

Illustrations of the Exposition show an exhilarating mix of avant-garde structures, primarily along the Esplanade des Invalides and, perched like a cramped medieval Italian town, along the Alexander III bridge.

The 1925 Paris Exposition was, despite its transitoriness, the premier showcase for Art Deco architecture. Although many of the structures bore vestiges of an earlier monumental style dating from about 1900, several pavilions were strongly Modernist, some in overall design, but most in terms of such added elements as gates by Edgar Brandt, stylized figural bas-reliefs or floral and geometric embellishments. Although they were not created to be practical, they were in themselves excellent show pieces. Robert Mallet-Stevens' *Pavillon du Tourisme*, for instance, was a handsome rectilinear building with a numberless — indeed faceless — clock topping a cruciform tower.

The pavilions of the four Parisian department stores, the Louvre, Au Bon Marché, Au Printemps and Galeries Lafayette, were all stunning Art Deco designs. Au Bon Marché's, created by Louis Boileau, was a squat, squarish, stepped building, gloriously dominated by a leaded-glass panel at the entrance, which was alive with arcs, zigzags and other geometric shapes; these were echoed on the stairway, in the ironwork and on the bas-relief cement cladding. Galeries Lafayette's was even more dramatic, with a long flight of steps leading to a doorway topped by a massive Jacques Gruber sunburst panel in leaded glass; this was framed by four columns surmounted by figures symbolizing feather, fur, lace and ribbon.

Without doubt, the most striking structure at the Exposition, and the most controversial in terms of its then-and-future significance, was Le Corbusier's *L'Esprit Nouveau* pavilion. Stripped of what he considered abhorrent decorative art — 'a dying thing', he termed it — it was instead filled with mass-produced standardized objects. The furnishings were rather boring and awkward, but the structure itself lived up to its title, *The New Spirit* — flooded with light and high ceilinged, its rooms and spaces practically designed.

Others were working along the same Modernist, functional lines, among them Robert Mallet-Stevens, Gabriel Guévrékian, Djo-Bourgeois, André Lurçat and Eileen Gray in France, as well as Walter Gropius and Mies van der Rohe in Germany and such architects as Walter Reitz and Adolf Rading elsewhere in northern Europe.

LEFT Although never intended to be permanent, the pavilions and other structures at the 1925 Paris Exposition have had a lasting impact on architects and designers. On the left is a view of the *Porte d'Honneur* entrance to the Fair, featuring Edgar Brandt's ornamental metalwork.

Paris architecture of the 1920s was generally traditional and restrained, not at all resembling the bold, innovative and indeed often startling confections at the 1925 Paris Exposition. The Champs-Elysées building, above, is conservative yet modern, with its two-toned façade, *moderne* ironwork and clean lines.

N ON-**E** XPOSITION **A** RCHITECTURE **I** N **E** UROPE

In France, curiously, the Parisian Art Deco style, which dominated the annual decorative arts salons from the end of World War I until the 1925 International Exposition, was applied only infrequently to buildings.

Examination of contemporary reviews, such as *Art et Décoration* and *Art et Industrie*, shows a random selection of boutiques – typically perfumeries, bakeries and shoe stores – adorned with the new idiom. Interpretation varied between decorators and architects. Süe et Mare applied an opulent array of bas-relief baskets of fruit and swagged flower garlands to the façades of chic small shops, such as the Parfumerie D'Orsay, the Robert Linzeler jewellery shop and the Pinet shoe store. Materials were characteristic of the firm's interiors: yellow marble ornamented with ormolu, blue stucco, wrought-iron and sculpted gilt-wood.

Elsewhere in the heart of Paris's most fashionable boulevards on the Right Bank, the decorating firms of Siegel and Martine generated a similar range of colourful Modernist shop façades, while the architects, René Prou, Djo-Bourgeois and Jean Burkhalter designed a more restrained and angular form of shop-front decoration.

Art Deco architectural ornamentation did not extend far beyond the French capital. Unlike the United States, which experienced a building boom in the 1920s, Europe was in a quiet period of retrenchment following the devastation of World War I. In addition, its rich architectural tradition leaned heavily towards renovation rather than demolition. Old buildings were restored rather than replaced. In England, the style took root, with modifications, in such period classics as the Savoy Theatre (1920), distinguished by its Egyptian-revival statues and urns; the Strand Palace Hotel (1930), literally dazzling with its angled illuminated glass panelling, and the Hoover Factory (1932) at Perivale, a curved, streamlined white sprawl, dotted with colourful Egypto-Aztec motifs. The isolated existence of such examples, generally standing out vividly amidst a sea of comparatively anonymous urban sprawl, tended to stress the style's absence, however, rather than its pervasiveness.

A RCHITECTURE **I** N **T** HE **U** NITED **S** TATES

Art Deco architecture, unlike other areas of Art Deco design, was dominated not by the French but by the Americans. Although most of the buildings created for the 1925 Paris Exposition were of course Art Deco by their very nature, they were only temporary and thus ephemeral. Later designers and architects know them only through photographs and drawings, but purists argue that they represent history's only true Art Deco architecture. The buildings that have come so gloriously to epitomize Art Deco – or, more appropriately, Modernism – are still very much in evidence today, scraping the skies of New York, Chicago and other American cities with their pointed turrets, stepped elevations, decorative finials and geometric friezes. Less lofty structures, too – cinemas, department stores, hotels, private homes – contain elements of Art Deco; examples abound in the United States, Britain, Germany, France and wherever else the design principles of Le Corbusier and the Bauhaus school, and the design elements of high-style French Art Deco, were adopted or adapted.

The most complete expression of Art Deco architecture is, of course, the skyscraper, that symbol of success, industry and capitalism which began to define the skylines of Chicago and New York at the turn of the century. The Chrysler Building, the Empire State Building, the Chanin Building, Rockefeller Center and Radio City Music Hall are supreme examples of the Art Deco style in urban America, although nearly every major town or city once boasted at least one Art Deco structure – post office, cinema, department store, or office building.

The landmark 1923 Chicago Tribune competition, in which a first prize of $50,000 was offered for a modern office building 'of great height', to symbolize the power of authority of the newspaper, drew 260 entrants from the United States and abroad. The first prize was awarded to John M. Howells and Raymond M. Hood of New York, for a building which, paradoxically, evoked the past rather than the future in its selection of Gothic ornamentation. A cathedral tower, replete with flying buttresses and a pinnacle, crowned a structure which appears today as an anachronism in downtown Chicago.

The jury's choice seems extraordinary – especially as the second prize, a soaring set-back Modernist structure by Eliel Saarinen, quickly became the prototype for the numerous Modernist skyscrapers which sprang up across America in the next ten years.

The Tribune Tower became the rallying-point for the proponents of avant-garde architectural ornamentation. The competition helped the architectural community focus on a self-evident fact: for the country's architecture to come of age, it had first to divest itself of all traces of past foreign influence. The period revivalism of the Tribune Tower and Cass Gilbert's Woolworth Building were now out of place. Suddenly, all neo-classical decorations were seen as *passé*, stylistic remnants of a bygone era. Architects began to search for a new form of decoration, one in symphony with the 20th-century building materials.

The Chrysler Building, at 42nd Street and Lexington Avenue, was designed in 1927 by William Van Alen for a real-estate developer, William H Reynolds, who later sold the lease and plans to Walter P Chrysler, the automobile magnate. The highly ornamented, 1046ft (319m) structure was completed in 1930, its soaring tower dramatically sheathed in shiny, nickel-chromed steel, in a design of overlapping arcs, punctuated by triangular

LEFT One of the highlights of London's plush Park Lane Hotel, opened in 1927, is the Art Deco ballroom. Palmette, shell and swag motifs embellish the cream-coloured room, which is dominated by an overdoor painted-plaster relief of Bellerophon and his glittering steed Pegasus.

windows. Just below this gleaming icing, at the 59th floor, an octet of stylized steel eagles play the roles of Modernist gargoyles; considerably lower, at the 31st storey, exterior brickwork forms patterns of streamlined automobiles. The interior was deemed an unbalanced hodge-podge by many critics, but its individual elements – onyx lighting fixtures, handsome bronze mail slots incorporating a majestic eagle in their design, elevators with stylized flowers veneered in several types of wood, ceiling painting by Edward Turnbull – are all well-thought-out and exquisitely realized masterpieces in themselves.

For one brief and glorious moment in the early 1930s, the Chrysler Building soared above all others. Today it remains the period's most exhilarating structure and romantic symbol. Stripped of its ornamentation, the building provides a characteristic example of late 1920s commercial architecture, one intended as a financial investment, with 77 floors of rentable space. Its massing, studied use of fenestration as an element of design, and surface treatment are similar to those of many buildings under construction at the

TOP LEFT The grandiose Reception Hall of London's Daily Express building, on Fleet Street, is decorated with sheets of shiny white and yellow metal. The 1931 entrance hall, designed by Robert Atkinson, was admired by John Betjeman for its 'wonderful rippling confections of metal'.

LEFT This elegant and luxurious bathroom was designed by Rateau for Jeanne Lanvin between 1920–22 and incorporated the use of marble, stucco, wrought iron and patinated bronze.

ABOVE: Although fast disappearing from American byways, petrol stations, like the Gulf one in Bedford, Pennsylvania, were once a delightful commonplace. The 1930s structure resembles an Egyptian temple, and the geometric and neo-classical motifs on its terracotta tiles are typical of much commercial architecture of the time.

RIGHT: The ebullient decoration on the façade of the present-day Kansas City retail store dates to c. 1929 (McKecknie & Trask, architects). The salient feature is the glazed terracotta tiling in a busy floral, geometric and neo-classical pattern. Note the three lighting fixtures and the clever rayed design in coloured clay below them.

time. With its Modernist ornamentation, however, it became a classic. The excitement lies primarily in the seven floors that comprise the elongated dome, each of tiered arched form with triangular dormer windows enveloped in shimmering nickel-chromed steel. Even today, surrounded by a host of taller midtown buildings, the dome still draws the eye unerringly.

Diagonally across from the Chrysler Building stands the 54-storey Chanin Building, which was erected in 1928 in a mere 205 days for the real-estate developer and architect Irwin Chanin. Chanin, one of two sons of an immigrant from Poltava (in the

Ukraine), had, like Chrysler in automobiles, built a substantial private fortune from scratch as an architect and land developer. Although its boxy, stepped shape (designed by the firm of Sloan and Robertson) was neither especially remarkable nor innovative, its decoration, inside and out, was, celebrating the theme 'City of Opportunity'. The lobby features bronze allegorical relief-panels and radiator grilles, designed by René Chambellan and Jacques Delamarre, all rich with stylized figures and skyscrapers and embellished with a blaze of ziggurats, spirals, lightning bolts and starbursts. Piles of coins appropriately adorn the ornamental-ironwork entranceway to the top-floor executive suite.

At this point it is important to stress that the term 'Art Deco architecture' does not relate to a specific style of 1920s architecture, but to the distinctive type of Modernist decoration applied to new structures at the time. Skyscrapers such as the Chrysler and Chanin Buildings qualify as Art Deco not because they are tall and terraced, but because of the fanciful decoration with which they were embellished to emphasize that they were new. As in traditional architecture, Modernist decoration was used as a transitional device to alert the eye to changes in the building's contour. Stepped vertical decoration was found to accentuate a skyscraper's height; horizontal decorative bands brought out the rhythmic ascent of its recesses. In addition to its exterior use in this manner, Art Deco ornamentation was concentrated principally on that part of a building seen and used most by its occupants – its entranceway – exterior grill-work, doors, lobby and bank of elevators. Often a sumptuous combination of stone, terracotta and metal transformed a bland commercial structure into one of great civic pride. On smaller buildings the same range of ornamentation was pared down for use as decorative accents.

The Empire State Building, on Fifth Avenue between 33rd and 34th streets, was completed in 1931 in a comparatively spare and modest style. Almost devoid of ornamentation, it is sheer height (1250ft, 412m), and the skilful massing of its 102 storeys that give it its rightful claim to fame. It is not, though, a classic Art Deco structure. The building's Modernist ornamentation is restrained, even cautious, both in the lobby and on the exterior.

The Rockefeller Center complex, including Radio City Music Hall, was designed by Raymond Hood, who was responsible also for the Chicago

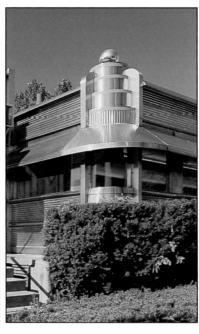

Tribune Tower, as well as for New York's American Radiator, Daily News and McGraw-Hill Buildings. The three-block-long complex provided numerous Art Deco sculptors, designers, painters and other artists and artisans with glorious empty space to fill with bas-reliefs, figures, metalwork and wall and floor coverings. Radio City Music Hall, whose decoration was overseen and in large part undertaken by Donald Deskey, constitutes one gigantic tribute to Art Deco, with a wealth of metal-dominated Modernist furniture and lighting fixtures, exotic-wood panelling, geometric ironwork, lavish painted murals, lively wallpaper and panels of carpeting. It is unabashedly opulent and exuberant.

Elsewhere in New York, skyscrapers, residential buildings and smaller office buildings bore decidedly *moderne* elements, including the Chanin Corporation's Century and Majestic apartment complexes on Central Park West (1930–31), the early New York Telephone Company building, now known as the Barclay-Vesey (1923), the Western Union Building on West Broadway (1923–30) and Ely Jacques Kahn's Film Center, 111 John Street, 120 Wall Street, Lefcourt Clothing Center and Squibb Building, all of which are marked by entranceways, lobbies, elevator doors and post boxes with geometric elements.

The most extravagant Art Deco façade in New York was that of the Stewart & Company Building on the east side of Fifth Avenue at 56th Street, now the site of the Trump Tower. The architects Warren & Wetmore conceived of a monumental entrance comprising six doors beneath a vast rectangular frieze flanked by two matching panels. The theme – to show that the building housed a series of women's speciality shops – had been common in Paris some years earlier: stylized draped nudes within lavish borders of tiered fountains, baskets of flowers and fruit, flights of birds, etc. A mixture of *repoussé* aluminium, polychromed faience and verdigris bronze brought the images sharply into relief, as revealed by the sun's rays or, at night, by a battery of lower, concealed lights.

With the marked exception of Ely Jacques Kahn, Ralph Walker, Stiles Clements and Frank Lloyd Wright, very few architects concerned themselves directly with the content of the ornament applied to their buildings. The initial selection of decorative trim was usually left to the firm's draughtsmen, for later approval. There are countless commercial buildings, factories and shops across the United States with terracotta and bronze ornamental friezes, spandrels and entranceways that are practically identical. Contemporary architectural reviews and trade journals provide the answer to their authorship. Manufacturers advertised portfolios of Modernist designs from which the architect could select any number of stock items with which to adorn his building.

The motifs were decidedly Parisian, covering the entire vocabulary of French ornament: stylized fountains, cloud patterns, sunbursts, tightly packed fields of flowers, chevrons, etc. By shuffling available patterns, one could create one's own 'unique' design. Precise detail did not matter, for it was the colour rather than the specific decorative components which provided the definition to the passer-by far below.

Towards 1930, however, architects began to comprehend that new building materials – specifically metal and glass – were more in harmony with new architecture than were traditional ones. Modern man's imagination was stirred now by the enormous tensile strength and brilliant sheen of steel, science's newest building aid. The age of metal began to phase out the terracotta and stone age in architecture, as it was doing in the decorative arts.

ABOVE Sculptor Lee Lawrie collaborated with English-born ceramicist Leon V Solon on the triptych, surmounting the entrance of 30 Rockefeller Plaza, part of the massive Rockefeller Center complex in Manhattan. In the middle is the figure *Wisdom*, who is flanked by *Sound* and *Light*. Solon's expertise was used in polychroming the reliefs. The subtly decorated wall below the figures, comprising blocks of glass bonded by Vinylite (a type of polyvinyl chloride, or PVC) and reinforced by steel rods, was made by Steuben Glass.

From the mid-1920s, Modernist architectural ornament gradually worked its way into every corner of the United States. New York's skyscrapers (and their decoration) were recreated in numerous small urban communities, to the chagrin of many, including Frank Lloyd Wright, who railed against the senselessness of large structures in sparsely populated areas. Regionalism played a surprisingly small part in the movement's growth; the same Parisian sunbursts and chevrons feature on factories in San Diego as on shops and banks in northern Michigan and Seattle.

The new Union Trust Building in Detroit stands unquestionably as America's premier Art Deco bank building, the theme and scale of its Modernist decoration justifying the soubriquet acquired when it opened in 1929, the 'Cathedral of Finance'. The Union Trust Company had originally commissioned Smith, Hinchman & Grylls, Associates, to build their new offices, but the $12 million project was turned over to Wirt Rowland, who had dressed his most recent architectural commission, the City National Bank Building (the Penobscot) in Detroit, with Modernist ornamentation. The Union Trust

Company, a new banking group anxious to project a concerned and public-spirited image, gave Rowland broad latitude to develop a decorative theme which would impart this messsage.

Within the building, the main lobby's vast vaulted ceiling repeated the beehive theme in bright Rookwood ceramic tiles. Imported Travertine marble columns, Mankato stone, Belgian black marble, and red Numidian marble walls compounded a kaleidoscopic effect further set off by the glistening Monel metal elevator doors, cashier desks, and trim, and a vast Monel ornamental grille centering a star-shaped clock.

Within six months of the building's completion, the Union Trust Company failed in the wake of the stock market crash. The Company reorganized in March 1930, under the name of the Union Guardian Trust Company. In 1949, following a second bankruptcy, the building was sold at public auction to the Guardian Building Company of the Michigan Corporation.

Kansas City has, until very recently, been America's unheralded Art Deco centre. Unlike St Louis – which is fundamentally a 19th-century city –

Kansas City underwent a building boom in the 1920s and 1930s. The result has provided a bonanza for Art Deco devotees: a wide range of well-preserved architectural elements on parking garages, apartment houses, and commercial and municipal buildings. The prize is the Kansas City Power and Light Company Building, which has retained its spectacular illuminated tower and almost all the metalware in its lobby. Kansas City's real Art Deco charm, however, lies in the scores of glazed terracotta friezes which adorn its commercial buildings. It is extraordinary, considering the attrition rate of similar factories and shops across the country, how many have survived.

On the West Coast, Los Angeles' grandest Art Deco building, both by day and under floodlights at night, was the Richfield Oil Building (known now as the Atlantic Richfield Building) at 6th and Flower Streets. Begun in 1928 by Morgan, Walls & Clements, the 13-storey structure was surmounted by a double recessed tower, itself topped by a 130-ft (40-metre) beacon tower. The building's novel aesthetic impact lay in the architect's decision to sheathe it in glazed black terracotta intersected by vertical terracotta gold ribbing.

In San Francisco, the movement found a most gifted disciple in Timothy L. Pflueger, of the architectural firm of JR Miller & TL Pflueger. Pflueger designed several important commissions in the new idiom, in particular the Medical and Dental Building at 450 Sutter Street.

The KiMo Theater (Carl and Robert Boller, architects, 1926–27), in Albuquerque, New Mexico, provides a rare example of a direct regional influence, its colourful terracotta frieze fusing Pueblo and Navajo motifs on a Spanish Mission-style building.

Elsewhere in the United States, Frank Lloyd Wright was designing houses that complemented, rather than imposed upon, their natural setting. They were fine examples of practical domestic architecture, made largely of wood and glass materials which integrated themselves better into their often wood surroundings than did the stark-white finishes of Gropius, Mallet-Stevens and Eileen Gray.

An interesting architectural sideline here is the whitewashed, pastel-highlighted architecture of Old Miami Beach, Florida, much of it featuring combinations of curved and flat walls, circular or polygonal windows offset by rectilinear frames, cantilevered sections and profuse metal railings, often 'bent' – all of which could be found on Modernist structures by

LEFT The door of the Gulf Building in Houston clearly takes its inspiration from high-style Parisian design, notably that of ironworker Edgar Brandt.

FAR LEFT William Van Alen's glittering Chrysler Building is still a jewel on Manhattan's skyline. It is crowned by a 27-ton nickel-chromed steel spire, comprising five gradating haloes studded with triangular windows. The 1930 skyscraper also boasts eagle gargoyles at the 59th-storey setback and winged radiator caps on the 31st floor.

the likes of Le Corbusier and the Bauhaus figures. But Miami's architects – about whom little is known except their names, Albert Anis, L Murray Dixon and Henry Hohauser among them – also incorporated unmistakable tropical elements, such as jalousied windows, marine motifs, and daubs, stripes and even huge blocks of colours into their structures, with some hotels and houses taking on distinctly nautical looks, portholes and all. Stylized flowers and leaves and geometric designs were found in relief on concrete over-door panels and in wrought-iron on gates, fences and doors. All in all, these delightful buildings took the pragmatism of modern architecture and coupled it with the romance and fantasy of holiday living – resulting in a unique urban district – which is thankfully well preserved for enthusiastic visitors today.

Art Deco shapes and ornamentation characterized not only buildings throughout the United States in the 1930s and 1940s, but also such vast engineering projects as the Hoover Dam, the towers of the Bay Bridge in San Francisco and the entrances to the Lincoln Tunnel, which connects New York to New Jersey.

The swansong of Art Deco architecture was spelled out, perhaps, with the 1939–40 World's Fair in New York, called 'The World of Tomorrow' and dominated by its symbol, a massive geometric spear and globe, the Trylon and Perisphere. But in any case, by the end of the 1930s, Art Deco was already on the wane, its liveliness and decoration soon to give way to a pared-down, purely functional style which had been presaged in the designs decades earlier of Le Corbusier and the Bauhaus school, and in the straight, boxy structures of the American Modernists.

C INEMA **A** RCHITECTURE

ABOVE The circle of the Liverpool Forum (now a Cannon cinema) is dominated by a peach-coloured relief panel of a hybrid landscape with two Manhattan-style skyscrapers flanking a curving river. The fluted pilasters (rectangular columns) around the pane are also architectonic.

Cinemas, too, were designed in the Art Deco style in the United States, and in Britain, where a clutch of Odeons still stand, paying tribute to the once-young art of movie-making with their geometric lighting fixtures, stylized murals and curtain designs, and other *moderne* elements. California movie theatres are, appropriately enough, the largest and most lavish examples of Art Deco cinemas, for example, Catalina Island's Avalon Theater, with its proscenium fire curtain depicting an angular Hermes symbolizing 'The Flight of the Fancy Westward'; Los Angeles's Wiltern Theater, with its lavish star-studded ceiling and wildly over-decorated interior; the Pantages Theater, also in Los Angeles, rife with myriad floral, figural and geometric elements, mostly highlighted with gold leafing, and Oakland's Paramount Theater, designed by Timothy L. Pflueger, sheathed all over with ornamental ironwork and sculpted plaster in the 'zigzag moderne' style, as some termed it. Indeed, the influences on cinema architecture were probably the most far-flung, eclectic and eccentric of all: Moorish, Egyptian, Aztec, American Indian, high-style French, mile-high New York and of course Hollywood itself.

The local cinema provided most of the American population with their only first-hand exposure to the modern style. It was not by accident that in the 1920s cinemas were termed 'movie-palaces'. Aware that most of the working class eked out a drab livelihood far beneath the American dream, owners erected glittering theatres across the nation as a palliative to life's daily grind. Here one could retreat for an hour into a fantasy world portrayed on the silver screen, propelled along the way by the most lavish and exotic surroundings conceivable.

Extravagance became the keynote to 1920s cinema and theatre design. To this end the entire building – its façade, marquee, entrance vestibule, lobby and auditorium – was transformed into a palatial fairyland. Designers switched from one national style to another with equal facility. The actual theme of the decor did not matter, only the degree to which it was romantically applied. Cinema theatres were designed as the Alhambra, Granada, Tivoli and Coliseum. Others, such as the Avalon, Palace, Paradise and Ritz, offered an equally grand, but less specific, flight into fantasy.

To the cinema or theatre manager, the arrival of the Modernist idiom, based on the prevailing French Art Deco style, simply meant that there was another choice in his decorative vernacular. That it was modern mattered considerably less than that it was lavish.

It was the advent of the sound motion picture, or 'talkie', that paved the way for Modernism, rather than any disenchantment by the public with period interiors. The attempt to recreate historic settings had led earlier to the 'atmospheric interior', in which buildings – palaces, temples, etc. – were reproduced

in plaster around the circumference of the auditorium. The entire façade of a Florentine palace, replete with balustraded balconies and niches enclosing statuary, gave the audience the impression of sitting down in the heart of Tuscany. The protruding walls of the make-believe palace tended to create acoustic problems, however, and 'atmospheric interiors' were suddenly regarded as encumbrances: trappings of the silent motion picture era which was itself facing extinction.

Streamline moderne cinema theatre design emerged gradually in the 1930s. Some of the designers who had earlier created the elaborate historical interiors, such as John Eberson and the Rambusch Decorating Company, switched readily to the new idiom. Decoration became more restrained. Emphasis was placed increasingly on curvilinear forms, as exemplified by the stepped contours of the auditorium in Radio City Music Hall and, ultimately, the bold sweep of Eberson's Colony Theater in Cleveland. Black glass, mirror and chromium-plated sheet-metal panelling provided the new mood.

CENTRE Interior view of a Paris cinema (movie theatre), the Rex. A perfectly-preserved and wildly baroque example of Art Deco. Designed as an inside-out cinema, the impression the spectator gets is of sitting out amongst the stars. During the intervals the ceiling is lighted with cloud effects. The red-lighted proscenium arch is reminiscent of Radio City Hall, New York.

RIGHT 1930s cinemas were often arresting architectural designs, appropriate to the fantasy worlds they offered behind their doors. This is a detail of the towering white mass of the Weston-super-Mare Odeon (T. Cecil Howitt, 1935).

ABOVE The façade of the Odeon in the Essex Road, London, a detail of which features Egyptian-Revival columns and stylized lotuses. The former cinema is now a bingo hall.

CENTRE RIGHT Carl Paul Jennewein: *Greek Dance*, a gilt-bronze figure of a goddess, about 1926, height 22¾in (52cm) including ebonized wood base. The work is inscribed 'C.P. JENNEWEIN' and stamped 'P.P.B.U.C° MUNCHEN MADE IN GERMANY'.

ABOVE Cormier: bronze figure of a nymph, 1925.

ABOVE Hollister: a bronze figure of Pan, about 1920.

BRONZE STATUARY

Sculpture in the Art Deco style was considerably more widespread than painting, especially in the variations on and imitations of the small decorative figures made mostly in Germany of ivory and cold-painted bronze, sometimes termed 'chryselephantine'. Ivory carving dates back to pre-biblical times, and by the 18th century the town of Erbach in Hesse had become its European centre. The greatest chryselephantine sculptor of the Art Deco period, Ferdinand Preiss, was a native of Erbach and descended from carvers on both sides of his family. In 1906, he moved to Berlin to found a workshop with Arthur Kassler, whose trademark, PK, became world famous. Preiss's figures were beautifully executed statuettes, usually female, often dressed in exotic costumes and leaping about energetically on elaborate marble or onyx bases. Their facial features were painted on to the ivory (in the manner of classical Greek polychrome) which had first been carved by hand and then polished. The cast-bronze sections were also painted or otherwise embellished, and the finished pieces, although designed to be merely decorative, and in part mass-produced, were none the less miniature masterpieces and are today much sought after.

Other sculptors worked in bronze or stone alone, such as Maurice Guiraud-Rivière, the brothers Jan and Joël Martel and François Pompon. Unlike the decorative ivory and bronze figures of Preiss *et al*, the works of these and other sculptors could usually be safely termed sculpture and not decoration, whether they were representational or abstract. The Martels and Pompon created animal sculptures which were sleek and highly stylized, even angular, constructions. Guiraud Rivière's figures – like those of Paul Manship, Boris Lovet-Lorski, William Zorach and Carl Paul Jennewein in the United States – were massive, often allegorical figures, sometimes cast as outdoor architectural elements, sometimes as small indoor sculptures. Their forms were essentially neo-classical, quite unlike those of the truly avant-garde Jean Lambert-Rucki (influenced by totemic African art); the Britons Eric Gill and John Duncan Fergusson; Josef Csaky, Alexander Archipenko, Gustave Miklos, Jacob Epstein, Jacques Lipchitz, Raymond Duchamp-Villon, and of course the Rumanian-born Constantin

BELOW Lenoir: *Abundance*, a bronze allegorical group, about 1925.

ABOVE Bernard: bronze group of two dancers, early 1920s.

Brancusi, whose sleek simplified abstract forms were inspired by African sculptures, but imbued with a strong sense of Machine Age modernism.

Gaston Lachaise's sculptures celebrated woman as a powerful, heroic Venus, not unlike Cycladic images of goddesses with unnaturally large breasts, thighs and bellies. Fellow American Elic Nadelman's sculptures could be classical bronzes – such as the gentle, monumental *Resting Stag* of c.1917 – or they could be humorous, painted-wood vignettes, like the dancing couple of *Tango* and the smiling *Woman at the Piano*, both of around the same time.

Alexandre Kéléty is another sculptor whose quality of design was impeccable. He modelled smaller-scale works, specializing less in the use of bronze and ivory than in exotic techniques for treating the bronze, such as damascening, a method much used in the Middle East (the name is derived from Damascus). This involves inlaying a precious metal into the surface of a base one in a decorative pattern – for example, flowers into the hem of a gown. Maurice Guiraud-Rivière and Marcel Bouraine also worked both with bronze and ivory, and with metal alone. The house of Etling, which edited most of the better models created by these artists, appears to have cornered the top end of the market for decorative sculpture.

John Storrs was perhaps the most eclectic American Art Deco sculptor of all: his monumental *Ceres* presents a strong, Cubist-inspired allegorical vision, whereas *New York* and *Forms in Space* (both c1924–25) are strong architectonic abstractions. Planes and volume were Storrs' main considerations, and his various creations, whether figural or abstract, clearly show this.

Many of the decorative bronzes produced in Austria were made by the Argentor and Bergman foundries in Vienna. The most important Austrian manufacturer of the period, however, was Friedrich Goldscheider, whose firm produced cast plaster and ceramic versions of the bronze and ivory dancers designed by sculptors such as Zach and Lorenzl.

Goldscheider established a branch in Paris in 1892 to 'commission, manufacture and sell bronze, plaster and terracotta sculpture'. The bronzes were made at an in-house foundry which was organized as a separate French company. When the Austrian-based parent company was forced to close after World War I, the Parisian foundry survived and, under the guidance of Arthur Goldscheider, developed into an *éditeur d'art* of considerable merit.

RIGHT Josef Csaky: *Adam and Eve*, bronze, signed and inscribed with the name of the foundry (Blanchet). The group was conceived in 1933. The present bronze is an estate cast.

ABOVE Kéléty: a bronze and ivory figure of a girl with a fan.

RIGHT Christa Winsloe Havatny: a bronze figure of a fawn, height 15in (38cm), early 1920s.

RIGHT *Kora*, a gilt and cold-painted bronze and ivory figure of an exotic dancer by Demêtre Chiparus. His speciality was the heavily-worked detailing of costume that this figure so aptly reveals.

ABOVE In 1932 Constantin Brancusi created the polished bronze, *Jeune Fille Sophistiquée.* The Rumanian-born sculptor moved to Paris in 1904, where he produced abstract forms, usually comprising one or several ovoid or cylindrical shapes. Simplicity and purity were paramount to Brancusi, who abhorred realism.

ABOVE Harders: a figure of a Japanese fan dancer from the Preiss-Kassler workshop, about 1929, height 16¾in (42cm).

ABOVE Pierre le Faguays: *Faun and Nymph*, bronze with a dark patina, inscribed 'Le Faguays' and impressed with the Goldscheider 'La Stèle' foundry seal. 1925, height 22¾in (52cm) including the green marble base. As indicated by the foundry stamps, the present model was exhibited at the Paris 1925 Exposition at the Goldscheider Pavilion. The 'La Stèle' stamp refers to this exhibition, in which objects shown by the foundry were divided into two categories: 'La Stèle' and 'L'Evolution'.

Arthur Goldscheider merited his own pavilion at the 1925 Paris Exposition. The firm's roster of contributing artists reads like a Who's Who of Art Deco design. Participants were divided into two groups. Sculpture was listed under the heading *La Stèle*, in which objects were identified with a small rectangular seal inscribed in stylized block letters. Other works of art, including glass and decorative objects, were listed as *L'Evolution*. Among the sculptors who exhibited under the *La Stèle* umbrella were Max Blondat, Bouraine, Fernand David, Pierre le Faguays, Raoul Lamourdedieu, Pierre Lenoir, Charles Malfray, Pierre Traverse and the Martel brothers. Artists such as Jean Verschneider exhibited in both groups.

One of Goldscheider's most highly stylized, and probably most successful, sculptures was Pierre le Faguays's group of a lecherous satyr in pursuit of a voluptuous nymph. The zigzag tresses of the maiden's hair, trailing at right angles from her head, and the highly stylized two-dimensional poses of the two figures, which are almost Egyptian, have become recognized as trademarks of the Art Deco style.

Art Deco's vocabulary of geometrical motifs and stylized floral patterns, repeated in all disciplines of the decorative arts, took their cue from the pervading themes of the era. Interest in the Middle East, specifically classical Greece and Egypt, had grown stronger after World War I, culminating in the discovery in 1922 of the treasures of Tutankhamen's tomb. Increasingly, Egyptian motifs and horizontal patterning crept into European styling.

MASTERPIECES IN CHRYSELEPHANTINE

Within the discipline of 1920s and 1930s sculpture, the category of chryselephantine (bronze and ivory) statuary has become synonymous with the term 'Art Deco'. Active throughout Europe, chryselephantine sculptors worked primarily in Paris and Berlin, where two very distinct styles evolved.

ABOVE
Chryselephantine sculptures of ivory and cold-painted bronze such as the *Dancer* by Rumanian-born Demêtre Chiparus, above, captured the drama and exoticism of theatre and dance, the Near and Far East, and Woman herself in a sensuous manner now synonymous with Art Deco.

LEFT C. Mirval: a silvered, gilt and cold-painted bronze figure of a stylized Mexican dancer, late 1920s, height 24½in (62.25cm), including elaborate green onyx and veined black marble base. The figure is inscribed 'C. Mirval'.

Ivory had been readily available in Europe as an inexpensive material for carving since the late 19th century, when the Belgian Congo was opened up and the colonial government pushed to develop it as an income-producing export. The 1897 Colonial section of the Brussels Exhibition in Tervueren, near Brussels, is credited with the first official public display of modern chryselephantine sculpture. The term had previously referred to the gold and ivory statues, often embellished with precious and semi-precious stones, produced by the ancient Greeks. The sculpture produced in Paris and Berlin during the 1910s, 1920s and 1930s imitated the classical models.

In Berlin, Ferdinand Preiss and his company Preiss-Kassler added Robert Kionsek of the Gladenbeck foundry in Berlin, and two ivory carvers from Erbach, Ludwig Walther and Louis Kuchler to the firm in 1900. In 1929, the company expanded further in its acquisition of Rosenthal und Maeder, a rival firm that monopolized the talents of certain designers.

Preiss himself designed most of the models produced by his firm. Early works, small in scale, were of classical figures. The firm closed during World War I, to re-open in 1919, when its style began to shift away from the classical towards the depiction of contemporary children, acrobats, dancers and athletes, for which it is now best known. As with their French counterparts, these figures often represented well-known personalities. For example, Preiss's dancer holding aloft a blown-glass beachball is Ada May, a member of CB Cochran's revue *Lighter Than Air*. Likewise, many of the athletes were modelled after Olympic stars, such as the ice skater Sonja Henie.

Among the artists who provided models for the Preiss-Kassler firm were Paul Philippe, 'Professor' Otto Poertzel, RW Lange, Harders and, surprisingly, the avant-garde artist Rudolf Belling. The styling of

ABOVE *Sunburst* by Demêtre Chiparus in cold-painted bronze and ivory. The sun symbol is often used in Art Deco design, and here sits boldly on the sheet of drapery falling from the woman's outstretched arm.

each of these artists' work was in such harmony with the existing PK style that it is often virtually indistinguishable. This applies particularly to Poertzel. *The Aristocrats* and *Butterfly Dancers* models, for example, have been known to carry both his and Preiss's signatures. Whereas there are differences between the two versions, these are so slight that it was assumed until recently that Preiss and Poertzel were one and the same man.

Demêtre Chiparus is considered the French master of bronze and ivory sculpture, choosing as his subjects the gods of contemporary society rather than the gods of Olympus. Ida Rubenstein and Vaslav Nijinsky of the Ballets Russes became the models for his *Russian Dancers*; two cabaret performers popular in Paris at the time inspired *The Dolly Sisters*, and a chorus line of cabaret girls in cat-suits were transformed into his five-figure group, *The Girls*. Many similar examples by Chiparus reflect the interest in the French capital at the time in the Orient – Bakst's

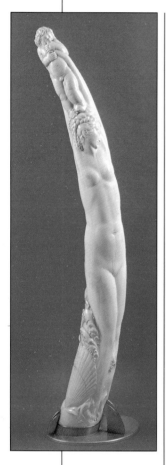

ABOVE Emile Just Bachelet: *Vénus et L'Amour*, a carved ivory tusk, height 3ft 10in (123cm).

LEFT Paul Philippe created the *Group of Dancers* in ivory and cold-painted bronze. The lithe, lively women sport short, wavy hairstyles in the *garçonne* mode, but their bodies, clad in form-revealing gowns, are anything but boyish. Philippe's sculptures are usually more elegant, attenuated and *moderne* than those of most of his contemporaries, which often tend to the theatrical, garish or sentimental.

LEFT The serene ivory face of Gerdago's harlequin dancer is nearly lost in all her sartorial splendour. Gerdago's dancing figures often were clad in elaborate, exotic costumes and head dresses, many of which were polychromed and then finished with lacquer.

LEFT One of the great chryselephantine sculptors was Rumanian-born Demêtre Chiparus, who worked in Paris. His charming *Pierrot and Pierrette* were inspired by the Ballets Russes, like many of his works.

ABOVE Demêtre Chiparus: *Semiramis*, a rare silvered gilt and cold-painted bronze and ivory figure of an Assyrian Queen. Height 26½in (67cm), including elaborate variegated onyx base signed 'Chiparus'.

costumes, Poiret's dress designs, and the night clubs and dance crazes of the new Jazz Age.

Chiparus designed on a fairly large scale. His forte lay less in the quality of his carving than in the jewel-like surface treatment applied to the bronze costumes of his figures. He was careful in his choice of ivory for limbs and faces, however, to ensure that its grain followed the natural line of their features in order to increase the realistic effect which he sought. Figures were mounted on interesting bases, the shapes of which became a vital part of the entire sculptural composition. Some of these were inset with bronze plaquettes cast with figures.

Very few – if any – of these figures were unique, although editions of the larger, more elaborate, models were probably limited. Chiparus's pieces were produced by foundries and manufacturing houses who likewise marketed ('edited') the work of his contemporaries. The Parisian firm of Etling is thought to have edited his early works, and the LN & JL foundry his later works. As with *Dancer of Kapur-thala*, models were produced in two or more sizes, or in a variety of materials, to accommodate a range of expenditures. In contrast to today's values, ivory in the 1920s was less expensive than bronze, so the more it was included in a model, the less expensive the finished piece was likely to be.

As the foremost sculptor working with bronze and ivory, Chiparus produced few works in inferior materials. The same applied to Claire Jeanne Roberte Colinet, a Belgian sculptress active in Paris, whose styling and choice of subject matter were similar to those of Chiparus, but whose costumes and drapery were rendered in a far more fluid style. Her pieces depicted exotic figures and dancers associated with countries such as Egypt, Mexico and Russia, rather than those associated directly with the theatre and cabaret popular in Paris at the time.

Whereas Chiparus concentrated mainly on the posture and intricate finishing of the bronze-work on his figures, the Berlin makers were concerned more with the quality of the ivory carving. An adaptation of Achille Collas' pantograph enabled the carved ivory detailing on these figures to be duplicated almost exactly, even down to the expression on a figure's face and the angle of its fingers. Figures were assembled like puzzles along a central core pin. As in the French technique, the surface of the bronze was chased and then cold-painted. The costumes on Preiss' figures required far less chasing, however; emphasis was provided instead by soft cold-painted metallic lacquers, often shaded to provide depth. The ivory faces of the models were also painted naturalistically, and the hair stained.

Austria, specifically Vienna, developed its own style of bronze and ivory statuettes and small decorative bronzes. These represented a marriage of the French and German styles – a combination of the more theatrical poses of the French and the softer surface treatment and scale of the Germans. Viennese artists such as Lorenzl Gerdago and Schmidtcassel provided representative examples.

Bruno Zach was another Austrian sculptor active at the time, one whose work was more overtly erotic than that of his peers.

 B RONZE **A** NIMALIERS

In the 19th century, animal sculptors such as Antoine-Louis Barye, Pierre-Jules Mêne and Isidore Bonheur, had concentrated on the realistic depiction of beasts wild and domestic. In the early 20th century, however, sculptors such as the Italian Rembrandt Bugatti and the Belgian Alberic Collin, led the movement

away from a strictly realistic interpretation of animals towards a more impressionistic portrayal, despite the fact that both artists modelled from life at zoos. It was the French, however, who developed the stylized hard-line form and pose which have come to be associated with Art Deco *animalier* sculpture. François Pompon whose walking polar bear created a stir both at the 1922 Salon d'Automne and in the foyer of the Ambassade Française pavilion of the Société des Artistes Décorateurs at the 1925 Exposition – is perhaps the best known Modernist *animalier* sculptor.

Edouard Marcel Sandoz, Simone Marye, Georges Hilbert, Sirio Tofanari, L Schulz, Paul Jouve, Maurice Prost, Louis Albert Carvin and the Spanish artist Mateo Hernandez all also exhibited *animalier* sculpture in Paris between the wars. These sculptors used a variety of materials, including bronze, ceramic, stone and marble, to produce large garden statuary and smaller, more intimate, table-top

RIGHT The ivory and bronze bust, is of the chryselephantine type popular in the Art Deco era. The woman wears an elaborately decorated cloche hat, with black and gold triangles adorning the centre of the cap, as well as the draped collar. This anonymously created bust is unusual for such sculptures, which tended to be full length.

ABOVE Bruno Zach: *The Black Leather Suit*, a bronze and ivory figure, inscribed 'Bruno Zach' and 'Made in Austria'. About 1930, height 72.5cm including the black marble base.

RIGHT Maurice Guiraud-Rivière: *The Comet*, a gilt and cold-painted bronze allegorical female figure, height 27in (70.5cm) including stepped black marble base. Inscribed 'GUIRAUD-RIVIERE' and 'ETLING PARIS'.

RIGHT Georges
Lavroff: a silvered
bronze figure of a
crouching tiger,
inscribed 'G.
Lavroff' and
stamped '8591'.
Length 24in (61cm)
including shaped
Belgian marble
base.

BELOW Georges
Hilbert: a polished
granite figure of a
bulldog, signed
'Hilbert 1926',
height 31.75cm.

BOTTOM Marye:
bronze group of a
rooster and hen,
mid-1920s.

ABOVE Paul
Howard Manship:
King Pengouin, gilt-
bronze, 26–27in
(78–75cm) high
including base. This
is one of the animals
on the Paul J. Rainey
Memorial Gateway
at the New York zoo,
commissioned in
1923.

figures. As with figural bronzes, a single model could be reproduced in different sizes or converted into utilitarian decorative objects such as bookends and dinner bells.

Many of these sculptors specialized in direct carving, employing the Assyrian technique of leaving the stone between the legs of the animal rough (uncarved), which reinforced the strength both of the beast and of the sculpture itself. Sandoz imparted a whimsy which was unequalled among his contemporaries. In his series of dancing frogs each of the creatures has an individual character.

INTERACTION BETWEEN ART FORMS

Although the term 'Art Deco' should by definition be applied only to the decorative arts, a group of sculptors active in the early twentieth century straddled the all-too-arbitrary division between the 'fine' and 'decorative' arts. For the most part they included painter-sculptors associated with the School of Paris – friends of painters and sculptors such as Chaim Soutine, Marc Chagall, Constantin Brancusi, Fernand Léger, Henri Laurens and Archipenko. Two of these 'chameleon' sculptors – Josef Csaky and Gustave Miklos – had studios in the same building as their associates. Nicknamed 'la Ruche', or 'The Beehive', the building had been designed by Gustave Eiffel

RIGHT Alexandre Kéléty's bronze group of stalking panthers is both exotic and sensuous. Kéléty was a Hungarian-born sculptor who often produced figures of female subjects. This feline group is a stunning departure from those statues.

as the *Pavillon des Vins* for the 1900 Exposition Universelle. In 1902, the grandson of the 18th-century painter François Boucher arranged for it to be moved to 2 Passage Danzig in Montparnasse, where it became a true beehive of creative energy for these impoverished modern artists.

One of the most interesting developments in French decorative arts was this interaction between supposed 'fine' and 'decorative' artists – between artists who worked in a variety of disciplines. The most important sculptors within this category were Gustave Miklos, Josef Csaky, Jean Chauvin and Jean Lambert-Rucki.

The work of these four sculptors bears no aesthetic resemblance to the decorative works of the other artists mentioned above. Miklos modelled in a severely geometrical style. His towers are an exercise in architectural form. His animal figures are far less abstract, although still formed with intersecting planes that are not in the least realistically conceived. Csaky's work is also Cubist in inspiration. Many of his pieces from the 1920s resemble three-dimensional interpretations of paintings by Léger. Chauvin is the

most abstract of this group, and the most cerebral, whereas Lambert-Rucki's work is perhaps the most varied. He worked in a variety of media, mixing wood, glass and metal. Many of his pieces are in painted plaster assembled with bits of wood and wire. In this respect it must be remembered that these artists were extremely poor, and that the cost of bronze casting was often therefore prohibitive. For this reason, many original models were cast in bronze only posthumously.

The pavilion of the Société des Artistes Décorateurs at the 1925 Exposition included screens lacquered by Jean Dunand with drawings of wonderful African-inspired beasts by Lambert-Rucki. The animal sculptor Paul Jouve provided Dunand with additional designs for panels and screens. He also worked with the noted bookbinder, FL Schmied, on the illustrations for Kipling's *Jungle Book*. Miklos in turn provided Schmied with interior graphics and decorative motifs for book projects, such as *Creation* (1925), *La Vérité Parole* (1929) and *Paradis Musulman* (1930). Miklos also created figural pins executed in gold by Raymond Templier.

BELOW Shonnard: bronze figure of a heron, 1922.

FAR LEFT Moore: 'Black Panther', bronze, 1929.

LEFT Edouard Marcel Sandoz: a bronze group of fennec foxes with a rich brown patina, inscribed 'Ed. M. Sandoz 1930' and stamped with the E. Robecchi foundry seal. Height 16in (39.5cm).

RIGHT Edgar Brandt: pair of andirons, wrought iron, early 1920s – at which time the serpent was a popular motif.

LEFT Parisian Art Deco creations were often noted for their use of rich, exotic materials. This vase is an opulent confection of silver-inlaid ivory and onyx. It is by the Japanese Mme O'Kin Simmen, who often provided ivory or other precious touches for pieces by her husband, potter Henri Simmen, Ruhlmann and others.

LEFT Vladimir Tatlin's 1919–20 *Monument to the Third International* was the Russian Constructivist's homage to the 1917 Revolution. Although the mammoth tower he first designed was never realized, smaller, symbolic versions of the skewed spiral, such as the one shown here, were. Tatlin believed in a strong connection between design and engineering.

OTHER FORMS, OTHER MATERIALS

Architecture and the skyscraper became the final catalysts for bona fide Art Deco style which developed in the United States. The modern shape of these tall buildings demanded a corresponding Modernist decorative vocabulary, which sculptors such as Paul Manship, Paul Jennewein, and Lee Lawrie were ready to provide.

For many disciplines, the Rockefeller Center project represented the apex of Art Deco design. The sculptors involved both in the interior and exterior decoration of the project's buildings and public spaces produced some of their finest works, many of which have become indelibly engraved in the lexicon of the American decorative arts of this century. Manship's gilt-bronze figure of Prometheus, which dominates the skating rink at Rockefeller Center, and Lee Lawrie's figure of Atlas at the entrance to 630 Fifth Avenue, have become two of Manhattan's best-known pieces of sculpture.

There was, however a group of avant-garde artists in America who embodied the abstract prin-

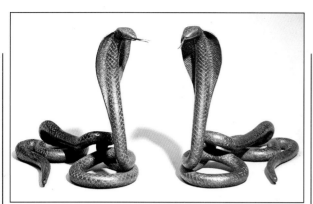

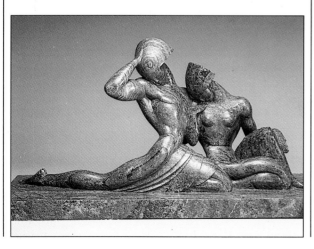

RIGHT *Le Joueur de Scie Musicale (Musical Saw Player)*, by Jan and Joël Martel, inspired by the musician Gaston Wiener. Comprising sheets of zinc, the 1927 sculpture is markedly different from the twins' colourful dancer, (**LEFT**). At the 1925 Paris Exposition, the brothers created concrete Cubist trees for the garden of their friend Robert Mallet-Stevens, who later designed Martel House for them in Paris.

LEFT The jaunty dancer is by Jan and Joël Martel, twin brothers who sculpted in a variety of materials. Best known for their animal carvings, the Martels also created Cubist abstractions and human figures — such as this 1925 piece inspired by a Swedish ballet dancer.

LEFT Boris Lovet-Lorski: *Rhythm*, Swedish marble, signed 'Boris Lovet-Lorski', and carved about 1936. Height 38cm.

ciples of Cubism and modern European art shown to the US public at the 1913 Armory Show. Some, such as the Chicagoan John Storrs, were native-born; others, such as Robert Laurent and Gaston Lachaise, were French immigrants who brought with them the inspiration of their homeland. Boris Lovet-Lorski, classically trained as a painter and architect in Imperial Russia, developed in the 1920s and 1930s a rigorous sculptural style which mixed his classical training and figurative modelling with Cubism and three-dimensionality through intersecting planes. His marble figures and groups incorporate elegance, sleek surfaces and dynamic design in a striking interpretation of both European and American Modernist sculpture.

The artistic diversity of the Art Deco period was nowhere more pronounced than in the field of ceramics. The wide range of wares made between World War I and World War II stands in marked contrast to the artistic sterility of the late 19th century and the technological conformity of the first two decades of this century. Added to a rigid geometric form, there could be a stylized floral design, a frieze of deer, or great whorls of bright colour. Sometimes those geometric patterns were to be found on irregularly shaped vessels – zigzagged vases and sugar bowls or cups with triangular (and hard to grasp) ears. Art Deco ceramics could also take the form of ebullient, sensuous or humorous figures: dancing couples in vivid costumes, earthenware female busts with corkscrew curls, smiling pigs with purple spots.

To understand the richness of the period, however, a survey of the evolution of the art in the late 19th century must first be made.

The emphasis by late Victorian reformers such as John Ruskin and William Morris on the virtue of handicraft was in part a reaction to the abysmal quality, both artistic and technological, of ceramics at the time. The production of vast quantities of cheap wares had been encouraged by the emergence of a large and prosperous bourgeosie. In reaction to this development, artistic reformers assigned a higher moral and artistic significance to handmade wares, elevating the status of the craftsman to that of artist and thereby enobling his creations. 'Art pottery' became a distinguished art form. The craftsman was seen as virtuous; the machine and its product as the root of evil. This orderly transformation of the potter's

TOP RIGHT A collection of the highly decorative pottery by Clarice Cliff.

BELOW RIGHT Gallé vase that replays the elephant theme so favoured by Deco designers.

CENTRE FAR RIGHT Stark yet successful design for a porcelain cup and saucer by the Russian Ilya Chashnik.

BOTTOM FAR RIGHT Suprematist porcelain cup and saucer from Russia by the designer Nikolai Suetin.

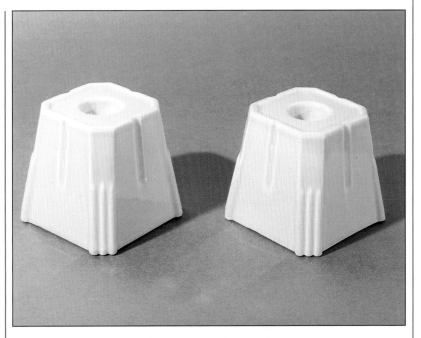

art coincided with the public's short-lived infatuation with Art Nouveau.

The disruption caused by World War I played a major role in arresting progress in the ceramics industry. Equally important was the gradual yet cumulative awareness within Europe of orientalism. The beginnings of this cross-fertilization with the Far East was apparent in the 'Japanesque' wares introduced by the Worcester Royal Porcelain Company in

LEFT A collection of the highly decorative pottery by Clarice Cliff. Simple forms are jazzed up through daring though sometimes less-than-successful colour combinations.

BELOW Three silver and thickly enamelled vases by Camille Faure, that owe much to abstract painting, and arguably manage to cross the slim dividing line between vulgarity and beauty.

the 1880s, and in the early 20th century's fascination with oriental glaze techniques in the work of Ernst Seger in Berlin, Auguste Delaherche and Ernest Chaplet in Paris, and the Rookwood Pottery in Cincinnati.

It would be simplistic in an examination of the ceramics of the Art Deco period to discuss only the high style which dominated the annual Paris salons and the 1925 Exposition. Characterized by the mannered female form, accompanied by the slender silhouettes of animals against a background of conventionalized flowers, volutes or geometric motifs, this element of inter-war decorative taste was certainly important, but it represented only one facet of the wealth of artistic talent found in Modernist ceramics.

To comprehend better the full range of Art Deco ceramics, it is possible to divide the ceramics of the 1918–1940 period into three more or less distinct categories. First, and most important, was the school of the artist-potter, direct heir to the reform movements of the late 19th and early 20th centuries. Second, there were the wares of the more traditional manufactories, some of which had been in continuous production since the introduction of porcelain into Europe in the 18th century. Third, and perhaps the era's most important contribution to the development of a distinct 20th-century aesthetic, came the birth of the industrial ceramicist, an artist whose wares designed expressly for serial production, became the fortuitous offspring of a marriage between art and industry unknown in 1900 but of considerable significance thereafter.

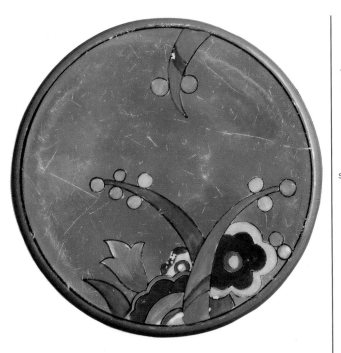

The hand-painted plaque, (**LEFT**), is by Noritake, a Japanese ceramics factory established in Nagoya in 1904. Much of the firm's export ware in the 1930s was decorated with distinctly *moderne* patterns, as the stylized floral design on this piece illustrates.

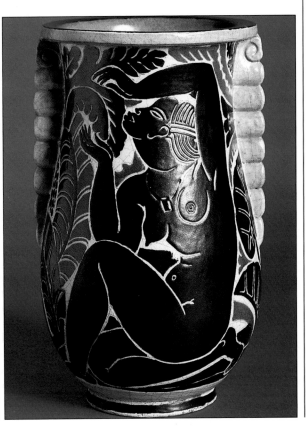

LEFT One of the premier ceramics designers in Art Deco France was René Buthaud, who created this stoneware vase with its exotic Negro figure. Buthaud executed this piece after attending the 1931 *Exposition Coloniale* in Paris, where much African art had been on display.

ARTIST **P**OTTERS

The artistic hiatus afforded by World War I redoubled the efforts of the individual studio potter. The 'war to end all wars' revitalized the market for hand-crafted wares as the public sought to replenish its inventory of household goods in the face of widespread devastation. The potter was effectively involved in all phases of production – design, modelling and glazing – in a manner often hard to distinguish from that of his immediate forebears of the Arts and Crafts Movement. At no time were greater levels of technical virtuosity achieved than in French ceramics of the late 1910s and 1920s. The mastery of glaze became paramount. This preoccupation with technical perfection, however, came at the expense of artistic innovation, and it was left to the British and Viennese-inspired Americans to breathe new life into this aspect of the medium.

The work of the French potter André Metthey provided an important link between the reformers and the early modern period. Although the great body of his work was executed prior to World War I, his wares incorporated many of the conventional Near-Eastern motifs which became a standard vocabulary for Art Deco artisans. Working initially in stoneware and then in faience until his death in 1921, Metthey invited prominent artists of the School of Paris – Pierre Bonnard, André Derain, Henri Matisse, Odilon Redon, Maurice Denis, Auguste Renoir and Edouard Vuillard, among others – to decorate his wares.

More significant, from a technical standpoint, was the work of Emile Decoeur. His stoneware and porcelains were noted for a pronounced unity of form and decoration. Working at first in exquisite *flambé* glazes with incised decoration carved into rich layers of coloured slip, his style evolved gradually in the 1920s towards monochromatic glazes which by their brilliance obviated the need for any further type of ornamentation. These were sometimes mottled, sometimes tinged with darker hues at the rim, but always applied to traditionally shaped vessels.

The work of Emile Lenoble was strongly reminiscent of Korean and Sung (*cizhou yao*) wares. Mixing kaolin to produce stonewares of exceptional lightness, Lenoble created geometric and conventionalized floral motifs suited to simple forms. Such decoration, incised into the vessel or its slip, was often used in conjunction with a refined celadon glaze. The glazes on his stoneware were often earthy in tone – greens, reds, browns, whites – but the stylized decorations, whether subtle or strong, distinguished the pieces from the works of his contemporaries. Lenoble's son Jacques likewise became an accomplished potter.

The work of George Serré was profoundly influenced by a sojourn in the Orient. On his return from Saigon in 1922, he established a studio where he produced massive vessels incised with simple geometric motifs and glazed to resemble cut stone.

Henri-Paul Beyer was noted for his revival of salt-glaze for stoneware, drawing on native European traditions for vessels and figures of simple form. Jean Besnard was also inspired by native traditions for his distinct glazes, some of which he developed to resemble the fragility of lace. Other models incorporated moulded or incised animals and birds in a more robust technique applied with a thick glaze. Séraphin Soudbinine, a Russian émigré and protégé of Rodin, worked in porcelain and stoneware, producing vessels which were highly sculptural.

In Boulogne-sur-Seine, Edmond Lachenal began to work with *flambé* glazes in the early 20th

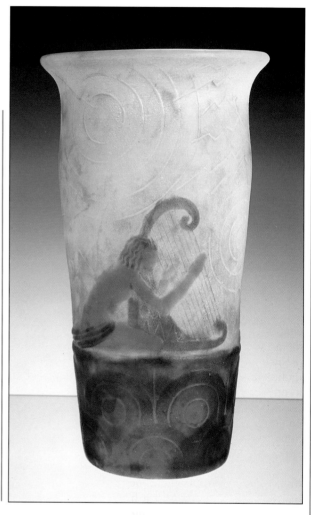

ABOVE *Pâte-de-verre* vase by Gabriel Argy-Rousseau, France, c.1925.

RIGHT Although its strong geometric design looks very 1920s, the coffee service here dates from 1911. The set is an example of Czech Cubism, a movement which permeated design in that Eastern European country in the 1910s. It is signed 'Artěl'.

LEFT Britain's best-known ceramics designer, Clarice Cliff, created patterns that were bold, lively and extremely popular in her own day – as they are with collectors today.

century, gradually developing a technique in which the glaze was manipulated to resemble the geometric precision of *cloisonné* enamel. His choice of colours included a brilliant turquoise blue often imposed on a crackled ivory or beige ground. A student of Lachenal, Henri Simmen used incised decoration to enhance his glazes. His Japanese wife, Mme O'Kin Simmen, sculpted stoppers and handles from ivory and horn to embellish his pieces.

Jean Mayodon's faience wares were noted for their painted figural technique and crackled glazes, many designed for him in a high Art Deco style by Marianne Clouzot. The simple, bulbous forms used by René Buthaud invited a similar type of figural decoration. Working in the provincial capital of Bordeaux, Buthaud's neo-classical imagery has often been linked to Jean Dupas' work in the same city. Painterly qualities notwithstanding, his technical capabilities were evident in the thick *craquelure* or *peau-de-serpent* glazes that he mastered in the 1930s. Also outside the French capital, Félix Massoul, at Maisons-Alfort, worked with a bright palette of metallic glazes, often in collaboration with his wife.

In Britain, studio potters were also strongly influenced by the ceramic arts of the Far East. Most significant was the work of Bernard Leach. Born in Hong Kong of English parents, Leach subscribed to the Oriental belief in the inseparability of the artist and craftsman. He was apprenticed to a traditional Japanese potter, Ogata Kenzan Vi, before returning with the ceramicist Shoji Hamada to England, where he founded the St Ives pottery in Cornwall in 1920. Leach's deft brushwork and understated style reflected his debt to Japanese folk traditions.

His appreciation of the tradition of English slipware influenced Michael Cardew, his first and most gifted student. For further inspiration, Cardew turned to the slip-decorated wares of folk potters in central Africa.

William Staite Murray was another highly significant figure in the British pottery tradition of the 1930s. Unlike Leach, Murray was not interested in bringing beauty to functional wares. He regarded ceramics as an art form equivalent to painting or sculpture. His work showed a pronounced Chinese influence, as did that of his disciples, Henry F Hammond and Thomas Samuel Haile.

Another of Leach's students, Katherine Pleydell-Bouverie, produced wares of extreme simplicity. Her aim was to unify form, colour, and texture. In partnership with Norah Braden from 1928 to 1936, she pursued the special effects of glazes produced from wood and plant ash.

The artists Duncan Grant and Vanessa Bell, in addition to the work commissioned from them by Clarice Cliff for the Arthur J Wilkinson & Co factory, also decorated pottery. Coming from the painterly traditions of the Omega Workshops which had been dissolved in 1921, they decorated available blanks as well as copies of peasant crockery produced for them by the potter Phyllis Keyes.

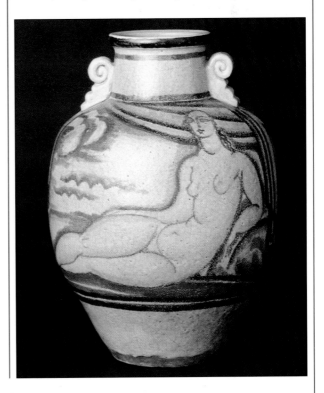

RIGHT Faience vase by René Buthaud, France, 1925.

A RT **D** ECO **C** ERAMICS AND THE **U** NITED **S** TATES

The influence of early 20th-century Vienna was felt profoundly in American studio pottery of the 1920s and 1930s. Whereas Germany took the abstractions of the 1905 years in the Austrian capital as an early manifestation of the Art Deco vocabulary, it was the more expressionist ceramics of Vienna's potters that had the most pronounced effect on American ceramicists, such as those of the Contempora, Sebring and Cowan potteries.

The Wiener Werkstätte, founded in 1903, provided a forum for artisans in a variety of different fields. With the hope of providing a commercially viable enterprise true to the ideals of reformers everywhere – the union of artists with craftsmen and the elevation of the decorative arts – the Wiener Werkstätte's early style was severe and uncompromising. Perhaps in reaction to the deprivations of World War

BELOW The glazed-ceramic figures are by American Waylande DeSantis Gregory. In the centre is *Salome*, and on the right is *Radio*, bearing a lightning-bolt (a common symbol of communication in the 1920s and 30s).

I, a spontaneous style evolved in the Werkstätte's ceramic workshop. Throughout the 1920s, Susi Singer, Gudrun Baudisch-Wittke and Valerie (Vally) Wieselthier, among others, worked in a highly idiosyncratic style characterized by coarse modelling and bright discordant drip-glaze effects. At the 1925 Exposition, Wieselthier exhibited both independently and through the Wiener Werkstätte. Also at the Exposition, Michael Powolny and Josef Hoffman showed modern ceramics through the Wiener Keramik workshops. In 1928 the Wiener Werkstätte potters participated in the International Exhibition of Ceramic Art which toured seven American cities, a seminal event which contributed to the later decision of Singer and Wieselthier to emigrate to the United States. Singer established herself on the West Coast after her husband's death in the 1930s, while Wieselthier, whose reputation grew rapidly in importance after she moved to America, was retained both by Contempora in New York and the Sebring Pottery in Ohio.

The impact of the Austrian school was also felt through the teachings of Julius Mihalik, who emigrated to Cleveland. A number of his students found employment at the Cowan Pottery in Rocky River, Ohio, west of Cleveland. Viktor Schreckengost, Waylande DeSantis Gregory, and Thelma Frazier Winter survived the economic reversals and demise of the Cowan Pottery in 1931 to pursue independent careers as studio potters.

Among Cowan's stock items were sleek Art Deco figurines designed by the artist Waylande Gregory after his return from Europe in 1928. After Cowan's closure, Gregory's sculptural style began to mature. Sensual forms, in biscuit or washed in a monochrome glaze, became characteristic of his monumental works in the late 1930s, such as his 'Fountain of the Atoms' at the 1939 New York World's Fair. A touch of humour – another Viennese legacy – was evident in the lithe and sprightly figures which he designed throughout the decade. Characteristic Viennese levity was also evident in the work of Cleveland artist Thelma Frazier Winter, whose figures and groups expressed her search for a sculptural ceramic style expressive of metal or stone.

Viktor Schreckengost's exposure to Viennese ceramics was direct: he studied under Michael Powolny at the Wiener Keramik in 1929. A part-time jazz musician, his figures displayed a typically Austrian 'feel' for the material. He is best known for his

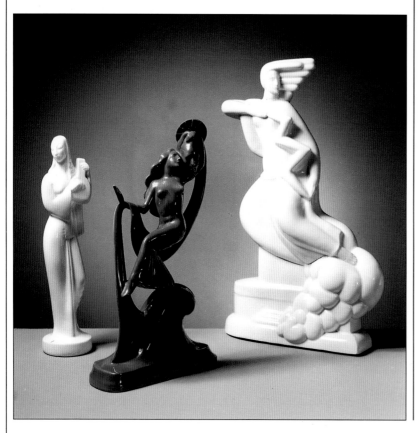

'Jazz' series punchbowls, the first executed in *sgraffito* for Eleanor Roosevelt, who was so elated by his design that she commissioned a second example for the Roosevelts' impending move from the New York Governor's mansion to the White House. The studied vitality of the bowl's decorative motifs – champagne bubbles, gas lights, musical notes, neon signs, etc – recalls the spirit of such artists as Charles Sheeler and Walter Demuth.

Trained as a painter with Robert Henri at the Chase School in New York, Carl Walters turned late to ceramics (in 1919), producing models with glazes derived from sources as diverse as American folk art and Egyptian faience. His clever animal figures, produced in limited editions, relied on strong modelling techniques.

Wilhelm Hunt Diederich, better known for his elegant metalwork, also executed pottery. Characteristic were animal forms in silhouette, reminiscent both in style and technique of the transparent washes found in early Mediterranean earthenwares.

Henry Varnum Poor, better known as a painter, turned to pottery in part from economic necessity. Inspired by primitive ceramics, Poor at first produced simple tableware. Although his emphasis gradually shifted toward more profitable architectural commissions, his style remained basically unchanged, relying on the decorative value of slip and *sgraffito* decoration.

The interwar period in the United States witnessed the growth and maturity of the Cranbrook Academy, founded in 1932 in Bloomfield Hills, Michigan. The Academy is best known as a catalyst of the post-World War II Studio Movement. Remarkable are a cool and elegant dinner service by Eliel Saarinen for Lenox, and the serene and austere creations of Majlis 'Maija' Grotell, both distinctive contributions to Cranbrook's reputation for progressive design. Grotell's ceramics of this period exhibited a tactile quality and careful glaze manipulation which showed her mastery of Oriental kiln techniques.

E UROPEAN **P** OTTERIES **1** 920s – 1930s

The state manufactories of France and Germany experienced general artistic stagnation in the 1920s and 1930s. Throughout the 19th century such manufactories had become bastions of conservatism, creating wares for those who could afford to indulge their taste in expensive ornaments, rather than trying to promote a Modernist idiom. On the whole, the national manufactories never recovered the vitality they lost in reproducing a seemingly endless repertoire of popular 18th-century forms. It was left in part to the Scandinavians, whose boundaries between art and craft were less rigid, to integrate the aesthetics of the potter's wheel with the grammar of Modernist ornament.

Other potteries, with widely varying capabilities, turned their attention to the possibilities of the modern style. These ranged from the French-inspired interpretations of Belgian firms, to the dichotomous efforts of the British, who produced both modern wares and period reproductions, and to various other European and American firms whose products showed a thinly veiled attempt to capitalize on the 1925 style. Ironically, it was the last-mentioned which served most to popularize the Art Deco style and, through such vulgarization, to precipitate its decline.

Rather more successful, in a Modernist context, were the stylish tablewares produced by Théodore Haviland et Cie, of Limoges. Commissioned from such artists as Suzanne Lalique, the *maître-verrier's* daughter, and Jean Dufy, brother of Raoul, there was an obvious attempt to adapt a contemporary decorative vocabulary to traditional forms. Marcel Goupy, a successful glass designer, created dining ensembles in porcelain and glass which were retailed by Georges Rouard. These displayed a fairly conservative mixture of floral decorations. Jean Luce, another artist whose designs in glass overshadowed his achievements in ceramics, designed tablewares for Haviland in a light Modernist style. A delightful selection of small *animalier* porcelain figurines by Edouard M Sandoz was similarly issued by the firm.

In the 1920s, the large Paris department stores generated a wide range of household ceramics designed by their own studios. At Pomone, Charlotte Chaucet-Guilleré, the director of the store's Prima-

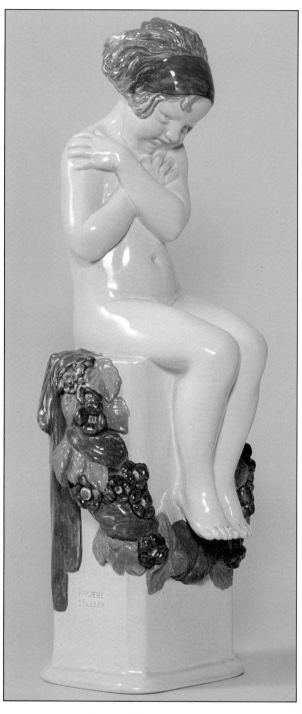

LEFT The white-glazed earthenware figure was made in the 1920s by Ashtead Pottery, Surrey, which employed disabled World War I veterans. The overall appearance of the girl and the floral-swagged plinth are similar to Viennese pottery of the same time.

vera studio, Madeleine Sougez, Marcel Renard and Claude Lévy, created lightly-decorated tablewares and accessories to complement their furnishings. At the Galeries Lafayette, Maurice Dufrêne, the director of the store's La Maîtrise studio, Jacques and Jean Adnet, Bonifas, and Mlle Maisonée, offered a similar line of household pieces executed for the store by André Fau & Guillard, and Keramis, in Belgium.

Louis Süe and André Mare's firm, La Compagnie des Arts Français, rivalled in prestige the

RIGHT The English tea service dates from 1934 and was designed by Clarice Cliff. One of the *Biarritz* line, the minimally decorated set is perhaps her most geometric. She was better known for her brightly hued, exuberantly painted ceramics, in part influenced by the colours and designs of the Ballets Russes. The spare, hand-painted black and red lines perfectly complement the pure rectangular and round shapes.

BELOW The Belgian pottery Boch Frères, a branch of the German firm Villeroy & Boch, established the Keramis factory at La Louvière in 1841. In the 1920s Keramis produced vessels decorated in the Art Deco style, such as this group, some of them by Parisian designer Marcel Goupy. The *craquelure* grounds were deliberate technical devices, adapted from oriental ceramics. The vivid eggyolk-yellow glaze of the same three pieces is quite modern, however.

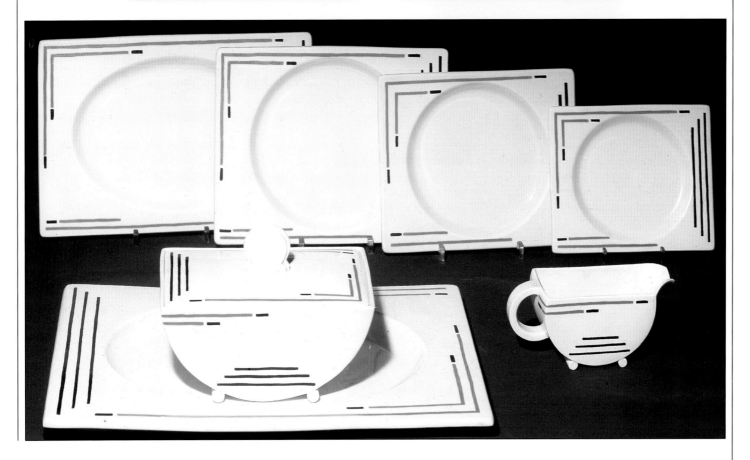

department-store pavilions at the 1925 Exposition. The pair designed heavily scrolled and floral table-wares such as tureens and vegetable dishes which evoked Louis-Philippe opulence, for their dining room ensembles. At the Exposition, Paul Véra and José Martin were retained to enhance the firm's pavilion with a series of ceramic friezes.

With the closure of the famed Vienna manu-factory in the 19th century, only the Augarten firm founded in 1922 by Franz von Zülow, and the firm of Friedrich Goldscheider, remained to play a signifi-cant role in Austria's production of modern-style porcelain wares.

In Czechoslovakia, the firm of Royal Dux, whose languorous nymphs of the Art Nouveau epoch had been extremely popular, generated a limited selection of new designs after World War I.

In Belgium, the modern style was vigorously adopted by the firm of Keramis, owned by Boch Frères, in La Louvière. Charles Catteau, born in Douai, designed a wide selection of Parisian high style ceramic wares in which leaping gazelles and flowers predominated. His choice of brilliant tur-quoise glazes on crackled ivory grounds evoked Lachenal's earlier palette. The firm shared its success in this line of bright commercial wares with the Primavera department store in Paris.

In Germany, the Meissen State Porcelain Manufactory was under the direction of Max Adolf Pfeiffer from 1926 to 1936. Little of any artistic innovation was produced.

The decorative genius of the architect Gio Ponti reversed the fortunes of the declining Società Ceramica Richard-Ginori factory in Doccia, Italy.

His work, in its attempt to link the decorative voca-bulary of ancient Rome with the modern period, dis-played a penchant for neo-classicism in both form and decoration. His wares included a prodigious range of crisp, delicate ceramic forms with highly mannered decoration. Ponti also produced wares of strictly modern decoration – sporting scenes, gro-tesques, geometrical forms, etc – with an easy affi-nity. In Turin, Eugenio Colmo, the founder of the review *Numero*, created ceramics as a hobby under the name of Golia. He purchased white porcelain blanks to which he applied a forceful range of Art Deco images in vibrant colours.

The English firm of Josiah Wedgwood & Sons was among the first in the 19th century to commission graphic artists to decorate their wares, a technique which the firm again pursued from 1935 under the artistic directorship of Victor Skellern. The well-known engraver and painter Eric Ravilious was re-tained to decorate blank ceramic vessels designed by the architect Keith Murray through the transfer-printing process.

Relatively few British artists took the trouble to transpose the modern decorative idiom into manu-factured wares. Among the foremost were Eric Slater, responsible for design and decoration of tablewares for Shelley potteries, and Susie Cooper, who produced her own simply decorated services. Initially a deco-rator of blanks at the firm of AE Gray & Co. Ltd in Hanley, Cooper accepted an offer in 1931 from Wood & Son's Crown Works to execute shapes of her own design. She produced dozens of tableware designs,

The flambé earthenware vase, (**LEFT**), was made by Royal Doulton at Burslem, c1925. Although its stylized-floral motif is not in the Parisian Art Deco vein, the Far Eastern-inspired red-flambé glaze is in keeping with French ceramics, which were richly decorated in the oriental manner.

of Patrick Nordstrøm. Later, a variety of neo-classical and Modernist themes were developed concurrently by designers such as Christian Joachim, Arno Malinowski, Knud Kyhn, Jais Nielsen, Axel Saltø and Gerhard Henning. At Bing & Grøndahl, the porcelain figures of Kai Nielsen and the powerfully modelled groups of Jean Gauguin, son of Paul Gauguin, were the most noteworthy.

In Sweden, Wilhelm Kåge was artistic director at the Gustavsberg porcelain works. His *Liljeblå* earthenware tablewares of around 1917, with restrained underglaze floral decoration in cobalt blue on a white ground, were based on traditional Swedish crockery designed to make good quality wares affordable to the working class. His *Praktika* tableware of 1933 showed the beginnings of the functionalist aesthetic while retaining elements of traditional design. Kåge's well-known *Argenta* stoneware is more decorative, with chased silver images applied to green-glazed grounds that resemble verdigris bronze. At the 1925 Exposition, Gustavsberg was joined in the Swedish pavilion by the Rörstrand Porcelain Manufactory, which displayed a line of understated floral designs. In Norway, the geometry of Nora Gulbrandsen's designs for Porsgrunds Porselensfabrik reflected very clearly the Modernist aesthetic.

decorated with subdued abstract or geometric 'jazz style' patterns in muted tones. Her perception of the British consumer's innate conservatism and her stringent attention to detail in both design and marketing rendered her wares a great success both nationally and internationally.

At the other end of the spectrum, Clarice Cliff's *Bizarre* tablewares, produced by the Newport Pottery from 1928, have come to symbolize the decorative exuberances and excesses of the Art Deco style. Her use of colour, geometry and eccentric shapes turned her wares into novelty items. Clever marketing schemes – including editions with fanciful names such as *Delicia*, *Biarritz* and *Fantasque* – and moderate prices helped to popularize her wares.

The Royal Copenhagen and Bing & Grøndahl porcelain manufactories continued after 1900 to apply a range of traditional Danish decoration to their commercial wares, perhaps in response to the enthusiasm at the time in England and France for similar iconography. In 1912 the Royal Copenhagen factory introduced a series of stonewares under the direction

The porcelain plate, (**LEFT**), was designed by Jean Luce for display at the 1925 Paris Exposition. Its simple floral/ geometric motif is highlighted in gold. A technical adviser for the Sèvres factory, Luce also designed glass and porcelain for the ocean liner *Normandie*.

INDUSTRIAL DESIGN AND MASS PRODUCTION

Perhaps most significant to the development of a 20th-century aesthetic was the birth of the professional industrial designer in the inter-war period. The profession is seen today as the inter-relationship between art and industry, the result of attempts in numerous fields – not the least of which is ceramic design – to prove that good design should be economical to produce and easy to sell, as well as functional. The true industrial ceramics of the 1930s, non-derivative in form and generally devoid of decoration, lost none of their character through mass-production. Throughout the decade, there occurred a gradual acceptance of functional forms coupled with modern industrial techniques. In this the machine, seen decades earlier as the antithesis of good design, now became the vehicle for its production.

The turning-point in this evolution can be traced to the establishment of the Bauhaus in Weimar in 1919. Although today nearly everything of functional form – from teacups to seat furniture – is said to be 'Bauhaus', the school was not founded to create a style but to develop a new approach to the applied arts. While no body of ceramic works evolved in the Bauhaus ceramic workshops to equal, for example, the metalware designs of Marianne Brandt or the furniture of Mies van der Rohe, the Bauhaus ceramicists are noteworthy for their wholehearted rejection of tradition, and for their artistic creativity amidst the chaos of the Weimar Republic after the defeat of World War I. The initial lack of adequate facilities for pottery in Weimar was turned to advantage when the workshop was established at nearby Dornburg, in 1921, under the technical supervision of Max Brehan. As the workshop received commissions from the local town, and as the need for pottery melded with the Bauhaus' artistic ideals, it is clear that the Dornburg workshop came closest to achieving the union of art and craft stated in Walter Gropius's original manifesto.

The only German manufactory to show a significant interest in functionalism was the Staatliche-Porzellanfabrik in Berlin. Its most direct link to industrial design occurred in the employment of ex-Bauhaus pupil Margarete Friedländer-Wildenhain,

who designed the simple, classic shapes of the *Halle* service of 1930, in which plain banding was the only form of decoration. Trude Petri's *Urbino* service of 1930 was more remarkable. In production for some 40 years, the service was among the first to rely neither on colour nor ornament for commercial success.

Also in the functionalist mode was Dr Hermann Gretch's *Arzberg 1382* for the Arzberg Porcelain Works. This form, again devoid of ornamentation, showed rather softer, more rounded, silhouettes than contemporary Berlin wares. First shown at the 1930 Deutscher Werkbund Exhibition, it won a gold medal at the 1936 Triennale in Milan and the Paris Exposition of 1937. These designs signified a growing interest in unornamented form as a characteristic of good design, without neglecting porcelain as a costly and formal material.

Eva Stricker Zeisel is one of the most noted 20th-century industrial designers, and although her most mature work generally belongs to the post-World War II period, her designs for the Schramberger Majolika Fabrik in the 1920s incorporated several geometrical motifs associated with Modernism. Throughout the 1930s her work in Berlin for Christian Carsten, in the Soviet Union for the Lomonosov Porcelain Factory and Dulevo Ceramics Factory, and in the United States for Bay Ridge Specialty and Riverside China, reflected a somewhat softening geometry.

In Britain, Keith Murray's designs for Wedgwood were very avant-garde. Trained as an architect and experienced in Modernist glass design at Stevens & Williams, in Brierley Hill, Staffordshire, Murray

ABOVE The jaunty teapot is by the Hall China Company, an American firm which mass-produced tableware. Covered in Chinese red glaze, the swag-like form is called *Rhythm* (1939).

FAR RIGHT Henry Varnum Poor: pottery tile mural, about 1930. Poor's style defies categorization, but his figural work, seen here in this panel for Edgar Levy's residence Littlefarm, is allied to the American Realist school both in the literal treatment and the choice of subject.

RIGHT Frederic Hurten Rhead for Homer Laughlin: *Fiesta Ware* pottery tablewares, about 1936. The meticulously crafted glazes of this tableware range originally came in these five colours. A clever marketing strategy was developed whereby the consumer was encouraged to purchase the pieces in open stock and mix colours at the table.

BELOW Russel Wright for Steubenville Pottery: *American Modern* pottery tableware, 1939. The subdued colours of coral, chartreuse, curry, cedar green and granite were particularly suited to the gentle organic forms of this range of ceramics. Such shapes seem to presage the postwar reaction to the more strident geometry of the interwar period.

joined Wedgwood in 1933. He designed large numbers of non-derivative shapes in which ornament consisted exclusively of turned or fluted motifs. Glazes provided textural interest. His wares were executed in black basalt, celadon, silken 'Moonstone' (1933) and matt green or straw (1935).

It was left primarily to the Americans to explore the phenomenal sales potential of mass-production. The most accomplished, and one of the best-selling tablewares, was Frederick H Rhead's *Fiesta*, designed for the Homer Laughlin Company, of which Rhead had become artistic director in 1927. Rhead, a Staffordshire potter who had emigrated to the United States in 1902, aimed at a mass-produced line of high-quality pottery free from derivative ornament, which would appeal to America's prosperous middle class. Introduced in 1936, *Fiesta*'s simple geometrical shapes were offered in five bright colours. In production for more than 30 years, the line was an overwhelming success, helping to precipitate a revolution in industrial design.

Russel Wright was another American whose ideas had a profound effect on the public perception of 'good design'. His *American Modern* dinner service, designed in 1937, introduced by Steubenville Pottery in 1939, and marketed by Baymor until around 1959, presaged in its biomorphic forms and subdued colours the work of post-World War II organic designers. It was a logical extension of the 'good design' theory by which Wright's *American Modern* became part of a larger scheme of decorative items entitled *American Way*.

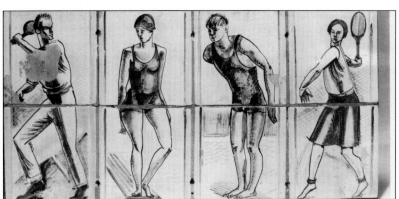

ART DECO
GLASSWARE
& LIGHTING

EUROPEAN GLASS

 The importance of glass to the development of taste in the 1920s and 1930s is often overlooked. The Art Deco glass that is collected by connoisseurs is often limited to the vases, glasses and lamps designed by René Lalique and Daum. Those pieces are of course particularly rare and beautiful, but they only represent a small percentage of the glass produced, and do not give a full picture of all the uses to which glass could be put. Glass was not only used for table ornaments or vases, or even jewellery, but was also an important part of a whole architectural project on the grandest scale. At its plainest, a glass sheet is transparent – almost invisible. It was that particular quality of glass that many of the Modernist architects exploited. Le Corbusier's *Pavillon de L'Esprit Nouveau* at the *Exposition des Arts Décoratifs et Industriels* stood as a statement against superfluous decoration. It also showed how to use the window as the only ornament and break in the structure of the building. Many architects, including Robert Mallet-Stevens, Mies van der Rohe, Walter Gropius and Le Corbusier himself used glass for its properties of transparency and the possibilities open therein.

Newly-invented types of glass compound allowed for a greater range of applications. Even within the traditional areas of glass usage such as for vases and lamps the Art Deco period saw a revival of many old techniques and the invention of some new ones, a number of them with stunning results.

France had kept alive the skill of working glass throughout the 19th century with the most exciting contributions to the medium coming from Baccarat and Emile Gallé. Gallé was the master of the Art Nouveau style, and René Lalique was his direct heir. Lalique, the master of glass manufacture, began to use moulds and casts in order to be able to manufacture large numbers of glass sculptures. Maurice Marinot discovered methods of catching bubbles between skins of glass in his vases; other makers used the etching and engraving techniques; while yet others exploited the *pâte-de-verre* technique. The revival of the *pâte-de-verre* and *pâte-de-cristal* techniques brought back the art of sculpting in glass.

The Swedish glass industry, comprising mostly small 'bruks' (industrial communities) in the heart of the Smaland forests near Kalmar, was the first to capitalize on the new movement. At Orrefors, the

ABOVE This English talcum-powder bottle sports a quarter-sunburst pattern. The motif – whether partial, half or whole – was found on glass of all sorts.

RIGHT The massive blue glass vase is by Daum Frères of Nancy. Its design, of stylized tropical birds perched on branches bearing square leaves with dotted centres, is curious.

LEFT Jean Luce: selection of vases with sandblasted and mirrored finishes, 1920s. Like Colotte, Luce applied powerful imagery to his designs by the use of deep and angular motifs.

RIGHT This selection of c.1920 Swedish glass shows the range of forms, techniques and motifs found on glassware from the Scandinavian country. The two pieces in the right foreground are examples of Graal glass by the Orrefors firm.

ABOVE This blown-glass vase comes from Murano, the famed Venetian glass centre. A stylized harvest scene has been applied to the rich plum-coloured body in strokes of black and gold.

owner, Johan Ekman, sought to expand the firm's first existing production of domestic wares – ink and milk bottles, and window panes – with a line of artistic glass. A fresh and innovative style evolved, particularly in the firm's Graal technique, an adaptation of the intarsia process that Frederick Carder had begun to develop in 1916–17 at the Steuben Glass Works in Corning, New York. Graal was a modification of the French Art Nouveau cameo technique popularized by Emile Gallé, in which superimposed layers of coloured glass were etched or carved with relief decoration.

In Copenhagen, functionalism was introduced into Danish glass in the appointment of the architect-designer, Jacob E Bang, as designer for the Holmegaard Glasværk, in 1925. Bang created glass tableware and vases for the firm in his simple engraved or etched 'Calligaglia' pattern until 1942.

In Norway, as in its neighbours, the production of Modernist glass in the 1920s was concentrated primarily in one factory, Hadelands Glassverk. In 1928 the firm employed the textile, glass and book designer, Sverre Pettersen, to design tableware with simple engraved patterns. Heavier, more functional models were introduced when Stale Kyllingstad joined the firm in 1937.

The production of Modernist art glass in Finland began in 1928 with the appointment of Henri Ericsson

RIGHT Marcel Goupy enamelled this vase c1926. Called *Les Baigneuses (The Bathers)*, its figures bear no resemblance to those on Cézanne's celebrated earlier canvas of the same name. The use of solid areas of colour – at times outlined by another hue, as on the bodies and water – is a striking device. Goupy also designed porcelain tableware for Haviland at Limoges.

as artistic adviser to the Riihimäki factory. In the 1930s he was joined by Arttu Brummer, who developed a series of moulded square and rectangular glass vessels entitled *Bubuki*. Of greater interest was the line of Savoy vases in clear coloured glass designed by Alvar Aalto in around 1936–37, at Karhula-Iittala.

In Belgium, the Val Saint-Lambert glassworks near Liège re-opened after World War I. During the

RIGHT
Delicately-shaped rectangular vase by E. Rousseau, with an image on the side of a grotesque figure.

early 1920s the firm introduced a series of vases decorated by Léon Ledru and engraved by Joseph Simon with high style motifs, entitled *Arts Décoratifs de Paris*, in which the crystal body was overlaid in transparent coloured layers cut with repeating geometrical patterns. Other noted Val Saint-Lambert designers included Modeste Denoel, Charles Graffart, Félix Matagne, René Delvenne and Lucien Petignot.

In 1912, under the direction of PM Cochius, Modernist glassware began to be produced at the Royal Dutch Glass Works in Leerdam, Holland. The architects Hendrik Berlage and KPC de Bazel were commissioned to create tableware items, bottles and ornamental stemware for mass-production. Berlage resigned in around 1925 to establish the Union Studio, and was replaced by Andries Dirk Copier, whose household glassware included the 'Unica' series of ornamental glassware.

In Austria, many of the Wiener Werkstätte were responsible for the production of handsome glassware from 1910 onward. Although these pieces often predate the 1925 Paris Exposition, they are none the less startlingly modern in appearance; typical are the various decanters, tumblers and other tableware made by the Lobmeyr factory.

Elsewhere in Europe, the Czechoslovakian glass industry produced Art Deco-style glassware, including lamps, vases and tableware, as well as lovely cameo-glass pieces with bold geometric motifs. Art Deco-type glass was produced, to a lesser extent, by Venini of Murano, Italy, which had hitherto made only transitional or revival pieces, reflecting its centuries-old heritage. A second designer, Ercole Barovier, like Venini, also reacted against Venetian revivalism by creating exciting new textures and processes, sometimes decorating simple, fluid forms with strong geometric motifs.

English glassware in the Art Deco period was produced by such old, established firms as Thomas Webb and Sons and Stuart and Sons, who hired well-known artists of the fame of Paul Nash, Laura Knight, Eric Ravilious and Graham Sutherland to design glassware for them. But the most highly regarded name in English glass design was Keith Murray, a New Zealand-born architect-designer who had also worked in silver and ceramics. He was a designer first for Whitefriars Glass Works and later for Stevens & Williams, for the second of whom he designed the so-called Brierley Crystal, which had a deeply engraved stylized-cactus motif.

Marcel Bouraine sculpted the drape-bearing figure, (**LEFT**), c1928. It was moulded in *pâte-de-cristal* by Gabriel Argy-Rousseau. The stunning sculpture has Cubist overtones, and the mottled amber glass is truly jewel-like. Bouraine also worked for the Etling firm.

F RANCE:
M ARINOT

In France, the two major names and influences were Maurice Marinot (1882–1960) and René Lalique (1860–1945). Marinot started and ended his working life as a painter, becoming a member of the renegade Fauve group, known for their wild and colourful canvases. But between 1911 and 1937, he devoted himself to the art of glassmaking. His most exemplary vases, jars and bottles – he produced some 2,500 in all – were thick-walled, stunning objects which

ABOVE This group of vases shows the range of colour, shapes and motifs found on the vessels of French glassmaker René Lalique. From left to right are *Archers, Ceylan, Sauge (Sage)* and *Ronces (Brambles)*.

elevated the medium of glass to new artistic heights. By emphasizing its actual physical qualities, by seeming miraculously to trap its fluidity in three dimensions, he produced pieces that captivated critics and public alike. What had hitherto been considered flaws in the medium – bubbles, specks of chemicals needed to produce colour and so on – he turned into primary decorative components. These elements, coupled with the traditional ovoid, spherical and squarish forms that so many Art Deco vessels assumed (metal and ceramic, as well as glass), resulted in some of the most beautiful *objets d'art* of the period. He also submerged pieces in acid baths to create deeply etched designs, and produced multi-layered works with various colours or streaks contained within the separate layers.

Many of Marinot's early pieces – produced from about 1912 to 1922 – were decorated with colourful enamelled designs, usually flowers, sometimes figures. Other Frenchmen, such as Auguste Heiligenstein, Jean Luce and Marcel Goupy (he also worked in ceramics), carried this type of design even further.

Other French glassmakers enthusiastically embraced Art Deco, including the esteemed Daum Frères which had produced Art Nouveau glass in the 1880s and 1890s in the naturalistic style of Emile Gallé. In the 1930s, the factory created etched-glass wares very much in the contemporary vein, with geometric and stylized-floral patterns often reminiscent of Marinot's vessels.

Born in Ay-sur-Marne in 1860 Lalique was one of the oldest practitioners of the Art Deco style. Turning to glass manufacture in 1902 he quickly recognized its expressive potential. It was in his jewellery shop in 1906 that Lalique's glass vessels first caught the attention of François Coty who, aware of Lalique's abilities as a graphic designer, is said to have asked Lalique to design labels for his various perfume lines.

Lalique's first designs for Coty were produced at Legras et Cie, in crystal and mostly unsigned. In 1908, Lalique rented the Combs-la-Ville glassworks, where he began to execute his own designs, and these premises were purchased in 1909, allowing him to go into serial production. Glass produced in Lalique's own factories was all in *demi-cristal*, a malleable and relatively inexpensive material suitable for moulding and mass-production.

Lalique was particularly important because not only did he achieve total mastery of the small ornament, vase and statuette, but in the 1920s he started to design glass furniture. Following the example of Baccarat's etched glass furniture in the mid 19th century Lalique reinvented the form in a totally modern way. He was followed in this by other designers, most notably Robert Block and Serge Roche.

The method of working that Lalique favoured for his ornamental pieces soon found wider favour. He would first shape the object in another material and then take a plaster cast and pour molten glass into the mould. Apart from the advantage of being able to cast shapes that could not be blown, moulds could be employed for mass production. The results could be varied slightly by using variously coloured glass, or in the finishing process.

Lalique's forms, techniques, designs and runaway success encouraged many to imitate him, including Sabino Verlys, d'Avesn, Hunebelle and Etling in France, Jobling in England, Val Saint-Lambert in Belgium, Leerdam in Holland, Barolac in Czechoslovakia and the Phoenix and Consolidated Lamp and Glass companies in the United States. But his peerless production methods could never be duplicated, and he guarded his technical secrets closely.

In Lalique's work other designers could see the unification of the disparate strains of Art Deco design.

He was at once luxurious, elegant, practical, interested in abstract design, showy, intimate and, above all, the supreme craftsman.

His repertory of subjects ranged from sentimental neo-classical nudes to bold, geometric patterns, and some of his finest Art Deco creations are his monumental coloured vases – for example, *Tortues*, with its pattern of billowing tortoises' backs approaching a stark abstraction, and *Tourbillons*, or *Whirlwinds*, a black-enamelled version of which was displayed at the 1925 Paris Exposition. His figures *Suzanne* and *Thaïs* are sensuous, scantily clad symbols of gaiety and abandon, while his mascot *Victoire*, or as it is known in English *Spirit of the Wind*, has become something of an icon of Art Deco.

PÂTE-DE-VERRE, PÂTE-DE-CRISTAL

The ancient Egyptian technique of *pâte-de-verre* – powered glass made into a paste with water and a fluxing medium, and then refired in a mould – had been revived at the turn of the century by Henri Cros, and several Art Deco glassmakers continued to employ the process. Foremost among them was François-Emile Décorchement (1880–1971), who was inspired in 1902, on seeing Dammouse's *pâte-d'émail* works, to experiment with *pâte-de-verre*. His first wares were typically Art Nouveau in style, with floral or symbolic motifs. Gradually, however, his style and technique changed. After returning from a travelling scholarship he won in 1908, he began to work in the *cire perdue* method of casting, producing thin-walled vessels with decorative details cut into the surface. By 1910 he also produced near-transparent *pâte-de-cristal* vessels by using a higher percentage of lead. Many of his massive, thick-walled pieces were decorated with stylized floral or faunal motifs and some had animal or figural handles.

He also made great use of colour and produced heavy vessels resembling marble or semi-precious stones, an effect he achieved by chemical streaking

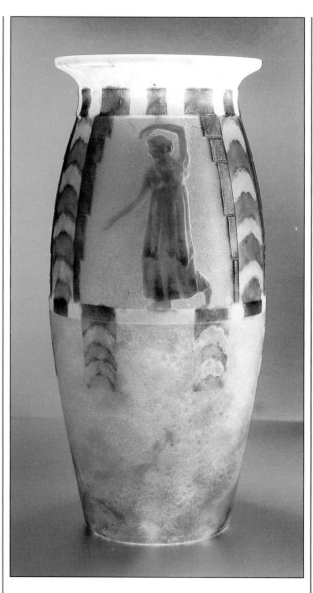

RIGHT This *pâte-de-verre* vase by Gabriel Argy-Rousseau, features a graceful classical dancer in its central panel. The cloudy russet, white and brown vertical designs make a lovely surround. Note the darker hues on the woman's hair, and on the bottom folds of her drapery.

LEFT The geometric pattern on the *pâte-de-verre* vase is unusually strong for its designer, Gabriel Argy-Rousseau. The zigzag design on the lower body of the piece has been refined and articulated at the top, to become a flock of angled birds in flight. The sandy quality of the moulded glass has been emphasized.

within the glass. Rich reds, oranges, mauves and blues blend delicately into each other without the strict demarcation lines that appear in other types of glassware. Jade green, turquoise and sapphire blue were streaked with black or purple to simulate semi-precious stones. He even simulated tortoiseshell with a lovely golden-brown glass.

In the 1920s Décorchement's style became increasingly bolder, progressing from the naturalistic floral motifs of his earlier works to the stylized asps and grotesque masks of the early to mid-1920s and, finally, the highly geometrical images of his mature

style. Of restrained elegance, his works in this later period are characterized by rigid, often cubic forms, with relief geometrical decoration. In the 1930s Décorchement became increasingly involved in the production of decorative window panels. From 1935 to 1939, for example, he worked almost exclusively on a window commission for the Sainte-Odile Church in Paris. In place of the traditional use of painted and leaded glass, Décorchement used *pâte-de-verre* to create a rich and intimate effect.

His grandsons, Antoine and Etienne Leperlier, have followed in his footsteps and are at work in France today as *pâte-de-verre* artists.

Gabriel Argy-Rousseau (1885–1953) also produced *pâte-de-verre* and *pâte-de-cristal* glass, including small lamps and three-dimensional neo-classical figures, usually of dancers, some modelled by sculptor Marcel Bouraine. Joseph-Gabriel Rousseau received his early training in ceramics, enrolling at the Ecole Nationale de Céramique de Sèvres in 1902. After his graduation in 1906, he became the manager of a small ceramics research laboratory and shortly afterwards opened his own workshop where he experimented with *pâte-de-verre*. He married Marie Argyriades in 1913, at which time he added the first part of his wife's family name, Argy, to his own.

Argy-Rousseau's vessels were less massive and more delicate than Décorchement's; indeed, floral and figural decorations on pieces dating from the 1910s were sometimes more reminiscent of Art Nouveau. However, the motifs he produced after the First World War – stylized female heads, classical masks, elegant gazelles or floral forms – were more in keeping with 1920s French style. His more notable works, executed in *pâte-de-cristal*, had neo-classical relief decoration, in keeping with the vogue for Egyptian revivalism spurred at the time by the discovery of Tutankhamen's tomb. Other models were rigidly geometric in form.

Alméric Walter (1859–1942) was another *pâte-de-verre* designer whose career spanned the Art Nouveau and Art Deco periods. He first encountered *pâte-de-verre* as a student, experimenting with the medium under the direction of his teacher, Gabriel Levy. In 1908, he moved to Nancy, where he found employment as a glassmaker at the Daum works, producing an array of *pâte-de-verre* vases, ashtrays, bowls and statuettes. His style was influenced by that of the firm's designer, Henri Bergé, and other

RIGHT This *pâte-de-verre* vase is by François-Emile Décorchement, most of whose creations contained evocations of classical Greece and Rome. Note the grape and volute frieze on this piece, as well as the two full-figure 'ears', found on ancient glass.

FAR LEFT Gabriel Argy-Rousseau designed this stunning *pâte-de-verre* vase. While studying ceramics at Sèvres, the designer began to experiment with *pâte-de-verre*. He soon devoted himself fully to this newly revived technique of glass-making, first exhibiting his work in 1914.

well-known local artists, such as Victor Prouvé and Jean-Bernard Descomps. Most of his works are highly sculptural, decorated with frogs, lizards, goldfish and beetles rendered naturalistically. Walter also designed *pâte-de-verre* medallions which could be used either as jewellery pendants or as decorative accents for furniture and lamps.

A waning public interest in *pâte-de-verre* from 1929 led to a gradual decline in production.

 ## **A** MERICAN **G** LASSWARE

The influence of the German Bauhaus was strongly felt in the United States, due primarily to the fact that many prominent German designers and architects emigrated to the United States in the interwar years. Mies van der Rohe, Walter Gropius, Marcel Breuer, Josef Albers and Laszlo Moholy-Nagy, among others, fled the increasing repression of a Fascist régime for the freedom and democracy of the new world. Under their influence, glass became a symbol of modernity for American designers. Mirrored and glass cocktail cabinets, frosted-glass panelling and glass-panelled chairs became fashionable among Modernist designers.

In the United States, in addition to the Art Nouveau genius Louis Comfort Tiffany, the leading name in glass in the 20th century was – and still is – the Steuben Glass Works. Founded in 1903 by the Englishman Frederick Carder, the firm was named

after a famous Revolutionary War hero, Baron von Steuben. The company was originally organized to produce crystal blanks for the Corning Glass cutters, of which it became a division in 1918.

Various types of colourful art glass were produced by Steuben during the Art Deco period. In the 1920s Carder added to his output, the *Cintra*, *Cluthra*, *Silverine* and *Intarsia* lines, which were mostly vessels made of layers of 'cased' glass characterized by internal air bubbles and designs, *à la* Marinot and other French glassmakers. One handsome Carder piece of the late 1920s, in the shape of a Chinese lotus bowl, and made of frosted glass acid-etched with a stylized flower, constituted more than a passing nod to French glassmaking of the time.

But it was not until the 1920s that Steuben Glass really began to take the lead with its modern wares, which included at least five patterns of elegant functionalist crystal stemware designed by Walter Dorwin Teague around 1932.

In 1933 Carder was replaced as the head of Steuben in an attempt to revive the company, which faced financial difficulties brought on by the Depres-

ABOVE Steuben's Frederick Carder designed this lily case, part of the firm's *Ivrene* line. The vase seems to shimmer with pearly iridescence.

BELOW This handsome centrepiece was designed by Walter Dorwin Teague c.1932, for Steuben Glass Works of Corning, NY. Teague was an industrial designer of note who directed his talents to several mediums, including glass.

sion. The company was reorganized, and radical policy changes were implemented under the presidency of Arthur Amory Houghton, Jr, who hired a new director of design, John Monteith Gates, and a principal designer, the sculptor Sidney Waugh. The coloured glass line developed by Carder was completely eliminated, and only items in clear transparent crystal were made.

Waugh's vases were highly reminiscent of Orrefors', engraved with monumental figures and sleek animals. Many were limited-edition pieces, one of the best known of which was *Gazelle Bowl*, a seven-inch (17.8cm) high engraved-crystal artwork of 1935 decorated with a frieze of these lithe leaping animals which, along with other graceful *biches*, figured highly in the Art Deco design repertory. Other Waugh bowls depicted mythological characters.

A wide variety of decorative and utilitarian glassware was produced by other American factories, perhaps the most noteworthy being the *Ruba Rombic* pattern of the Consolidated Lamp and Glass Company of Coraopolis, Pennsylvania (the firm also manufactured designs in the Lalique vein). The mould-blown, non-lead platters, pitchers, candlesticks, goblets, etc, introduced in 1928, were wonderfully geometric, with jagged, jutting-out angles in shades of grey, amber and lavender. The Phoenix Glass Company, also in Pennsylvania, likewise produced both Lalique-style and *moderne* glassware. Much of its output was identical to that of Consolidated, making for many identification problems today.

Among the other American factories, Libbey Glass Company created stunning modern glass, some of which was designed by Walter Dorwin Teague. There were also dozens of lesser companies which multi-mass-produced so-called 'Depression' or 'Carnival' glass. These were generally imitative, cheaply made coloured pieces which aspired to be art glass, several decades after such glass had gone out of fashion. Among the firms producing Depression glass were AH Heisey, Indiana Glass, Anchor Hocking and Fostoria and Federal. Some of these also offered more geometric lines, such as George Sakier's 'classic modern' vases of about 1930 for Fostoria.

Donald Deskey employed glass in a variety of ways: in architecture, he used glass bricks to create indirect lighting, and in furniture he employed glass tops and shelves to achieve transparency and planarity. His clock of 1926–27 provides a fine example of how he combined several European influences to produce a unified whole. Its use of textured glass panels recalls the work of Louis Barillet which Deskey saw at the 1925 Paris Exposition. The diagonal, geometric design evokes also the painting of the Dutch De Stijl artist Theo van Doesburg.

Many other designers in the United States incorporated similar principles. Among them were Gilbert Rohde (1894–1944) and Kem Weber, who used glass in their furniture designs.

Maurice Heaton (b. 1900), whose father, the stained glass artist Clement Heaton, emigrated to the United States from Switzerland in about 1910, produced a number of outstanding designs which stand out among American glass of the period. Like Marinot in France, Heaton was a studio artist who metamorphosed simple sheets of bubble-retaining glass into splendid modern abstractions by decorating them with geometric patterns of translucent enamels.

Among stained glass designs in the United States those of Frank Lloyd Wright stand out, including the boldly coloured, almost Mondrian-like windows he created for the Avery Coonley Playhouse in Riverside, Illinois. Many of Wright's stained glass pieces were executed by the Leerdam factory in the Netherlands.

Other decorative, architectural glass was made in great quantities in the United States in the 1920s and 1930s, much of it embellishing shop fronts, restaurants and cinemas, as well as the façades and interiors of Manhattan and Chicago skyscrapers.

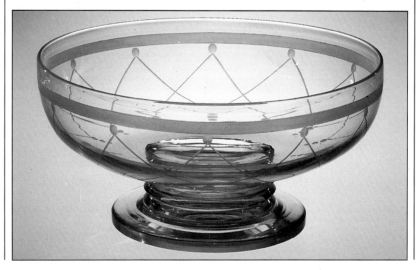

G LASS AND **L** IGHTING

The Art Deco period witnessed a profusion of decorative lighting devices, the inevitable result of the fairly recent discovery of electricity. They were sometimes adorned extravagantly in colourful, showy garb, sometimes more restrained – mostly in the United States – in streamlined, *moderne* dress. Lamps of all shapes and sizes – table and floor models, sconces and chandeliers – appeared in the modern interior, often as a subtle, subdued element, but at other times (as during the Art Nouveau period) as a highly visible, significant *objet d'art*.

BELOW Daum Frères designed this table lamp, its base and matching creamy shade of glass decorated with vertical ribs and squares on a rough, granular surface.

Modern lighting capitalized on metal and glass, which science had demonstrated to be the most efficient transmitters and reflectors of light. Instead of hiding the glass bulb between layers of silk and brocade, modern designers succeeded in investing the bare materials themselves with artistic qualities. The resulting designs made use of simple lines, angles, juxtaposed squares, circles and triangles, and were completely in harmony with the new style of interior decoration. The design and manufacture of decorative equipment for interior lighting became a vast area for experimentation and innovation. Designers and artisans from all areas of the decorative arts, and with every design orientation from traditionalism to Modernism, were drawn to the challenging new field of lighting design.

It was the French who created the widest range of decorative lighting devices. The glassmakers René Lalique, Daum Frères and Gabriel Argy-Rousseau, the metalworker Edgar Brandt, and numerous sculptors and furniture designers – Pierre Legrain, Pierre Chareau, Desny, Armand-Albert Rateau, Jean Goulden, Eileen Gray, Jean Lambert-Rucki among others – applied their creative skills to this new marriage of science and art. They designed glorious night lights, standard lamps, ceiling lights and chandeliers.

It was probably Maurice Dufrêne, a French furniture designer and interior decorator, who first had the idea of suspending basins of alabaster or glass from the ceiling by means of a simple cord. (This was an improvement over what was then being done in Austria and Germany, where designers had also adopted the use of cords, often criss-crossing

them into a decorative network.) René Lalique used this simple idea of a suspended basin as the point of departure for his extraordinarily successful lighting.

The lighting devices of René Lalique ran the gamut from sculptures to table lamps with beautiful crescent-shaped tops, and to ceiling, wall lights and chandeliers, with floral and geometric motifs. Even his automobile mascots could be fitted to light up. His *Grande boulle de gui* (literally, a large ball of mistletoe) comprised 10 pieces of convex glass moulded with a mistletoe design and attached to each other with metal rings to form a massive sphere. The quality of Lalique's glass and his varied, original, and always tasteful designs put him far ahead of others. His simplest designs consisted of shallow bowls in frosted or tinted glass; peach and yellow tones were favoured because they blended well with most décors and were flattering. These simple shapes were moulded in high relief with a variety of fruit and floral motifs, some quite true to nature, others stylized. As Lalique responded to more Modernist trends, he created strong, geometric forms for his hanging fixtures.

Lalique liked to play with the transmitted effects of light through glass, and experimented with ways in which it delineated forms which were either moulded as figures, cast in high relief, or moulded in intaglio. Strikingly effective, the concealed light source defined all the subtleties of the moulding to create an object that seemed to float in space. This was fully exploited in the *surtouts-de-table* that Lalique began to produce around 1925, comprising a thick slab of glass moulded in intaglio. When illuminated from within their bronze bases, the effect was

impressive, although not altogether practical, for they did not give off much light.

For other glass artisans who sought to create lighting with their own personal stamp, the major difficulty was to avoid repeating what Lalique had already done.

Ernest Sabino, who was one of Lalique's most successful competitors, favoured motifs of flowers and branches in intaglio and relief, and sought to vary his designs and compositions to produce something original. His firm took several stands in the Grand Palais at the 1925 Exposition, where it displayed numerous hanging fixtures and sconces in colourless pressed glass. For the occasion, Sabino designed everything himself, and the glass was pro-

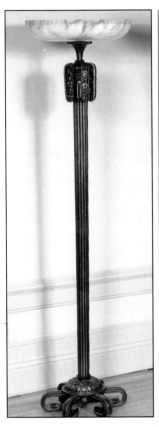

ABOVE Edgar Brandt: *Les Crosses*, wrought iron and alabaster, early 1920s.

RIGHT Georges Le Chevallier: table lamp in brushed aluminium, late 1920s. Like Chareau, Le Chevallier stressed the industrial, machine-made aspect of his fixtures by leaving their screws clearly visible.

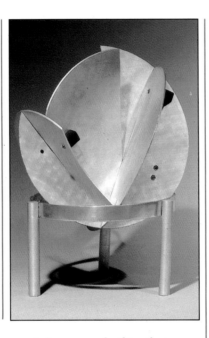

duced in his own workshops – a facility that gave him an edge over much of the competition because he did not have to rely on collaborators. Furthermore, his designs were meant for mass-production, which made the prices very attractive.

Simonet Frères was one of the oldest bronze houses in the Archives quarter of Paris. Their strong, solid reputation, earned through years of doing fine restorations, did not keep them from being among the first drawn into the currents of new design. Indeed, Albert Simonet was one of the first to realize that electricity required new designs for lighting, and not simple a reworking of gas and candle fixtures. In 1925, Simonet Frères completely overhauled their operations. Bronze became secondary, and they devoted their attention to the design of glass elements for lighting fixtures. They abandoned their earlier forms, and commissioned the sculptor Henri Dieupart to design sections of pressed glass, modern in concept, that would give off a flattering play of light from their surfaces.

Jacques Adnet and his brother Jean, who frequently worked together, were important figures in the Art Deco movement. Their designs for La Maîtrise and Saddier et fils were exhibited in the annual salons, and in 1928, Jacques was made director of La Compagnie des Arts Français, where he produced his own designs. He was in complete agreement with the philosophies of Le Corbusier,

and this orientation is clearly present in his lighting, which contains the simplest possible elements. Where others sought to hide the light source and create a diffusion, the Adnet brothers were bolder, and used the bare bulbs as their major design element, making their lighting among the most inventive and controversial of the period.

Perhaps the most popular lamps were the small table models, produced by Daum Frères and Schneider/Le Verre Français among others. They usually had mushroom-shaped shades topping round, cylindrical or oval vases and were made of either white or coloured glass with etched geometric motifs. In addition to the well-known French firms who turned out these decorative and practical pieces, there were numerous anonymous companies – French, Dutch, Czechoslovakian, German – who marketed them. The Bauhaus also designed functional lighting devices, including Marianne Brandt's revolutionary Kandem bedside lamp of 1928, which was the basis for many lamps in wide use today.

Jean Perzel, a designer who had studied painting and glassmaking in Munich and settled in Paris in 1910, specialized in lighting, not only creating wonderfully geometric shades, sconces, ceiling lamps and such, but also sensitively relating these objects and the light they emitted to their environment. Although Perzel's light fixtures were calculated to provide both direct and indirect lighting, he did not favour the kind of indirect lighting that eliminated planes and shadows, feeling that this effaced the life of the room. To avoid this, he carefully balanced the light reflected from the ceiling with the direct light coming from below. Perzel succeeded in making lighting a plastic element. His genius was in his ability to distribute light so that it seemed to have an almost tangible volume. His lamps, often of brass with frosted white or pink glass, had strong yet subtle angular forms; they were similar to those of Desny, devoid of the ornamentation which characterized other lamps of the period.

Foremost among the ornate lighting devices are the standard lamps of Armand-Albert Rateau and Edgar Brandt. One of Rateau's, made of green-patinated bronze, had tripod feet of birds echoed by a frame of avian heads which held the bulb at the top. The screens, vases and lamps that Brandt constructed were beautifully illuminated by the glasswork of Daum and sometimes Schneider. The famous 'Cobra' lamp, made predominantly of bronze, was in

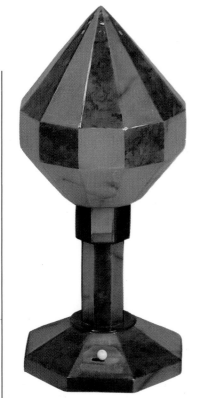

LEFT This 1920s table lamp is sheathed with mottled plastic, in two shades simulating tortoiseshell and horn. The chalice-like design is reminiscent of early Austrian pieces.

RIGHT This plastic table lamp comprises several pieces, in tones of cream and russet, which have been either fused together or sewn at the joint. The overall geometrics combine to create a smart – and inexpensive – 1920s accessory.

ABOVE Emile-Jacques Ruhlmann, the Parisian *ensemblier* known best for his furniture, designed this lighting sconce. The alabaster shade, with its subtle striations, is perched on a smart metal mount, its top dotted with silvery beads, its bottom gently fluted.

the shape of a tall, coiling cobra in whose neck nestled an etched-glass bowl by Daum. It could not only be bought in three sizes, but had a variety of coloured glass lampshades by Daum, enabling it to fit into the overall decorative and colour scheme of the client's home. The contrast of translucence and opacity was further heightened by the tactile contrast of solid metal supporting fragile glass. When Edgar Brandt manufactured doors and gates for specific settings such as the Paris shop for Paul Poiret, clear glass filled the spaces, so that the metalwork looked like sculpture suspended in air. When Brandt designed overhead lighting and chandeliers he would also draw on the talents and expertise of René Lalique.

The firm of Décoration Interieure Moderne – better known by its acronym, DIM – established itself as one of the major lighting studios in Paris, and sought out designers who were in sympathy with its design principles of clean, spare lines. DIM also undertook interior design, and it is ironic that René Joubert and Philippe Petit, heads of the firm, eventually eliminated all but concealed lighting in their interiors. A number of notable designers worked for DIM. Among them were the firm of Venini in Murano, Jean Prouvé, Gabriel Guévrékian and Le Chevallier.

Le Chevallier's work is often compared to that of Maison Desny. He too used flat planes of metal,

with no ornamentation to spoil the drama of form on form, but his pieces almost unfinished quality gives them the directness of seeming to be cut from the metal in a single burst of creative energy.

Jean Goulden's table lamps, usually of silvered metal and enamel, were quite sculptural and Cubist, while those of Jean Lambert-Rucki, although often also carved and sculptural, paid homage to tribal Africa with their stylized figures. Eileen Gray designed several lamps, including a standing model in lacquered wood with a parchment shade which she created for the 1923 *Salon des Artistes Décorateurs*. Both base and shade sport numerous jutting triangles and angles, making the creation both highly futuristic and extremely whimsical.

In the United States, many industrial designers directed their talents to lighting fixtures, among them Walter von Nessen, Raymond Loewy and Walter Dorwin Teague. Furniture/interior designers, such as Donald Deskey, Kem Weber and Gilbert Rohde, also produced table and standard lamps, or *torchères*, as did Frank Lloyd Wright. On the whole, American lamps were ultra-modern, streamlined and/or geometric, composed of contemporary materials – bakelite, Lucite, Formica, steel, brushed chromium and aluminium. Often reminscent of Jean Perzel's Parisian output, they tended to be primarily lighting devices – and 'decorative' only secondarily.

METALWORK

Adaptability and inventiveness flourished in Art Deco metalwork. Metal was often used on its own for gates and doors, but it could also be employed in conjunction with almost any of the other favoured materials. The history of Art Deco metalwork is also the history of changing materials. The 1920s was the period of wrought iron, bronze and copper. By the early 1930s these had not been completely replaced, but designers favoured the more modern aluminium, steel and chrome. The 1930s were remarkable, not for any single colour preference, but for the lack of any colour at all. Glass and shiny metals complemented each other; both were reflecting and anonymous, sparkling and transparent. The typical 1930s room had mirrored walls, with discreet metal borders, repeated in the bent metal furniture. It was stark, and ideally suited to university professors in pursuit of the pleasures of the mind. There were no distractions, except for their own reflections, twice or even 10 times at the corners where the mirrors met. Such ideas were a long way from those involved in the initial resurgence of metalcraft.

Art Deco metalwork was dominated by Parisian design, notably by Edgar Brandt, Jean Dunand and Jean Puiforcat. They worked in three entirely different manners, however, each producing distinctive metalwork which inspired designers in France, the rest of Europe and the United States.

Edgar Brandt (1880–1960) was an ironworker of immense talent and breadth who created jewellery, vases, lamps and firedogs, as well as grilles, doors, panels and screens. He often collaborated with architects and glassmakers, as at the 1925 Paris Exposition, where his several successful exhibits gained him worldwide recognition. His designs – also executed in copper, bronze, gold and silver – often combined animal and human forms with floral and/or geometric patterns. Many of his surfaces were hammered in a decorative manner, as that of a lovely bronze platter which featured seaweed and other marine motifs.

Jean Dunand (1877–1942) was a designer *extraordinaire* who trained first as a sculptor. He directed his talents to various mediums, but finally made his name as a lacquerworker, applying the coloured resin to wood and metal surfaces and creating jewellery, bookbindings, vases, tables, panels, screens and mantelpieces of the utmost beauty.

LEFT The pewter tobacco box is by Britons AR Emerson and AE Poulter. Its engraved floral motif and fluted knob are handsome *moderne* elements.

ABOVE The lacquerworker Jean Dunand created this slender copper vase c.1920–25. It has been gilded and patinated with refined geometric designs.

Jean Puiforcat (1897–1945) also worked in metal, and his stunning creations in silver and silvergilt, often with semiprecious stone and glass embellishments, occupy a unique place in Art Deco design. He and his work are described more fully in the section in this book on Silver and Jewellery.

The battle between a revamped French traditional approach to metalwork and the Modernist tendency was short-lived. It started and finished with Art Deco, which, for a brief moment, managed to contain both opposing forces. The Modernists, however, won the day.

WROUGHT IRON: EDGAR BRANDT

As wrought iron has few limitations beyond that of the craftsman's skill, it broke through the confines of use in one specific area. Art Deco metalwork pieces ranged from the intimacy of a commemorative

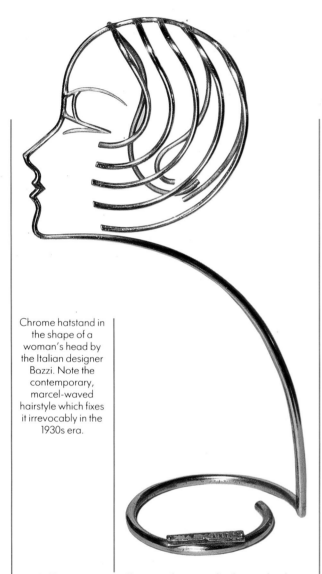

Chrome hatstand in the shape of a woman's head by the Italian designer Bazzi. Note the contemporary, marcel-waved hairstyle which fixes it irrevocably in the 1930s era.

ABOVE Radiator grille reproducing the exterior of the building in brass by Jacques Delamarre for the Chanin Building, New York, 1929.

medallion or a small mantelpiece clock, to the huge entrance gates for the *Exposition des Arts Décoratifs et Industriels*. Almost all these outstanding craftsmen/designers worked across this wide range, spreading their time and creativity between all the possible applications of the material.

New developments in technology made wrought iron indispensable where scientific innovation introduced into the home or building required decorative camouflage. Radiators begged to be covered, and wrought iron was ideal for this purpose because it neither obstructed the flow of heated air nor was adversely affected by it. Lift cages became decorative focuses in building lobbies, coordinated in design with railings and entrance doors to create an overall unity that was modern, practical and often stunning in its impact. The combination of wrought iron with other metals such as copper, silver, bronze, steel and aluminium expanded the opportunities for dramatic effects.

The movement now known as Art Deco was broadly defined by two predominant styles. The first and most strongly 'traditional' made extensive use of stylizations of nature: of birds, flowers and animals; natural phenomena such as clouds, waterfalls and sunbursts were subject to varying degrees of geometrification. An almost Mannerist elongation of proportions and an exaggeration of round volumes were also much in evidence, and there was a predilection for choosing animals and plants that naturally exhibited some of these qualities. Greyhounds, gazelles, pigeons and ripe fruit were among the motifs that came to be associated with the Art Deco style. After 1925, decorative wrought iron also began to reflect in its images the more simplified geometric lines of the 'rationalists' and sleek lines of machinery, aeroplanes and steamships. The beauty of the straight line had become the new aesthetic.

Edgar Brandt was born in Paris in 1880 and, through his father's involvement in an engineering

BELOW These wrought-iron gates by Edgar Brandt, date from c. 1929. They were once located at the entrance to a building on Paris's rue Geynemer designed by Michel Roux-Spitz. The cast-iron medallions centreing each of the gates depict faces which may represent night and day or summer and winter. Brandt's triumph at the 1925 Paris Exposition, for which he designed much of the ornamental ironwork, led to numerous commissions both in France and abroad.

firm, he very early on developed an interest in working with metal. Most of his early work came from direct commissions by architects, who needed metal fixtures for private houses and hotels. Brandt never lost that willingness to work with others, and his best work was almost always the result of direct collaboration. Many of his commissions demanded a highly developed sense of detail and the ability to work to a very strict set of limitations. At the same time as sets of monumental doors, or wrought-iron staircases for the liners *Paris*, *Ile de France* and *Normandie*, Brandt would be designing more mundane work: grilles for indoor heating, radiator covers and other everyday objects. Some of his finest work was with the glass expert Antoine Daum. His cobra standard lamp, the coiling serpent acting as foot, stem and holder for its Daum glass shade, is one of his most striking creations.

Brandt had a deep respect for the aesthetic and moral heritage of French art, and he saw it as his duty to keep France in the forefront of contemporary decorative design. He felt that industrial processes

ABOVE This wrought-iron mirror was designed by Edgar Brandt in the 1920s. The floral swag is a rococo device, but stylized in the Art Deco mode. The *pâte-de-verre* lampshades are by Gabriel Argy-Rousseau.

could be well used to serve this end, and he sought constantly to ally art with industry. Many artists, on the other hand, feared that the introduction of industrial techniques would lead to mass-production, which they felt would debase their art. Brandt found this fear groundless. It was his conviction that artists could only benefit from an understanding of the mysteries and difficulties of production and of the processes and techniques of the machines. He had himself served a long apprenticeship not only in wrought-iron work, but in silversmithing and jewellery, in which he had won prizes at the salons of the Société des Artistes Français. He was also on the juries of the Salon d'Automne and the Société des Artistes Décorateurs. A man of phenomenal drive and energy, he executed both his own designs and those of others.

Although already well known prior to 1925, it was Brandt's varied and extensive work at the 1925 Exposition that catapulted him to the forefront of his field. He was commissioned, with Ventre and Favier, to design the Porte d'Honneur for the Exposition, which they designed in collaboration with René Lalique and Henri Navarre.

The Porte d'Honneur was made of 'staff', an inexpensive alloy, for the cost of iron in a project of this size and impermanence was prohibitive. Part of the challenge was to make the 'staff' look as fine as the material which it imitated. It was a great success, as were the other commissions he did for the exhibition. In particular he was responsible for the acclaimed metal furniture and furnishings for the Ruhlmann Pavilion. Another vital exhibit for Brandt at the Exposition was his own pavilion, for which he designed an ensemble that included the spectacular and monumental five-panel screen *L'Oasis*, a highly refined fantasy of stylized flowers, foliage and fountains executed in brass and iron.

The Brandt *ensemble* led to his first major commission in the United States, for what is variously known as the Madison-Belmont Building or the Cheney Building, on the corner of Madison Avenue and 34th Street in Manhattan where the exterior metalwork is still in situ. Cheney Brothers, a fabric house that occupied several floors in the building, also invited him to design their showrooms. This gave him the impetus to open Ferrobrandt Inc. in New York. He expanded his operations in Paris at the same time, taking full advantage of all the publicity that evolved from his work at the Exposition.

LEFT Edgar Brandt: detail of the *Oasis* five-panel screen. The brass chevron panels, applied paper-thin by electrolysis, have mellowed with age to their present golden hue.

Brandt's work was successful because he understood the delicate balance between the monumental and the decorative. His talent for balancing these two elements added great style to modern decoration. He was sometimes criticized for his use of industrial techniques, but his work was always redeemed by the beauty of the material, his meticulous attention to detail, and especially for the fine, finished appearance of his pieces. This finish was achieved by one of the industrial techniques that he perfected – oxyacetylene welding, which is all but invisible. In joining decorative elements, Brandt used hidden screws and bolts so that the eye was never distracted by details of construction.

Brandt's most popular designs by far featured attractive human and animal forms, usually in openwork floral or foliated surrounds. He also made small andirons in the shape of cobras and jardinières with cobra handles. The snake, taken from Egyptian art, was a popular Art Deco subject also used by Jean Dunand, René Lalique, François-Emile Décorchement and others.

Brandt exploited the tensile strengths of the material he used when designing furniture. Console tables, instead of standing solidly on four squat legs, could be treated more as open sculptures. Legs could be opened out with delicate filigree mouldings

ABOVE Classical volutes figure on this hammered wrought-iron urn by Edgar Brandt, which measures some 20in (50cm) across. Although on first glance deceptively simple-looking, the urn shows impeccable craftsmanship; the soft, ribbony quality of the bent metal could be achieved only by the most skilful of metalsmiths.

CENTRE Stone and wrought-iron column supporting a glass vase and a wrought-iron vase by Edgar Brandt and Daum, Nancy.

of fans and thistles filling the gaps, yet still have enough strength to support the heavy weight of a thick slab of marble. Fire screens and doors could be reinterpreted to look almost like drawings suspended in air. Curling lines and leaves in door fronts seemed exquisitely delicate but had a strength and solidity fit for the purpose. Brandt also collaborated with Henri Favier on a series of screens for which he provided the framework.

Another reason for the great success of Brandt's designs was his understanding of the relationship of each piece within an ensemble – such as a grille, staircase or chandelier – to the whole. Other objects – trays, paper-knives, pendants, brooches and small items of jewellery – are testimony to the same inventiveness and sureness of hand as his more monumental works.

Other French metalworkers included Raymond Subes, Paul Kiss, Armand-Albert Rateau (whose work is treated in the Furniture section), Louis Sognot and Nics Frères. Their console tables, lighting fixtures, grilles, doors and screens were beautifully executed and featured various motifs from the Art Deco repertory. Pierre-Paul Montagnac and Gaston-Etienne le Bourgeois, a painter and a sculptor respectively, successfully allied modernity and tradition in wrought-iron design. But in the end it was Brandt's *oeuvre* which set the standard not only for French but for other European and American ironwork as well.

Raymond Subes was second only to Brandt in the scope and quality of his work. In 1919, at a relatively young age, he was appointed successor to Emile Robert as the director of the firm of Borderel et Robert.

Subes endeavoured to create an impression of richness and elegance in his work, but with great simplicity of technique. This aim was completely in accord with the economic and social conditions of the time, for (as now) the public demanded the maximum effect for the lowest price. Subes' solution was similar to that arrived at by Edgar Brandt: the marriage of artistic design with industrial technique. He found through his research that industrial techniques could be used with very satisfactory results both in furniture and more massive architectural works. This philosophy journeyed a long way from that of his mentor, Emile Robert, who had stubbornly scorned the use of anything but hand-tools.

Subes devoted a great deal of time to the technical problems of his trade: how to produce the finest work, keep costs within reason, and yet maintain artistic integrity. In particular he aimed much of his research to the uses of sheet steel, which could be formed by machine into any desired shape. Subes was also ingenious at using flat iron pieces to create works in series.

The intelligent use of machines allowed Subes to produce pieces as cheaply as by casting. At the same time he understood that unique pieces must still be produced by hand, and he himself often took up the hammer to create powerful bas-reliefs for a door. A new metalwork had been born which allowed for production in series, and also made possible works too monumental to be executed at the forge.

Paul Kiss (sometimes spelled Kis) was born in Rumania and went to Paris to study, where he eventually became a naturalized Frenchman. His work explored the lyrical and expressive qualities that he saw in wrought iron, but was quite different in character from that of Edgar Brandt, with whom he collaborated early in his career. He exhibited a comprehensive range of wrought-iron furniture and lighting at the salons of the Société des Artistes Décorateurs and the Société des Artistes Français.

Jules and Michel Nics were Hungarian-born brothers who worked in Paris under the name of Nics Frères, producing a complete range of decorative ironwork from furniture to architectural decoration. Their work was characterized by a highly conspicuous *martelé* (hand-hammered) decorative finish and a rather excessive use of naturalistic forms even after these had gone out of fashion. They rejected as heresy die-stamping and file work, and affirmed themselves as masters of the hammer, proud of their ability to make any piece by hand in a technique comparable to the finest artisans of the past.

Although the United States lagged behind France in its adoption of metalwork for interiors, the influence of the 1925 Paris Exposition and the opening of Edgar Brandt's New York office stimulated a taste for this highly versatile area of the decorative arts. By the late 1920s it had become immensely popular, and there were a number of American designers and craftspeople who produced a great variety of both interior and exterior ironwork.

Oscar Bach was perhaps the only craftsman in this field who could match the technical mastery of the great French ironworkers. Born in Germany, he enjoyed a successful career there before coming to the United States in 1914. He opened a studio in New York, where he was soon flooded with private and commercial commissions. Proficient in many metals and styles of metalwork, he used copper,

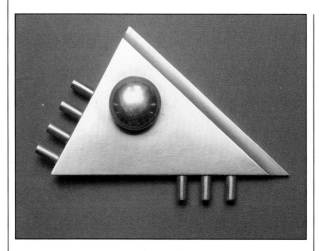

aluminium, bronze, chrome, and nickel silver to provide colour and textural contrast in the decorative elements he designed. His contribution to many of New York's most outstanding buildings was immeasurable.

William Hunt Diederich emigrated to the United States from Hungary when he was 15, and took up residence in Boston with his grandfather, William Morris Hunt, who was an artist. Diederich was a successful designer in several areas, but was particularly attracted to metalwork. His simple two-dimensional figures and animals seem snipped out of the iron. With their sharp, jagged edges and minimal surface decoration, they have a lively vitality that reflects their creator's personality and love of animal subjects.

OTHER ARTISTS, **O**THER MATERIALS

Although Brandt was clearly the leader of the more traditional metalworkers, men like Subes, Adnet, Kiss, Rateau and Szabo produced work of great beauty. The most eccentric of this group by far was Armand Albert Rateau. He constructed a bronze chaise longue for Jeanne Lanvin's boudoir that rested, almost comically, on the backs of four deer. A washstand and mirror was modelled from two peacocks standing back to back, their two heads holding the mirror. With metal, anything was possible, but the bizarre examples of Rateau were way out of keeping with the clean and practical furniture of Le Corbusier or the Irish designer Eileen Gray.

Elegance was not just the domain of the intricate foliage of a Brandt screen, a Kiss cabinet, or a Subes mantelpiece clock: it could be seen to even greater effect in an oak table top supported by just two sheets of bent metal by Louis Sognot. It was minimal, reduced to the contrast between the two materials used; the shiny cold metal, and the rich patina and grain of the wood.

There were also various Art Deco medallists working in silver, bronze and other metals, not only in France, but in England, Germany and the United States. The Hungarian-born Tony Szirmai, who was based in Paris, specialized in commemorative pieces. Pierre Turin produced bronze, copper and silvered-metal plaques, often octagonal, which featured stylized figures and flowers. André Lavrillier created a handsome medal depicting Leda and the Swan, one of which is presently on exhibition in the British Museum.

At the Bauhaus, Wilhelm Wagenfeld, architect and industrial designer, was associated with the metal workshop from 1922 to about 1931, when he left to work with glass and ceramics. He fashioned a hammered-copper coffee machine in 1923 which is so futuristic in appearance that it could be a prototype for a spaceman's helmet.

Marianne Brandt (b.1893) of the Bauhaus is perhaps the best-known German metalworker. Surprisingly, she turned her supreme design skills to rather mundane objects, such as ashtrays, shaving mirrors and cooking utensils. The most celebrated is her Kandem bedside lamp, which, with its push-button switch and adjustable reflector/shade, is the forerunner of so many lamps today.

ABOVE FAR LEFT
Georges Fouquet, one of Paris's foremost jewellers, fashioned this gold brooch. Many of his creations, with their crisp geometric styling, displayed a Machine-Age sensibility far removed from his early Art Nouveau-period works.

ABOVE LEFT This wrought-iron table with a top of grey granite is attributed to Raymond Subes who, like Edgar Brandt, served an apprenticeship with the ironworker Emile Robert. Like Brandt, he also produced a variety of works for the 1925 Paris Exposition.

The Chase Brass & Copper Company in Water-bury, Connecticut, which employed famous as well as obscure designers, produced a wide range of useful ware known for their 'beautility' – cigarette boxes, ashtrays, cocktail shakers, wine coolers, kitchen utensils, candlesticks, vases. Their designs were wonderfully *moderne*, architectonic, Cubist and crisp. A bud vase of 1936, one of which is in New York's Metropolitan Museum of Art, consists of four chrome pipes attached to each other at uneven angles and resting on a circular base.

Kem Weber (1889–1963) was born in Berlin, but settled in California by the 1920s. His designs for clocks (including digital ones in the 1930s!), lamps, tea and coffee sets and furniture were sleekly *moderne* but wholly functional. Even the smallest of items, like a stepped clock case of brass and chromed metal, was impeccably designed, undeniably Machine Age. Weber was also a voracious writer on modern design, publishing several thoughtful articles in contemporary journals.

Large-scale metal works in America – gates, architectural elements and such – were much influenced by the Parisian designs of Edgar Brandt, Subes and other *ferronniers*. Brandt himself opened a New York outlet in 1925, Ferrobrandt, and exhibited widely in the United States. The impact of his work can be clearly discerned on the designers at the Rose Iron Works in Cleveland, Ohio, whose screens and tables are blatant imitations.

Many American metalworkers were engaged in gigantic architectural projects for which they often turned to materials other than the traditional iron, bronze, brass and copper. Aluminium, chromium,

ABOVE Rustic 1920s marriage between glass and wrought iron. The wrought ironwork is by Majorelle and the glass bowl by the firm of Daum, Nancy.

LEFT William Hunt Diederich: candelabrum, wrought iron, 1920s. Diederich applied the same sharp silhouetted imagery to his work in other media, especially ceramics.

ABOVE Paul Kiss: wrought-iron gate with gilt-bronze applications, about 1926.

BELOW Although these sunburst-patterned compacts look precious, they are examples of the inexpensive enamelled- and paste-encrusted metal variety. The one on the left is English, by Stratton, and the rectangular one by Elizabeth Arden.

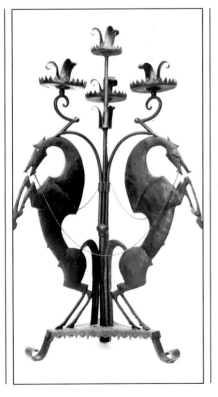

ABOVE RIGHT Jean
Dunand: group of
lacquered objects,
all but one with
coquille d'oeuf
applications, 1920s.

FAR RIGHT This box
features graceful
gazelles leaping
amid stylized leafy
forms. Deer,
gazelles, elands,
stags and various
other *biches* (does),
as they were
collectively called,
appeared on a
wide variety of Art
Deco objects,
especially
metalwork. This
yellow-metal
container is actually
a powder compact-
and-cigarette case,
and was made by
the Elgin American
firm in Illinois.

cadmium and 'Monel' metal (a nickel-copper alloy), among others, all came into play, sometimes used as thin sheetings (or plates) over another metal. Numerous components of New York skyscrapers — elevators, mail boxes, doors, etc — were made of these new metals, used either on their own or in combination with other materials. Some of these (often anonymous) creations, with their geometric, floral and figural grillework, have come to be considered the most outstanding examples of Art Deco in the United States. Distinguished examples are to be found in New York's Chanin and Daily News buildings, as well as in countless other structures throughout the country.

D INANDERIE

Work in non-precious metals is called *dinanderie*, a term which derives from the Flemish town of Dinant, where quantities of brassware were made during the Middle Ages. Many of the techniques of metal incrustation were of ancient origin, and by returning to old traditions and applying them in a new way, 20th-century artists were able to produce works of a singular vitality.

The interest in Japanese art that began in the late 19th century had much to do with the resurgence of interest in *dinanderie* and lacquer. Jean Dunand, who was to become the most important artist to work

in these techniques, was introduced to the medium by the Japanese lacquerer, Sougawara, who approached him with a metalwork problem. Dunand agreed to help if Sougawara would in return teach him the techniques of lacquer work, and this was to have a profound effect on his life and career. He quickly mastered the technique, and his skills brought him so many important commissions that he had to extend his *atelier* and was soon employing as many as a hundred people. Dunand's fascination with these techniques produced some of the most extraordinary objects of his or any other time.

Obviously the lacquer had to be applied to a surface, and Dunand began with vases, all made by hand in the *dinanderie* technique. His earliest vases derived their shape from gourds and other vegetal forms, and he often worked the surfaces with repoussé, chiselling, patinas of browns and greens, and inlays of other metals either to highlight the naturalistic form or to produce organically inspired motifs such as scales and peacock feathers. His forms gradually became simpler and his designs more geometric, relying on surface ornamentation and applied metal for effect; some of his later vases were little more than spheres or cones of colour.

Jean Goulden (1878–1947) created clocks, lamps, boxes and other *objets* in metal, often embellished with coloured enamelling, a process he learned from Dunand, with whom he sometimes collaborated. His avant-garde, highly angular works often resembled Cubist and Constructivist sculpture.

Camille Fauré (1872–1956) also worked with enamel on metal, but, unlike Goulden's pieces, Fauré's vessels were dominated by the coloured enamel, sometimes in stylized-floral designs, but more often in geometric configurations in the style of abstract paintings. He worked in Limoges for over 50 years.

Claudius Linossier was a master of the art of *dinanderie* whose inspiration flowed from a different source. He was an apprentice metalworker in his native Lyons when only 13 years of age, and mastered embossing, engraving, enamelling, metal incrustation, repoussé and all the other metalwork tech-niques. The outstanding element of Linossier's work is his use of metal incrustation. He was a great admirer of Etruscan pottery, and this served as a departure-point for his designs, painstakingly executed in the techniques of metal incrustation. He loved the subtle play of one tone against another, and as silver and copper provided only a limited palette he began to develop his own alloys, using ingots he cast himself, and fashioning thin plaquettes that he graded by tone.

Another silversmith who on occasion worked in base metals, often with silver inlays, was Jean Serrière. His objects, mainly trays and bowls, are massive in feeling and of extremely simple design, enlivened by traces of the hand work that formed them. Paul-Louis Mergier, an aeronautical engineer who painted, designed and made furniture, also found time for *dinanderie* work. His vases are simple in form, and his preferred subjects were stylized figures and animals defined by various patinas, inlaid silver and lacquer often executed by the well-known Japanese artist Hamanaka.

Maurice Daurat was an artist who chose to work in pewter. Pewter is a soft metal, ductile and extremely supple, and Daurat exploited its almost flesh-like surface and its potential for sombre shadows and irregular reflections of light from hammer marks, finding that these imparted a warmth more appealing than the cold gleam of silver. His designs became increasingly refined, until they were almost a series of exercises in form and simplicity. His minimal concessions to ornament were a ring of beads at the base or an interestingly designed handle. He intended his pieces to be admired rather than used, and in fact their very weight often rendered them impractical, rather flying in the face of Modernist theories of functionalism.

SILVER
AND
JEWELLERY

Since time immemorial, rare and precious materials have symbolized luxury, gold and silver taking pride of place among them. Gold, because of its expense and weight, was impractical for making any but the smallest useful objects, such as snuff-boxes; silver-gilt, also known as *vermeil*, was far more practical, and gave a similar look to gold. Silver shares many of gold's desirable qualities, being soft and easily worked and capable of being cut and hammered or cast into an infinite variety of shapes.

Since the invention of silverplating in the mid-19th century, the required look could be achieved for a less discerning audience at a more attractive price. Apart from the advantage that electroplating gave to the trade, high quality silverwork is a skill that seems never to have suffered.

There is a great variety of ways of working silver – the most painstaking, but also for many the most satisfactory, is hand-raising which is too time-consuming and cost-intensive to be practical for commercial production. Successful alternatives include spinning, stamping and casting, all of which had been greatly improved upon by early 20th-century technology, and worked well with the spare, uncluttered lines of Art Deco silver design.

Because of its colour, silver is sometimes described as a 'dry' material, and to give it life without the use of surface ornament the silversmith had to rely on an interplay of light, shadow and reflection created by contrasting planes and curves. Another way of relieving the soberness of form and colour was to incorporate semi-precious stones, rare woods, ivory and horn, and towards the 1930s gilded sections and thin plates of gold soldered to or inlaid into the surface were added to the repertoire. These materials, when used with restraint so that they did not over-

ABOVE: Stylish but somehow impractical cubist tea set in silver from the 1930s.

RIGHT Jean Puiforcat, who created this silver and jade soup tureen was France's foremost silversmith in the Art Deco period. His handsome, classic pieces were fashioned in accordance with his motto *Le beau dans l'utile* (Beauty in the useful), and his strict adherence to the Platonic ideal is shown by the perfect proportions and geometry of his work.

LEFT Examples from a discreetly designed, understated and highly functional silver cutlery service by the Art Deco genius Jean Puiforcat.

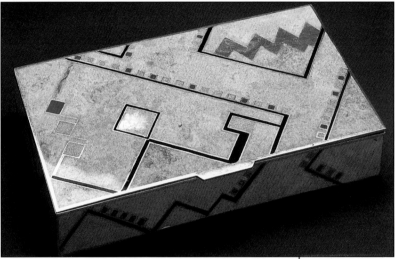

whelm the balance and purity of the design, added warmth, richness and textural contrast.

Items of luxury created solely to be admired need only concern themselves with aesthetics, but articles intended for use must respond to practical considerations as well. Silversmiths who sought to modernize silver design quickly realized the difficulties presented by drastic modifications of traditional forms which served their purpose well – styles change, but human bodies do not, and we must still grasp by handles, pour from spouts and cut with knives.

The Art Deco silversmith, who disdained influence from the past and relied only on creative inspiration, had to approach these technical problems in a new way. When designing a teapot he had to forget everything he knew about teapots and think instead about how to contain the greatest quantity of liquid in the smallest volume, how to facilitate pouring out at any angle, and how to unify the design so that it combined practicality with elegance.

The greatest of all the silversmiths was Jean Puiforcat who, along with Ruhlmann and Lalique, will be remembered not just as a practitioner of the Art Deco style, but as a true master of his respective crafts. Puiforcat, Georg Jensen, the Danish silversmith, and the American Kem Weber, each in their own way, extended the craft of silversmithing, and the language of Art Deco.

Puiforcat learnt his trade at his father's workshop; through Art Nouveau on to Art Deco, he rapidly outgrew him. The precursors to Puiforcat's

mature style were Josef Hoffmann and the other members of the Wiener Werkstätte. He adopted their example of radical austerity and perfected it into a new sensuous simplicity. After having seen the beauty and lustre of a plain sheet of silver, it is difficult to imagine that anything could improve it. Puiforcat recognized this, but also saw that the minimum of sophisticated detailing in another element could enhance the material's outstanding beauty through the power of contrast. The best examples of this were also the most minimal. Puiforcat produced dish after dish that was highlighted just by thick ivory handles, an ebony knob, or a ring-pull made from pale jade. The result was luxurious, made doubly so by the fact that the materials themselves seemed to do all the work; only seemed, because it was Puiforcat's inherent sense of the correctness of form that made it all possible. He was not just a craftsman but also a highly sensitive aesthete; he believed that, ultimately, some forms are right and others wrong. With his work it is possible to sense that he, above all the other contemporary designers, came the closest to that elusive goal which totally harmonizes form and function.

Other important craftsmen in silver were promoted in Paris by Christofle goldsmiths, who encouraged, among others, the talents of Cazes, and Süe, of the Süe et Mare workshops. Two outstanding examples in particular are the ice-bucket and champagne cooler modelled by Luc Lanel for the *Normandie*. They are not only superbly functional; they are, quite simply, right.

ABOVE A lively but spare geometric pattern has been enamelled onto this box by Jean Goulden. The zigzag, or lightning bolt, pattern is a common Art Deco device, as is the dentate row of squares, which here are painted in green and blue. Goulden gave up medicine to pursue a career in enamelling, a technique he learned from his friend and sometime collaborator Jean Dunand.

S ILVER IN **E** UROPE

As we have already seen, in France the art of the silversmith was dominated by the great Jean Puiforcat. He was born into a family of goldsmiths, beginning as an apprentice in their workshop and later studying sculpture. He first exhibited in 1922, and as the years went on his designs became pure geometric statements, devoid of nearly all decoration. He worked with silver in an attempt to attain a Platonic ideal of form through mathematical harmony and geometry. Gifted with a powerful originality, Puiforcat concerned himself with rejuvenating silver design, which had long been over-ornamented in response to the clients' love of ostentation and the silversmiths' desire to display their technical virtuosity. His elegant and simple designs proved that figures, flowers, chasing, repoussé and all the traditional embellishments could be eliminated without sacrificing either beauty or luxury.

His 1920s tea sets, dishes and bowls, which often included ivory finials, jade handles and the like, gave way by 1930 to purer, sleeker shapes – bold statements of form and volume with only the occasional touch of ice-green or salmon-pink glass, wood or crystal. Puiforcat's later works, amongst them silver *objets* for the liner *Normandie*, could also appear futuristic – a covered candy dish resembling a shiny UFO, for instance, or a cylindrical vase with a crenellated relief design.

The name Christofle is almost synonymous with silverplate in France. The firm was founded in 1839 by Charles Christofle, who invested his entire personal fortune plus money borrowed from friends to buy up the existing French patents for electroplating. By 1859 the firm employed 1,500 people. Christofle made a fortune and was awarded the Cross of the Légion d'Honneur. He also won high awards at the Paris exhibitions in 1839, 1844, 1849 and 1868, and received commissions from Napoleon III, the Empress Eugènie and the city of Paris. His nephew, Henri Bouilhet, was aggressive in marketing abroad, and the firm's work was shown in London, Vienna and Philadelphia. They were so proud of the quality of their production that they stamped their goods with the weight of silver used. Christofle produced every conceivable article of both utilitarian and decorative silverplate many of their pieces in the

1920s were designed by such notable artists as Gio Ponti, Maurice Daurat, Luc Lanel and Christian Fjerdingstad, among others. The company still flourishes today, and their flatware pattern *Baguette*, first produced in 1861, has remained one of the best-selling designs in Europe.

It is human nature to look for visual analogies in an artist's work, and because some of Jean Tétard's forms resembled the prow of a boat or the sleek lines of an automobile, it was concluded – wrongly – that he was inspired by boats and cars. In fact, Tétard tried to keep his mind free of pre-conceived ideas, and let the design flow according to his logic. A base, for instance, would enlarge to become the foot; the top, projecting at a sharp angle, would become the spout; and the rear would narrow and rise up on itself to become the handle. Tétard's teapots were not just cases with handles and spouts, they were the very essence of teapots.

Tétard was a latecomer to the field of silver, but the pieces he presented at the Salon d'Automne were audacious in their originality and of superb workmanship. He had abandoned simple geometric shapes and was fascinated by the challenge of more complex flattened forms made of two identical sections joined by a flat piece at the front. These designs required a high degree of technical skill but freed him from the restrictions of more conventional forms. Brief experimentation with surface decoration led him to abandon the idea immediately: his only concessions to ornament were lovely sculptured handles of rare woods that seemed to grow out of the silver.

ABOVE A beautifully sympathetic juxtaposition of silver and ivory in this tea service by the master craftsman Jean Puiforcat. The spouts and handles are reminiscent of the ocean liners of that age.

RIGHT English silversmiths in the Art Deco era wrought stylish, if conservative, pieces; some, however, sported the occasional geometric motif. At right are four round boxes by HG Murphy, each topped by a stylish finial; a cigarette box by CJ Shiner, and a nielloed bowl by Bernard Cuzner, all from the early 1930s.

LEFT Jean Puiforcat fashioned the seven-piece silver and ivory tea service c.1930. Paris's premier silversmith often embellished his precious-metal work with semiprecious materials, such as ivory, jade and lapis lazuli, as well as with more common materials like wood and glass. The attention Puiforcat paid to the geometric detailing of his pieces can be seen on the subtly fluted sides of the six vessels.

He finally set up his own company in Paris.

There was a ready market in France for fine silverware, and many smaller houses also flourished, among them Cardeilhac, Keller, Fouquet-Lapar, Chapuis, Linzler and Ravinet-d'Enfert, all of which produced quality articles. Boin-Taburet created elegant objects that, while traditional in style, showed a strong oriental influence, often incorporating jade carvings and wood sections inlaid with semi-precious materials in the Japanese manner.

Georg Jensen (1866–1935), although he was a Dane and worked in his native land, exerted much influence on Parisian Art Deco, as he had previously done on Art Nouveau. Not only were his wares shown to great acclaim at the 1925 Paris Exposition, but he was also admired and imitated by artists of the calibre of Puiforcat. He opened shops in Paris in 1919, London in 1920 and New York in 1923, the last having a marked influence on silver design in America. He himself often hand-worked his elegant and refined vessels – with hammered and chased surfaces and such decorative details as silver beads, leaves and openwork stems.

In Britain, many established silver firms employed designers who created works in the *moderne* style. Bernard Cuzner (1877–1956) worked in Birmingham and, although grounded in the Arts and Crafts tradition, his pieces – boxes, bowls, etc – in the 1920s and 1930s included those with stylized floral and geometric motifs. The Scot J Leslie Auld (b1914), who headed the silversmithing department at the Glasgow School of Art, designed among other things, commemorative works with Viennese and high-style French overtones, one of which he made for the 1939–40 World's Fair in New York.

 S ILVER IN THE **U** NITED STATES

The United States was chock-a-block with mass-produced and hand-crafted metalwork, as well as with precious objects made of silver. The latter were based primarily on European design, but to an extent less influenced by European styles than other areas of the decorative arts, although Puiforcat and other major designers exhibited their work at the Metropolitan Museum of Art, New York, in 1926 and 1928. Their designs were admired, but the conservative attitude towards silver design remained – silver,

being something passed down from generation to generation, hinted at inherited wealth, and most silver design was intended as 'instant heirlooms'.

As in France and Britain, established silver firms hired talented designers. The Danish Erik Magnussen (1884–1961), for instance, worked, among others, for the Gorham Manufacturing Company in Rhode Island. Gorham, an important name in American silver, was under duress both financially and stylistically in the period following

LEFT German-born Peter Müller-Munk, who emigrated to the United States in 1926, designed this silver-plated pitcher *Normandie.*

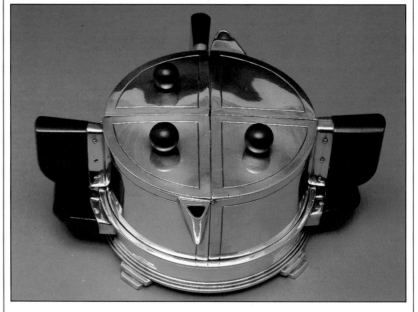

ABOVE This handsome silver-plated metal and ebony tea service was designed by Gilbert Rohde for Internationl Silver in Connecticut; it was made by the Wilcox Plate Co.

FAR LEFT
Commemorative silverware was a popular souvenir in the 1920s and 30s. Here are four spoons from a set of 12 celebrating the 1939 New York World's Fair. The architectural theme of the Fair, the Trylon and Perisphere, appears at the top of each handle, and the different exhibition buildings on the bowls. The spoons are silver-plated, and were made by the Wm Rogers Mfg Co., which was connected with International Silver of Meriden, Connecticut.

LEFT The designer of this lovely enamelled metal powder compact is unknown; it was made for the American cosmetics firm Richard Hudnut. Its incised design, of a stylized Egyptian lotus, is simple yet stylish – but for its mundane materials, it could have been designed by a skilful silversmith.

World War I; indeed 1920 was the worst year in their history. The situation improved in 1923, when Edward Mayo came to head the firm. Gorham's chief designer, William Codman, rejected all aspects of 'modern' silver design, and Mayo may have attempted to inspire Gorham by hiring Erik Magnussen, who worked for the firm from 1925 until 1929. Codman continued to design silver in various academic and revival forms, but Magnussen produced contemporary designs that took their inspiration from Constructivism, Cubism and the skyscraper.

His output was sometimes fairly restrained and classic, sometimes exuberantly *moderne*. He produced a covered cup in silver and ivory which is quite Jensen-like; at the other extreme, he created a burnished-silver coffee service with gilt and oxidized angular panels, entitled *The Lights and Shadows of Manhattan*, which is bold, witty and architectural in form. Among his other audacious – possibly rather extreme – designs for Gorham were the serving pieces, similarly architectonic in inspiration, which caused considerable controversy. They were also much imitated, most notably by two *Skyscraper* tea services in nickel-plate produced by Bernard Rice's Sons, Inc. for Apollo and skyscraper-inspired tea services by the Middletown Silver Company and the Wilcox Silver Plate Company, both in Connecticut. Norman Bel Geddes designed a *Skyscraper* cocktail set and a *Manhattan* serving tray, but these were in a restrained, linear design that was almost Scandinavian in feeling; in fact Scandinavian design was more successful than French in the United States, and Magnussen's subsequent work was considerably more conservative.

Tiffany & Co, one of the largest and most prestigious showcases for fine silver, executed few pieces that incorporated contemporary design trends, but even these did not make an appearance until the 1930s, and in the main they continued to produce fine, traditional silver for a wealthy and conservative clientele. Several of their attractive Art Deco designs, principally the work of AL Barney, were exhibited at the 1939 World's Fair, but in the early 1920s Tiffany & Co was more interested in the designs of 18th-century masters such as Paul Revere than those of Jean Puiforcat.

Unlike many American silver companies whose success was based on traditional designs, International Silver of Meriden, Connecticut, hired outside designers such as Gilbert Rohde, Eliel Saarinen and Gene Theobald to design a wide range of hollow- and flatware in silver, silverplate and pewter that reflected new trends in the decorative arts.

One of the most noteworthy silversmiths working independently in the United States during the 1930s and 1940s was the German-born Peter Müller-Munk. After coming to New York in 1926, he worked briefly for Tiffany before setting up his own studio in 1927. His designs were modern without being extreme, and reflected a European sophistication that attracted many private clients. Müller-Munk produced wonderful silver designs for many years (his epony-mous industrial-design firm still exists). Essentially simple and neo-classical, but with subtle tinges of modernism, his works were supremely crafted. A rectilinear silver tea and coffee service in the Metro-politan Museum of Art has ivory handles that resemble tusks, and is engraved with linear patterns reminiscent of Mayan or Aztec motifs. Other objects, although more rounded and traditional, always contain some unique, modern touch – a wavy gold line, an exaggerated spout, an architectonic pedestal.

O BJETS D'ART **A** ND JEWELLERY

Jewellery and *objets d'art* are two closely linked fields, and several jewellers saw artistic possibilities in larger objects. Jean Despres, for instance, made silver-plated or pewter bowls, boxes, tureens and flatware, starkly simple, almost brutal, in design, with heavily hammered surfaces and boldly hewn bolts and rivets. Gérard Sandoz produced a small number of distinctive objects often incorporating lizard skin, *galuchat* and ivory, and the American designer William Spratling designed small objects characterized by a primitive elegance. Cartier, Van Cleef & Arpels, Marchak, Mellerio, Tiffany and, in fact, all of the major jewellery houses produced an amazing variety of *objets d'art*, some of which are really more jewellery than object, with elements carved in semiprecious stones set in silver and gold often elaborately lacquered. Influenced by Chinese, Japanese, Persian and medieval art, these *objets d'art* combined coloured gemstones, precious stones, marcasite, enamel and lacquer. The small cigarette-cases designed by Gérard Sandoz introduced a further type of decoration in its use of crushed *coquille d'oeuf*. Whether a vanity case, cigarette-case, com-

pact, lighter, lipstick case, mirror or handbag, each item was intended as a miniature work of art. Cartier's famous mystery clocks are perhaps the most extreme examples.

France was on the whole less dominant in the area of *objets d'art* than in other arts during the Art Deco period; some extraordinary work was being done throughout Europe in this field. In Brussels, Marcel Wolfers, son of the Art Nouveau jeweller and silversmith Philippe Wolfers, became as famous as his father. Like Puiforcat, he studied sculpture while working in his father's *atelier*, and also mastered the techniques of enamelling and stone carving. He was fascinated by Chinese decorative techniques and used them extensively in his work. In England, Charles Boyton produced many interesting articles,

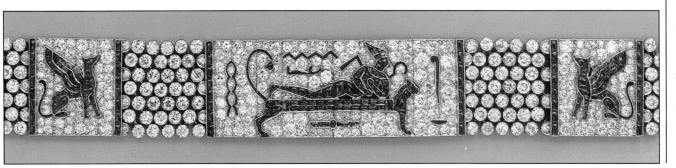

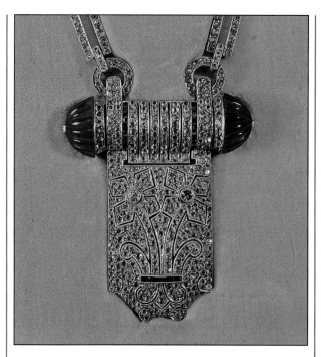

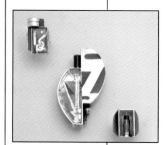

elegantly geometric in design. But some of the most exciting designs were produced in Germany by Bauhaus designers – Marianne Brandt, Christian Dell, Wilhelm Wagenfeld, Wolfgang Tümpel and Otto Rittweger – and by Bauhaus-influenced designers, such as Theodore Wendte and Emmy Roth.

Denmark's Georg Jensen was a major figure in 20th-century silver. Through the efforts of Jensen and his colleague, the painter Johan Rohde, Scandinavian modern silver came to be a practical realization of the ideals of William Morris and the British Arts and Crafts Movement. Jensen and Rohde did much of the firm's designing, but they also hired a number of distinguished artists to design for them. One of the most important was Harald Nielsen, who joined the firm in 1909 and brought with him a functional style derived from the Bauhaus. Two decades later, in the 1930s, their most influential designer was Sigvard Bernadotte, son of the King of Sweden, whose hard-edged pieces were often characterized by incised parallel lines.

Jewellery is one of the most exciting disciplines of the 1920–30 era. The Art Nouveau movement freed jewellery design from the antiquated influences of the 19th century. Art Deco took this evolution a step further, introducing geometrical forms and brilliant colour schemes. All of the major jewellery

houses, both in Europe and the United States, embraced the new style to some degree, but it was due primarily to Parisian artist-jewellers, such as Jean Fouquet and Raymond Templier, that jewellery design became an art form.

The style which later became known as Art Deco traces its origins to the period before World War I. In the first decade of the 20th century many factors caused an abrupt change in fashion. The couturier Paul Poiret, for example, revolutionized dress design, freeing the female figure from constricting layers of clothing. Serge Diaghilev's performances of the Ballets Russes in Paris in 1909 and in the United States in 1916, provided another influence, both through its introduction of bright colours into the drab world of fashion, and its emphasis on the Orient. New art movements, such as Cubism, Futurism and Neo-plasticism, helped further to create a new vernacular for art, which in turn initiated new concepts of jewellery design that were taken up with renewed interest after World War I.

The abstract qualities of Art Deco jewellery can be traced to various avant-garde art movements in the first decade of the 20th century. Picasso's *Demoiselles d'Avignon*, painted in 1907, launched the Cubist movement in its division of the human figure into flat, overlapping, geometric configurations. In 1909 the Italian poet Marinetti published the Futurist Manifesto, which heralded the machine, urban life and speed as the pictorial expression of a new reality. The Dutch De Stijl painter Piet Mondrian took Cubism a step further, into Neo-plasticism. Through abstraction, he freed forms from any suggestion of objective reality.

As early as 1913, several of these new concepts were evident in jewellery design, particularly in France. In the United States, where Modernism in jewellery design was resisted fiercely for many years, a critic for *The Jewellers' Circular Weekly* (on 26 March 1913) asked, 'Will the new movement in painting and sculpture be reflected in the forthcoming jewelry?' The article went on to conclude, concerning Cubism and Futurism, that 'whether the exhibits appeal to us or not the vital impulse toward something new and simple is apparent on every hand . . .'

As in most disciplines of the decorative arts, French jewellery was well represented in the 1925 International Exposition in modes that celebrated the culmination of the high Art Deco style. Beyond France, the style had few adherents. In the Japanese

RIGHT Diamond pendant brooch, a diamond calibre, ruby and enamel Coldstream badge brooch by Cartier, and a diamond and emerald bracelet and brooch by Lacloche.

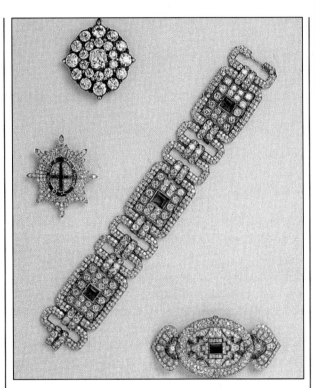

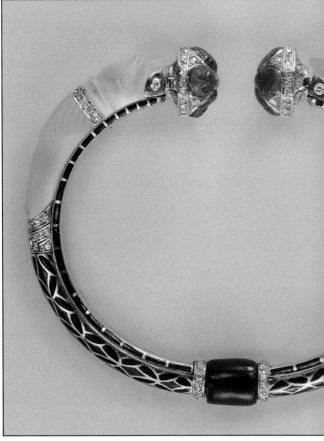

display, for example, Mikimoto filled a showcase with loose strands of cultured pearls. Great Britain was represented by one jewellery firm, Wright & Hadgkiss, which exhibited items influenced by Gothic metalwork. Similarly, Italy and Spain sent exhibits that were more traditional than modern. On the whole, foreign entries did not reflect the current geometrical style which had prevailed in Paris since World War I.

The principal exhibitors were Boucheron, Chaumet, Dusausoy, Fouquet, Lacloche, Linzeler, Mauboussin, Mellerio and Van Cleef & Arpels. Cartier chose to exhibit in the *Pavillion de l'Elégance* with the fashion designers.

The artist-jewellers Raymond Templier, Paul Brandt and Gérard Sandoz contributed outstanding examples in new and original materials. La Maison Fouquet was represented by the architect Eric Baggé, the graphic artist André Mouron (called Cassandre), the painter André Leveillé, Louis Fertey and Georges Fouquet's son Jean, who had joined the family firm in 1919. André Leveillé and Louis Fertey received Grand Prix awards, and Cassandre and Jean Fouquet received honourable mentions. Leveillé's designs recalled the overlapping images in Picasso and

Braque collages, while Cassandre adopted the mandolin, a motif popularized on canvas by Picasso, into the design for a brooch. The Exposition was very well attended, which allowed the general public to become familiar with the new trends in French jewellery design.

By 1929 the abstract creations seen at the 1925 Exposition had evolved into mechanistic forms based on industrial design. The design principles inherent in motorcar and aeroplane construction inspired a new decorative vocabulary for jewellery. A remote but real influence could now be traced to the Bauhaus.

Jewellery design had evolved from the thin, delicate creations of the early 1920s into bolder, larger designs with sharp outlines. The rainbow palette of bright colours gave way to muted tones. Stark contrast was achieved with black and white, epitomized with onyx and diamonds.

From 1930, the effects of the Depression were felt in luxury items. After the Crash of 1929, multiple-use jewellery (jewellery comprising two or more components which could be dismantled and used separately) became popular. Pendants could double as brooches or be attached to lapels. The

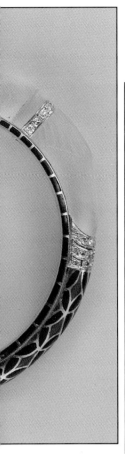

ABOVE Paris' Lacloche frères created this stunning bangle, a suitable complement to the revealing new fashions of the 1920s, which often bared the arms, necks and legs, begging them to be covered with jewels. Of rock crystal, diamonds, rubies and coloured enamel, the armpiece features facing dolphins. The sea animals were a motif drawn from classical Greece and Rome. Interestingly, Lacloche took over Fabergé's London shop after the Russian Revolution.

LEFT Pearl and diamond necklace by Cartier, and a delicate pair of Art Deco emerald and diamond earrings by Van Cleef and Arpels.

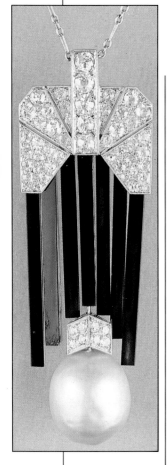

double barrette, formed from two linked parts, could be separated and worn in two places.

As the economic effects of the Depression deepened, firms were hesitant to produce new items which might prove difficult to sell. Tiffany's in New York, the leading American jewellery establishment in the 19th century, created traditional objects in the new style, but never with the clear geometrical elements found in pieces by Boucheron or Mauboussin. Other jewellery firms such as Black, Starr & Frost and Udall & Ballou in New York; JE Caldwell & Co and Bailey, Banks & Biddle in Philadelphia; and CD Peacock and Spaulding-Gorham, Inc. in Chicago, produced jewellery in the new style, but again not with the panache of their counterparts in France.

M OTIFS IN **A** RT DECO **J** EWELLERY

The principal motifs in Art Deco jewellery design were simple geometric forms, such as the square, circle, rectangle and triangle. These shapes were often juxtaposed or overlapped to create complex linear configurations. Abstract patterns, derived from the architecture of ancient civilizations, such as Babylonian ziggurats and stepped Mayan and Aztec temples, likewise found their way into the contours of jewellery design.

As with furniture, the use of exotic new stones and metals was promoted. No longer limited to the traditional precious stones and metals, the jewellery designers made full use of new materials. The adoption of platinum as a setting meant that the other elements could be accentuated. Platinum is a far stronger metal than gold or silver and the settings for stones could therefore be reduced to just two or three retaining teeth. Other new materials were onyx, ebony, chrome, plastic, lapis lazuli, lacquered metals, agate, coral, bakelite, rhinestones, jade, tortoiseshell, jet and moonstone. Used in conjunction, these materials offered up a riot of colour and contrasting textures. Faceted and flat stones provided additional contrast in their different surface treatments.

By the end of the 1920s, jewellers refined gem cutting further by the introduction of several new shapes, such as the baguette, trapezium, table and square cut. Jewellers also engraved emeralds, jade,

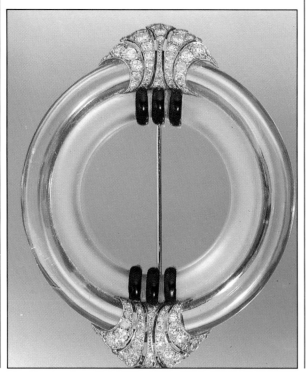

played the most up-to-date creations at the French Exhibition at the Grand Central Palace in New York. Although American jewellery design did not directly derive models from this exhibition, it later became more geometric, and objects in the new style were termed 'modernist'.

One new stylistic development can be discerned in American jewellery at this time. The stepped outline made its début on the contour of a few pieces of jewellery, coinciding with the emergence of skyscrapers, which were transforming the skylines in major cities across the country.

Elsewhere, the style was neither widespread nor much imitated, although occasional pieces were produced in Italy, Germany and Britain during the late 1920s. Switzerland's watchmakers, whose designers were often French, created cases with subtle geometric motifs.

The Art Deco period also spawned thousands of cheap anonymous designs, many of which are highly sought after by collectors today. These included bracelets, brooches, barrettes and clips – for ears, shoes, lapels – in coloured bakelite, celluloid and other synthetics, often in geometric shapes or carved as stylized flowers. Czechoslovakia, long a producer of glass beads, made inexpensive necklaces, pins and other bits of jewellery which were sometimes quite striking, with strong angles and colours.

coral and lapis lazuli in imitation of Oriental jewellery (the stones were often carved in the Orient and shipped to the West for setting). Cartier, Black, Starr & Frost, JE Caldwell & Co and Van Cleef & Arpels mixed engraved stones in figurative compositions, such as animals and baskets of fruit and flowers, that took their inspiration from Japanese and Egyptian prototypes.

Sir Flinders Petrie's archaeological excavations in the first decade of the century started an Egyptian craze. Howard Carter's discovery of Tutankhamen's tomb in 1922, and the press coverage which this generated for 10 years, ensured a continuing interest in Egyptian art. The clean lines in hieroglyphic calligraphy reiterated the linear concepts which had begun to emerge before the war. Van Cleef & Arpels, among others, introduced stylized pharaoic motifs into a series of bracelets, shoulder clips and brooches. Diamonds, rubies, emeralds and sapphires were interchanged with neutral stones such as onyx.

Towards the end of the decade, large, massive pieces, worn in quantity, became popular. In 1924, the major French houses of Boucheron, Cartier, Mauboussin, Sandoz and Van Cleef & Arpels dis-

J E W E L L E R Y **A** N D F A S H I O N

Fashion influenced the style, size and shape of Art Deco jewellery. The rise and fall of both the hemline and neck-line precipitated a wider need for different types of jewellery. Colour, which had been reduced to subdued shades in clothing, suddenly came alive with Diaghilev's Ballets Russes. The sets and costumes, designed by Léon Bakst, radiated with oranges, bright blues and greens, generating a sudden craze for anything Eastern. Oriental stones such as coral, jade, onyx and crystal became popular and remained so until after World War I. Paul Poiret brought this mania for the exotic into fashion, first by streamlining dresses and then by introducing the Empire waistline, which eliminated the need for tightly laced corsets.

FAR LEFT The three jewels, brooches at top and centre, ring below, were designed by Parisian Jean Fouquet, whose father, Georges, was also a jeweller. The combination of the semi-precious stones onyx and coral with diamonds and platinum is typical of the time.

BELOW Raymond Templier: earrings in gold, ivory and enamel, about 1925; ring in yellow and white gold, coral, carnelian and onyx, about 1925.

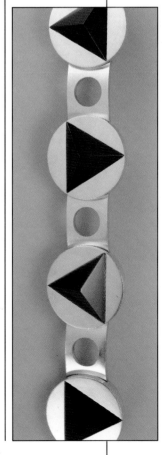

ABOVE Revealing
yet teasing photo of
Josephine Baker in
1926 at the Folies
Bergères, wearing
the barest amount
of Art Deco
jewellery.

bear the weight of a heavy piece of jewellery, necessitated lighter pieces of jewellery, now made possible with platinum.

Poiret's slim, high-waisted dresses were replaced in 1917 with a line of low-waisted models. Hem-lines fluctuated for the first five years of the 1920s, from ankle- to calf-length. Then, in 1925, skirt hems shot up to just below the knee (the length now generally associated with the 1920s), and dropped back to mid-calf-length in 1929. The silhouette of the body became long and flat, and suppressed all curves. The new look necessitated new jewellery with simple lines, minimum design and vivid colours.

Both the neck-line and the back of the dress fluctuated, the latter plunging to almost obscene depths. To accentuate the vertical line of the tubular dress, jewellery designers introduced long, dangling necklaces influenced by the multi-strand models of the Indian maharajahs. Women wore *sautoirs* and strings of beads in materials such as ivory, wood and semiprecious stones, either in the traditional manner, or hanging down the back, over one shoulder, or even wrapped around one leg. Necklaces, suspended with pendants and tassels, hung as far as the stomach or, on occasion, even to the knees. In the 1920s, long necklaces complemented short tunic dresses, fast dances and swaying movement.

Brooches were worn attached to hats, shoulders, straps or belts. The brooch-buckle was composed of a ring of onyx, crystal or coral, either in a circle or an ellipse, with decorative motifs at either end using diamonds, pearls or sapphires. Black, Starr & Frost advertised a typical example in 1926 with oxblood coral, diamonds and onyx. The brooch-buckle and the hatpin, another piece of jewellery which became popular in this period, could be worn either on a belt or attached to the cloche, the hat which became a symbol for the 1920s. Making its appearance in the winter of 1923, the cloche completely covered the head from the eyebrows to the nape of the neck. Long hair or hair pinned back in a bun distorted its shape, however, which prompted women to cut their hair in the new bobbed and fringed styles.

Such new cropped hair styles exposed the ear for the first time, and long, dangling earrings of diamond, jade, ivory, jet, onyx, crystal and amber became fashionable. By 1929 earrings were so long that they touched the shoulder, further emphasizing the verticality.

World War I introduced women into the workforce, helping to liberate them further from constrictive clothing. In 1917, Mrs Vernon Castle arrived in Paris and changed forever the concept of the ideal woman. Her slim, lithe figure glided across the dance floor, charming Parisian society with the latest ballroom dances and providing a preview of the energetic woman who appeared ater the war to challenge the staidness of her predecessor's role in society.

During World War I there was a need to conserve heavy fabrics for the troops. This hastened women's acceptance of a softer, slimmer silhouette. The introduction of rayon and muslin, materials too light to

In response to the new slender fashions at the beginning of the century, the bandeau had replaced the tiara and diadem. Still desired as an ornament worn in the evening, women in the 1920s wore the bandeau on the hair-line, or set back on the head, like a halo. In 1930 Chaumet designed an elegant diamond bandeau with three rosettes and stylized foliage. In the United States, Oscar Heyman & Bros., a jeweller's jeweller which still manufactures fine jewellery for other prestigious firms, designed a delicate diamond-studded example.

TOP The striking geometric design on this rouge box includes the cosmetics line's name, *Princess Pat*. A 1930s advertisement for the product promised to make customers 'all fragrant and beautiful – all charming – all serenely perfect'.

RIGHT Five pieces of jewellery by Raymond Templier and Jean Desprès.

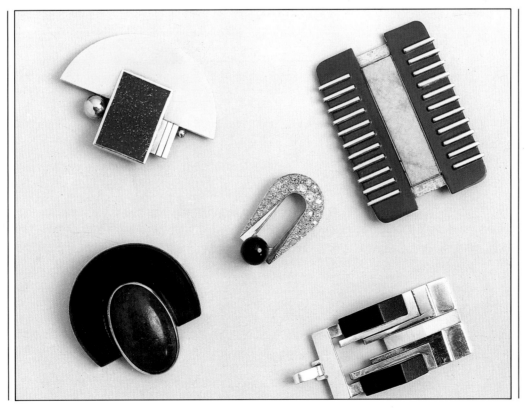

ABOVE These chrome necklaces are both strikingly set off by pieces of bright synthetic plastic. The chains are intricately fashioned, solid yet flexible and easily worn. The pendant on the right-hand piece is a miniature exercise in Cubism, and presages many contemporary designs of the recent past.

FAR RIGHT The Greek-key design on the frame of this handsome handbag fits nicely into the Art Deco repertory, being both classical and geometric. The metal and cloth bag is probably French.

ACCESSORIES **A**ND **A**CCOUTREMENTS

The typical Art Deco dress was sleeveless, which allowed the jewellery designer free rein to design creative jewellery to decorate the wrist and upper arm. There were several types of bracelets. The first were flat, flexible, narrow bands decorated with overall stylized designs of flowers, geometricized shapes and motifs from Egypt and Persia. Because these were narrow, four or five were worn together on the wrist. Towards the end of the 1920s they became wider. Big, square links of coral, rock crystal, onyx and *pavé* diamonds were accentuated with emeralds, rubies, sapphires and other cabochon gems.

Other types, bangles or slave bracelets, were worn on the upper arm or just above the elbow. (In England they covered the wearer's vaccination mark.) They were made out of gold, silver and materials

FAR RIGHT The Greek-key design on the frame of this handsome handbag fits nicely into the Art Deco repertory, being both classical and geometric. The metal and cloth bag is probably French.

RIGHT Powder compacts both bejewelled and non-precious were produced in vast quantities in the 1920s and 1930s. The enamelled metal quartet, here, are of French and American origin (the open one reveals a patent number). In actuality, the impeccable tooling and engineering of these feminine accessories were often due to the skills of a talented male industrial designer. The figures on the four here present attractive silhouettes, notably the red and black example with its musicians and dancing couple.

such as bamboo. Like flexible bracelets, several were worn at a time. Artist-jewellers such as Jean Fouquet, Raymond Templier, Jean Despres and Gérard Sandoz combined a variety of stones and metals. In Sweden, Wiwen Nilsson mixed silver with large pieces of crystal.

A third type, worn in the evening, consisted of loose strands of pearls, held together by a large pearl-studded medallion from which additional strings of pearls were suspended. Like the bangle, it was worn above the elbow.

With sleeveless dresses and the rage for sports, the watch bracelet became very popular in the 1920s. Jean Patou introduced the *garçonne*-type (the boyish woman) into fashion when he outfitted the tennis star Suzanne Lenglen, the ideal personification of the new woman. Every woman wanted to look the part of a sportswoman even if she did not participate. The wristwatch, worn during the day, was plain and strapped with leather or ribbon. The evening watch resembled a richly jewelled bracelet set with pearls and diamonds, either enamelled or in different colours of gold. An example from the period by Tiffany & Co was set with diamonds and onyx and mounted in platinum.

From 1925 to 1930 the pendant and châtelaine watch became popular. Suspended from a ribbon or silk cord, the face of the watch was upside down so

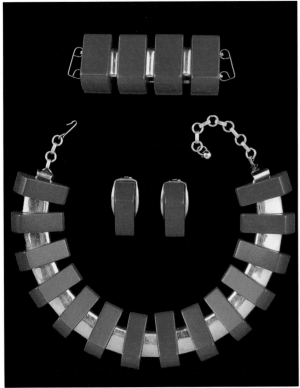

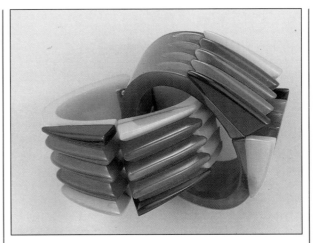

that the wearer could glance downwards to determine the time. An example by Van Cleef & Arpels shows the Eastern influence with jade, enamelling and Oriental motifs. The pendant watch, suspended from a sautoir chain, was worn in the evening. The chain was studded with pearls, diamonds and coloured gems. Its case was embellished with diamonds.

After the war, rings grew larger and bolder, dominating the finger. Surfaces were smooth, polished or in satinized metals. Stones could be either precious or semi-precious, set with *pavé* diamonds or a combination of two lacquered metals. Towards the end of the 1920s, gloves went out of fashion; muffs were preferred for the new fur-trimmed coats. Women started to wear massive rings to adorn their now gloveless hands. The popularity of the fan for evening wear gave them additional opportunities to show off the latest in ring fashions. Suzanne Belperron's large ring in carved chalcedony, set with a single Oriental pearl, captured the new mood. Other designers offered widely different solutions. Jean Despres combined crystal, gold and silver in abstract geometric patterns influenced by Cubism and African masks. Fritz Schwerdt, working in Germany, designed rings inspired by machines, one of which reproduced precisely the inner mechanism of a rotary engine in which an agate rod acted as the connecting pin.

Mauboussin, Lacloche frères, Fouquet, Boucheron, Cartier, Chaumet and Van Cleef & Arpels were some of the major jewellers whose output included not only standard jewellery items, but also powder compacts and cigarette cases. These became *de rigueur* in the 1920s for the bold woman of fashion,

who could now both smoke and powder her nose in public. Inexpensive versions of all these items were fashioned of paste, plastic and base metal. The application of coloured enamel to the metal pieces often made them, despite being cheap and mass-produced, every bit as handsome as the more expensive models.

The *nécessaire*, or vanity case, which held a mirror, compact, lipstick and comb, took its form from the Japanese *inrō* (a small case divided into several compartments). Although small in size, it accommodated all of the accoutrements that a lady might need. Vanities were mostly rectangular or oval, and hung from a silk cord. In 1930 the vanity case was enlarged into the *minaudière* by Aldred Van Cleef, who named it this after witnessing his wife simper (*minauder*) into the mirror. The *minaudière* replaced the evening bag and daytime dress bag.

The Art Deco handbag was made of luxurious fabrics or exotic skins with gold or platinum frames and clasps. Gemstones, accented with faceted or cabochon rubies, emeralds, sapphires and diamonds studded the frames. Semiprecious stones carved with Egyptian and Oriental motifs were used for the clasps. An evening bag designed by Van Cleef & Arpels was embroidered with sequins sewn onto the fabric. Mauboussin designed elaborate evening bags with diamond and emerald clasps that matched the brooches and bracelets worn on the bearer's evening gown.

Fans ranged from simple contemporary designs in paper (often with an advertisement on the reverse side) to delicate silk and satin fantasies on carved wooden frames. The mother-of-pearl fans created by

Frenchman Georges Bastard were perhaps the most lavish accessories of the time, their delicate ribs patterned with stylized flowers, triangles or other geometric shapes. Bastard also designed boxes, bowls, lanterns and a wide range of jewels – bangles, hatpins, haircombs – in mother-of-pearl, ivory, jade, tortoiseshell, horn, rock crystal and coral.

The Art Deco style was also reflected in men's jewellery, although never with the same flair as women's. Geometric forms characterized the dials of pocket watches which were mounted in platinum set with onyx, diamonds, pearls, emeralds, rubies and topazes. Watch-chains were made up of cylinder links enhanced with polished or faceted stones. Cuff-links followed the same general shapes. Jean Fouquet designed a notable pair with enamelled Cubist motifs. Black, Starr & Frost's selection included a pair in onyx with diamond borders.

C LOCKS

Clocks deserve a special mention in this chapter, partly because timepieces are such an important part of our daily lives, and partly because the 20th-century saw many innovations in the field of clock-making which freed designers from previous restrictions. With the new smaller movements clocks could now be made of a suitable size to sit comfortably on a table, and with an electric clock that required no winding, wall placement was not a problem either.

Nearly all French designers after World War I abandoned the round clock, as strongly vertical and horizontal shapes were more in keeping with current decorative tastes, and there was much radical experimentation with clock design. Some designers modified or even abolished the traditional needle-shaped hands, replacing them with balls on moving metal plates, or stationary points on a rotating dial of numbers. Great attention was paid to the design of the numbers themselves; the traditional Roman numerals no longer sufficed, even though they were more inherently geometric than the curved Arabic ones.

There were several noteworthy designers working in this field. Jean Trenchant experimented with radical designs in polished glass and metal directly influenced by Modernism. UTI, under the direction of George Meyer, produced clocks of varying degrees

ABOVE Geometric designs adorned jewellery and fashion accessories both precious and costume. The tiny timepieces, above, with Swiss-made works and elaborate frames, could be worn as brooches or pendants. Though of rhinestones and paste, their forms mimic those of expensive jewellers' works.

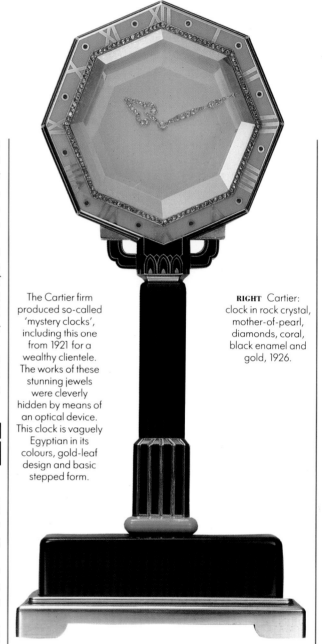

The Cartier firm produced so-called 'mystery clocks', including this one from 1921 for a wealthy clientele. The works of these stunning jewels were cleverly hidden by means of an optical device. This clock is vaguely Egyptian in its colours, gold-leaf design and basic stepped form.

RIGHT Cartier: clock in rock crystal, mother-of-pearl, diamonds, coral, black enamel and gold, 1926.

of distinction, the best deriving their interest from the interplay of black, triangular needles against the black circles that served for numbers. Gascoin designed some interesting models in curved wood and metal, elegant in their extreme simplicity, with the numbers always given an interesting treatment. Melik Minassiantz, among the most original designers, replaced the needles with balls which, attached to metal plates, moved along circular grooves, suggesting the solar system and giving an intriguingly mysterious air. Puiforcat also designed some extraordinary clocks, usually of silver-plated metal with glass, rock crystal or other semiprecious stones in dramatic geometric forms, and Jean and Jacques Adnet and Boris Lacroix were responsible for some clocks of rather stark design, primarily in metal.

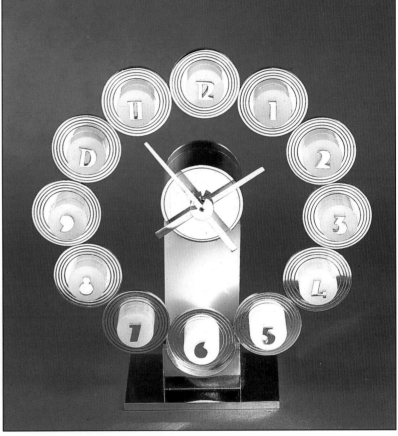

Clocks and other small table items were similarly embellished with elegant *moderne* motifs. Cartier epitomized splendour in their 'mystery clocks', which blended the world of myth and fantasy with stones, crystal and quartz carved with antique Chinese figurines, with creations by M Hirtz, M Masse and M Rubel. These mystery clocks seemed to run without any works; these were in fact hidden by means of an ingenious optical device. More progressive, Boucheron superimposed rectangles, triangles and squares in a gold clock.

In the United States, clock design was less extreme. Paul Frankl, Gilbert Rohde, Kem Weber and others produced designs in the streamlined, Machine-Age style that characterized the Art Deco movement in America. The sumptuousness of the materials — contrasting metals with brushed or polished surfaces, tinted glass, and new varieties of celluloid and other synthetics — substituted for the more innovative designs coming out of France.

ABOVE It was the great French silversmith Jean Puiforcat who made this unusual silver-plated and onyx clock.

LEFT J. E. Caldwell & Co.: clock in diamonds, jade, chalcedony and silver, about 1925.

FURNITURE
AND
INTERIOR DECO

RIGHT Sycamore sideboard by Jacques Adnet. The heaviness is lightened and relieved only by the chrome fittings, and by the drawers which look as if they were somehow magically held in suspension.

RIGHT One of the most exquisite and sensational examples in the whole canon of Art Deco furniture, this lacquered bed by Jean Dunand is the ultimate in design for luxury living between the two great wars.

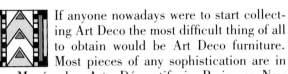

If anyone nowadays were to start collecting Art Deco the most difficult thing of all to obtain would be Art Deco furniture. Most pieces of any sophistication are in the Musée des Arts Décoratifs in Paris, or New York's Metropolitan Museum. A few other museums around the world have examples, and a few private collectors like Alain Lesieutre, Felix Marcilhac, and Mr and Mrs Peter M Brant have substantial collections. Scarcity is one of the obvious difficulties facing a new collector, but price is even more prohibitive. For a piece of furniture by Jean Dunand, Emile-Jacques Ruhlmann or Pierre Legrain the price would now be in the hundreds of thousands. Art Deco furniture is certainly one of the most interesting and inspired applications of the style. The high prices nowadays are certainly due to its rarity, but they also reflect another factor, that of the value of quality craftsmanship. Even when Emile-Jacques Ruhlmann sold his furniture in the 1920s, such pieces were only affordable by the wealthiest of wealthy clients, such as maharajahs and princes. If his work commanded such prices, it was not because of commercial greed but because of the months and months of skilled labour and the use of the most expensive materials as expressions of his genius. If such a piece of furniture were to be copied today it would be next to impossible to find a cabinetmaker capable of producing it. What men like Ruskin and William Morris had feared, the loss of the crafts due to industrialization, had become a reality. The 1920s and 1930s witnessed, among so many things, the dying of the old crafts. Skills like French polishing and marquetry had been passed down from father to son, and the apprentice system protected and maintained expertise. Even today, craftsmen jealously guard their secrets, and find it difficult to pass on the experience that comes from years of perfect co-ordination between hand and eye.

Art Deco furniture, therefore, more than any other expression of that style deserves preservation. It is the final chapter in the craft of cabinetmaking.

Within Art Deco furniture design, there were two distinct trends. On the one hand, there were the early experiments in what we have now come to recognize as modern furniture, using metals and plastics in forms which could lead to eventual mass production, and on the other the high-quality craftsmanship of which Ruhlmann was the greatest exponent. Purists would say that Art Deco furniture is truly only that of the highest quality production.

At the turn of the century, most quality furniture that was built to last was in the Louis XVI or Empire styles. Solid it might have been, but in no way was it modern. The achievement of Ruhlmann, Süe et Mare, Jean Dunand and others, was to re-evaluate the furniture styles, take the best and subtly alter and revamp them. Many of the people responsible for furniture design, including those just mentioned, were not themselves great craftsmen, but they were capable of running large workshops, and using the talents of their own and other studios' craftsmen to the best effect. They were virtuoso performers, and they showed off their abilities to the utmost. The materials they used were equal to their skills. France's vast empire provided them with the most exotic of materials: macassar ebony, mother-of-pearl, abalone, ivory, tortoiseshell, amboyna wood, burr

BELOW Chair from a pair dating from 1927 by the architect Robert Mallet-Stevens. The use of wood and fabric is a clever rethinking of the deckchair concept.

walnut, palmwood, silver and gold and the inspiration of oriental techniques such as lacquerwork.

Expensive and élitist as the luxury trade undoubtedly was, its resurgence depended on other factors. Apart from a few specialist shops, the outlet for contemporary furniture was limited. When the new department stores realized that design could be of great use to them, the situation altered. Au Printemps set up its Studio Primavera, Le Louvre set up Studium Louvre, Au Bon Marché set up Pomone, and Galeries Lafayette set up La Maîtrise. Customers soon realized that at these shops they could buy the most modern furniture at a reasonable price. The cream of France's young designers – Louis Sognot, René Prou, Robert Block and Etienne Kohlmann – were brought in to direct these studios and their modern furniture production. The public was easily persuaded that it was, at long last, getting what it wanted. Competition between the department stores spread to smaller firms, such as René Joubert and Philippe Petit's Décoration Intérieure Moderne (DIM), André Domin and Marcel Genevrière's Dominique, Michel Dufet's Meubles Artistiques Modernes (MAM), and Louis Süe and André Mare's La Compagnie des Arts Français. Furniture benefited by the competition, as designs and materials were modernized. At the 1925 Exposition, both the stores and firms were well placed to present a wide range of ultra-modern household goods to the public.

The further advantage of the studio system was that craftsmen were also allowed to accept private customers, as long as this did not interfere with the studio's work.

The whole furniture industry had a surprising openness of attitude, and ideas and skills were generously shared. In Ruhlmann's *Hôtel d'un Collectionneur* at the 1925 Exposition des Arts Décoratifs et Industriels, he included the work of sculptor Antoine Bourdelle, animal sculptor François Pompon, Jean Dupas, metalworker Edgar Brandt, silver designer Jean Puiforcat, lacquer expert Jean Dunand, and Pierre Legrain. It was an act of consolidation, an appeal for unity, which must also have displayed Ruhlmann's talents as an interior designer.

F RENCH **F** URNITURE

The period from 1905 to 1910 was a transitional one, during which the style now known as Art Deco began to evolve in Paris. Its major proponents seem to have had two primary objectives concerning design. The first was the desire to remove all traces of foreign influence in order to return to a purely French mode. Consequently, French taste in furniture was expressed by a return to 18th- and early 19th-century styles – Louis XV, Louis XVI, Consulate, Empire and Directoire – adapted to contemporary taste.

The second of the objectives in forming a new style was to abolish the obsession with the curve, which had been used as a primary mode of expression in Art Nouveau furniture at the turn of the century. Disciplined, stylized bouquets replaced the whiplash stems of Art Nouveau.

In 1912, Jacques Doucet sold off a fine collection of 18th-century French furniture and Old Master paintings, and sought out instead designs by such modernists as Paul Iribe, Clément Rousseau, Rose Adler and Pierre Legrain, as well as paintings and sculpture by Picasso, Douanier Rousseau, Miró, Ernst, Brancusi and Miklos, and even pieces of the traditional Negro art, which had had a great impact on, among others, Picasso and Legrain.

Similarly, in 1920 Jeanne Lanvin commissioned Armand-Albert Rateau, known for his emulation of classical antiquity and oriental art, to design her Parisian dwelling. His patinated-bronze, wood and marble furnishings were rife with elaborate floral and animal motifs – birds supporting a bronze coffee table; deer amid foliage on a bathroom bas-relief; marguerites entwining a dressing table.

ABOVE Clément Rousseau: occasional table in exotic woods, shagreen, ivory and mother-of-pearl, about 1921.

LEFT Atelier Martine: commode, silvered wood with incised decoration, 1923.

DIM: jewellery cabinet, Chinese red lacquer and *coquille d'oeuf*, 1926.

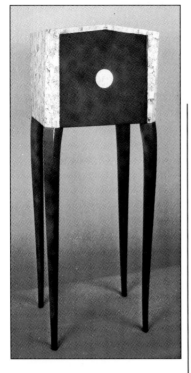

ABOVE Bizarre bronze and marble table by Armand A Rateau, with four encrusted stylized birds used as supports.

While Rateau's furniture and overall vision are among the most figurative and truly sculptural of the period – at times even whimsical – the heavily veneered, embellished and/or lacquered pieces of many of the others are much more handsome and restrained, often deriving from classical shapes. Classical scrolls, or volutes, were also used to decorate furniture, as well as stylized wings, animals, birds and human figures.

Designers embellished and sometimes even entirely covered furniture with such exotic materials as mother-of-pearl, sharkskin (also known as shagreen or, in French, *galuchat*), snakeskin, gold and silver leaf, crushed-eggshell lacquer and ivory. These might form a pattern – usually stylized flowers or a geometric motif – or they might take advantage of the nature of the substance itself, perhaps using the imbrication pattern of the shark's skin decoratively. The shapes of furniture ranged from overtly traditional – 18th-century *bureau plats*, petite ladies' desks, *gondole* or *bergère* chairs – to the strikingly *moderne*, severely rectilinear with not a curve in sight.

The greatest *ébéniste*, or cabinet-maker, of Art Deco France, Emile-Jacques Ruhlmann (1879–1933), produced forms both simple and elegant, usually traditional in shape and technique, but sleekly modern in decoration and detail. His desks, cabinets, tables and chairs were veneered in costly, warm woods, such as amaranth, amboyna, ebony and violet wood, and embellished with silk tassels and subtle touches of ivory in dentate, dotted or diamond patterns. The long, slender legs – sometimes torpedo-shaped with cut facets – were often capped with metal sabots, or shoes, a concept that was both decorative and practical.

There are two matching Ruhlmann cabinets dating from 1925 in the Metropolitan Museum of Art in New York and in the Musée des Arts Decoratifs in Paris which show an absolute synthesis of his ideas at work and amply demonstrate his absolute mastery of the medium. Made from rosewood, the cabinets are inlaid with macassar ebony and ivory. The floral display on the front is highly reminiscent of Art Nouveau, yet the strictly spartan lines of the vase containing the flowers displays a sensibility well in advance of the turn-of-the-century style. It is in all the detailing around the edges of the pieces that the Art Deco spirit comes to the fore. On the top edge, the ivory keys set into the macassar ebony suggest a modernized Greek decoration, or even a piano. The pieces are quite classical but in a modern vein. The slightly-offset and angled edging strips that run from the short legs to the white top edge are carefully finished with a small strip of ivory. The back legs, double the width of those at the front, are squared off, while the front legs taper elegantly down hexagonally. The pin-prick detailing on the front in ebony works as an open edge, marking out the floral pattern, but at the same time allowing the character of the rosewood grain to show through. It is the detailing on the front legs that exemplifies Ruhlmann at his best. The legs are clearly supports, but the scrolls stand proud of the cabinet and are also inlaid with ivory. They are pure ornament, extraneous to

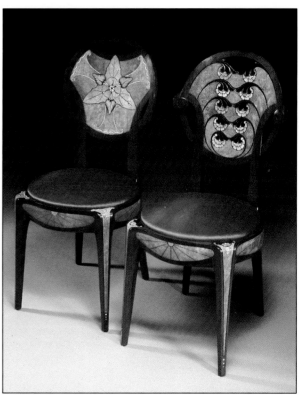

RIGHT Palissander-wood veneer and an etched-glass top comprise the elegant surfaces of this table by Pierre Chareau. Dating from c.1928, the table has a simple pedestal form. Note the horizontal and vertical directions of the veneer.

FAR RIGHT TOP The two chairs are by Clément Rousseau. Their frames are rosewood, their predominant material sharkskin (shagreen), with floral designs on the tops and sunbursts on the aprons.

FAR RIGHT BOTTOM Pierre Legrain and Jean Dunand collaborated on this red-lacquered cabinet. Commissioned by fashion designer Jacques Doucet, its doors open to reveal 24 file drawers lacquered in a red slightly lighter than on the outside.

the functionality of the cabinet, decorative yet discreet. The cabinet in the Félix Marcilhac collection in Paris also reveals Ruhlmann's ingenuity.

He even used chrome and silvered metal towards the end of his career, when many of his furniture forms became quite rectilinear; at the same time, his ivory dots and silk fringes gave way to chrome fittings, leather cushions and swivel bases. Ruhlmann was also the supreme *ensemblier*, designing rugs, fabrics, wallpaper and porcelain; in this guise he triumphed at the 1925 Paris Exposition with his *Hôtel d'un Collectionneur* – the imagined town house of a wealthy connoisseur. He was a fine draughtsman as well, and in 1924 he published a book containing watercolours of his interiors and detailed studies of sketches which followed the stages of his design from initial idea to finished product.

Jean Dunand (1877–1942), known for his *dinanderie* (the art of chasing and hammering metal) and for his lacquerwork, also designed and decorated elaborate furniture, including cabinets, panels and screens. These were often covered with figural or animal designs, either by Dunand himself or after a noted artist. The pieces themselves may have been designed by an *ébéniste*. An especially stunning black-lacquer cabinet in the 1925 Exposition, for instance, was designed by Ruhlmann and lacquered by Dunand with a charming scene of two fantastic animal-hybrids after a pictorial composition by Jean Lambert-Rucki. His huge screens, often of silver, gold and black lacquer, displayed massive geometric motifs, exotic oriental or African maidens, lush landscapes or elaborate mythological scenes. Among these last is a pair made of lacquered wood, designed

by Séraphin Soudbinine for the Long Island, New York, home of Mr and Mrs Solomon R Guggenheim, and depicting the *Battle of the Angels: Crescendo and Pianissimo*. They are now in the Metropolitan Museum of Art, New York.

Dunand was another of the designers who executed major commissions for the liners *Ile de France* and *Normandie*. His most famous single piece, however, was a bed made in 1930 for Mme Bertholet, in lacquer and mother-of-pearl. It is a beautiful yet almost completely absurd object. So beautiful, in fact, that it verges on the hideous. The actual construction must have been a nightmare of intricate modelling and shaping.

Irish-born Eileen Gray (1879–1933), another great Parisian furniture designer and *ensemblier*, started out fashioning exquisite handmade objects such as screens, tables and chairs. These were often embellished with Japanese lacquer, whose technique she studied with the master Sougawara. Even-

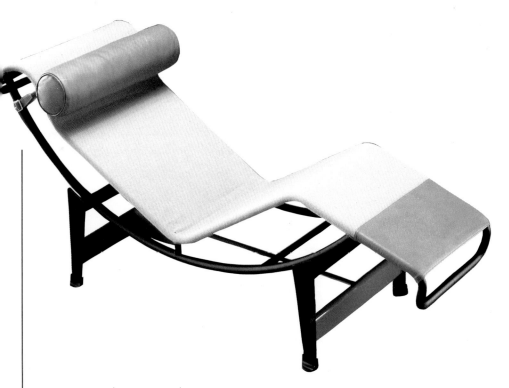

tually she moved on to more rectilinear and strongly functional furniture, as well as to architecture. For modiste Suzanne Talbot (Mme Mathieu Lévy) she designed a Paris apartment in 1919–20 which included a canoe-shaped chaise-longue in patinated bronze lacquer with subtle scalloped edges and a base comprising 12 rounded arches. By 1927, however, her chair designs were radically different and distinctly *moderne*. A padded-leather seat *Transat* armchair, set on a rigid lacquer frame with chromed-steel connecting elements, was more akin to Le Corbusier than to Ruhlmann, Dunand *et al*. Her case pieces, with built-in cupboards that featured swivelling drawers and doors set on tracks, and tables that moved easily on wheels, were considerably more practical.

Ruhlmann's furniture always allows for an uncomplicated appreciation of the qualities of each material. If not necessarily a strict follower of the truth to material ethic, his best pieces never disguise themselves. In this way his work was very different from the eccentricities of Pierre Legrain, who made the African chairs for Mme Tachard.

Born in 1887, Legrain initially made his mark as a designer of book covers for his wealthy patron Jacques Doucet. Legrain was like many of the other Art Deco designers in that he seemed to be able to apply himself with equal success to designing for a wide range of craft disciplines. It is important to stress again the value of having access to experts in many fields, which set designers like Legrain free to experiment at will. One of Legrain's most famous pieces of furniture was the *Zebra* chair, or chaise longue. His clear affinity to all things African could

hardly be more explicit than in this piece made in 1925. Compared to such representations of the opposite extreme of Art Deco as Eileen Gray's experiments in metals or, more directly, Le Corbusier's own chaise-longue, Legrain's is nothing short of bizarre. The zebra skin is imitated in velvet, the armrest which logic tells you should be against a wall is decorated on the reverse with abstract patterns, expensively executed in mother-of-pearl. The overall design is almost crude, appearing both clumsy and uncomfortable, the exact opposite to the Le Corbusier chair, which is probably the most comfortable piece of furniture ever invented. The arm rest is left open from the front in order to house a small shelf whose purpose could be nothing more than aesthetic. The whole chair exudes a feeling of gratuitous luxury and decadence, the kind of chaise-longue that Nancy Cunard or some other wealthy aesthete might have possessed, on which to lie back elegantly while puffing on an opium pipe.

Two artisans emerged as masters of Modernist materials. The first was Clément Rousseau, who designed and executed finely detailed furniture and precious objects in rare woods, tooled and stained leather, carved ivory and enamel. The other was Adolphe Chanaux, a virtuoso craftsman who executed furniture designs for André Groult, Emile-Jacques Ruhlmann, and Jean-Michel Frank, as well as for his own creations. Chanaux's importance lay in his mastery of all the period's most exotic and fashionable furniture materials – sharkskin, parchment, vellum, ivory, straw marquetry and hand-sewn leather – to which he applied his talents with equal facility.

Le Corbusier's best-known furniture pieces are his chairs, designed in collaboration with his cousin Pierre Jeanneret and Charlotte Perriand. His chaise-longues and armchairs often fashioned of tubular-steel frames and simple but comfortable and functional leather seats, were slightly more inviting than the spare, minimal designs of the Bauhaus school. These, especially the designs of Marcel Breuer and Mies van der Rohe, were even further removed from the plush, upholstered chairs of André Groult, Maurice Dufrêne and Dominique, all of which recalled a luxuriant past. Theirs instead clearly signalled a new era in design which still reigns today.

 ## FURNITURE ELSEWHERE IN EUROPE

In between the elegantly carved and veneered confections of high-style Parisian Art Deco and the near-antithetical, ultra-*moderne* tubular-steel and leather creations of Le Corbusier and the others were myriad pieces of furniture by Europeans and Americans that reflected either – at times even both – of the Art Deco design schools, with the occasional completely innovative design making its own waves.

In Great Britain, which had its strong native tradition of solid Arts and Crafts-style furniture,

ABOVE Around 1926 Rose Adler designed this table of ebony, sharkskin, metal and enamel, for couturier Jacques Doucet, in whose studio it was topped by Gustave Miklos's rock-crystal sculpture. Adler also designed bookbindings for Doucet. The sharkskin top sports a design of stairways and stepped buildings.

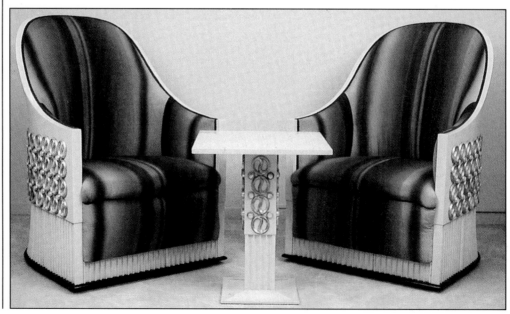

RIGHT The lacquered-wood and mother-of-pearl table and chairs were designed around 1921 by Viennese-born Joseph Urban. Urban's domestic furniture often reflected his theatrical bent (he was once a designer for the Ziegfeld Follies and the Metropolitan Opera), these three lavish pieces included. Urban was the head of the short-lived (1922–24) Wiener Werkstätte in Manhattan.

ABOVE Five-piece giltwood and Beauvais tapestry drawing room suite by Maurice Dufrêne. This type of application of tapestry to furniture, by no means unique, provided a boost to an ailing industry. Note in particular the giltwood layering down the stubby feet.

craftsmen such as Edward Barnsley designed sturdy, rectilinear pieces that bore no reflection whatsoever of *moderne* continental designs. Others, however, such as Betty Joel, Ambrose Heal, Russian-born Serge Chermayeff, Gordon Russell and the design firm PEL (Practical Equipment Limited) produced functionalist furniture with distinctly modern lines and, especially in the case of Chermayeff, occasional stylized-floral designs.

Russell designed a boot cupboard in 1925 in Honduras mahogany in a style very similar to French models introduced a few years earlier. And in 1929 Heal produced a desk and chair in weathered oak on which the perpendicular detailing again betrayed the influence of contemporary Continental models.

The general absence of furniture in England in the Modernist style was punctuated by a handful of spirited avant-garde models. Sir Edward Maufe, an architect known principally for the Guildford Cathedral, designed a range of furniture that appears to have been inspired by Paris. A typical example is provided by a desk manufactured by W Rowcliffe in around 1924, and exhibited at the 1925 Exposition. Made of mahogany, camphor and ebony gessoed and gilded with white gold, the desk had all the sumptuousness and ostentation characteristic of prominent French models. This was perhaps partly due to the influence of Maufe's wife, who worked for Sir Ambrose Heal.

Betty Joel, née Lockhart, was born in China in 1896. At the end of World War I she and her husband established their decorating firm in South Hayling, near Portsmouth, with a showroom in Sloane Street, London. Early designs revealed the fact that she was self-taught. By the end of the 1920s, however, she had developed a distinctive furniture style in which curved contours (described by her as silhouettes of the female form) predominated. Superfluous mouldings and projections were eliminated; ornamentation was achieved through a range of luxurious, contrasting veneers. Joel's firm won many commissions to decorate libraries, boardrooms, shops and hotels. Joel is remembered today primarily for an inexpensive line of furniture aimed at the working woman. Many of her designs were popularized by English manufacturers of modestly-priced furnishings. She retired in 1937.

Although most critics view German design of the 1920s in the context of Modernism embodied by the Bauhaus, many Germany designers now considered to be Modernists actually created furniture in the contemporary French style. For example, Bruno Paul, of the Munich Vereinigte Werkstätten and Director of the Berlin Kunstgewerbeschule, invariably incorporated an element of richness in his furniture designs. Well into the 1920s, he continued to design pieces in luxurious materials and thick, glossy veneers for the Deutscher Werkbund, a group known for its emphasis on the union of artists and industry. The furniture designed by Paul for the 1927 Cologne exhibition was more in keeping with the Modernist high style in Paris than the machine ethics of the Bauhaus.

German designers thus made expensive custom-made furniture in limited quantities. According to one commentator, 'Special attention is paid here to the wood used and to the finish. The simpler and more severe the piece the more attention is paid to the materials. Especially handsome inlaid pieces are preferred because it is possible by clever assembling of veneers to achieve beautiful patterns . . .'

That observation drew an obvious comparison with the well-crafted and sumptuous cabinetry of France's foremost furniture designers.

In Holland, De Stijl architect-designer Gerrit Rietveld created his famous *Rood Blauwe Stoel* (red-and-blue chair) in 1918. Just as the De Stijl movement's painters in Holland combined simple geometric shapes, primary colours and horizontal and vertical lines in their canvases, so this classic chair ably combined these same ingredients in a three-dimensional manner; the final result may have been uncomfortable, but it has none the less become an icon of modern design.

French-inspired furniture was also produced in Scandinavia. From the early 1920s, individual designers and companies in the industrial arts gathered forces in preparation of the 1925 Exposition. Denmark and Sweden each had its own pavilion, in addition to stands in the Grand Palais; Finland exhibited only in the joint facility. Erik Gunnar Asplund was perhaps the premier Scandinavian designer to work in the Modernist style. He designed an armchair made of mahogany, leather and ivory in about 1925, produced by David Blomberg of Stockholm, in a style which evoked the Paris fashion. The chair was part of a suite of furniture favourably reviewed by the critics at the 1925 Exposition.

THE TRIUMPH OF MODERNISM

No unified furniture aesthetic emerged at the Paris Exposition. Rather, there was an uneasy coexistence of contradictory images and styles. Varnished rosewood appeared alongside tubular nickelled steel; the Cubist rose competed with Constructivist geometry; and the brilliant colours derived from the Ballets Russes and the Fauves clashed with the subdued tints used by Modernists who embraced Le Corbusier's preference for achromatism.

Even before 1925 there had been signs of a reaction against the excessive ornamentation of Paris's high-style furnishings and *objets d'art*, opposition which gathered force increasingly after the Exposition closed. Amedée Ozenfant and Le Corbusier's *L'Aprés le Cubisme*, written in 1913, advocated a universal style stripped of ornament and even individuality, which owed its inspiration to the machine. The tenets of Russian Constructivism upheld by Nikolaus Pevsner, espoused similar concepts. The architecture of the avant-garde Russian Constructivists, such as Konstantin Melnikov's USSR

ABOVE Mornington & Weston: baby grand piano and stool, lacquered wood, about 1930. As the fashion for inner-city living grew, the scale of most pieces of furniture, such as this piano, was reduced to accommodate them in small flats or town houses.

pavilion at the Exposition, contrasted sharply with the prevailing Beaux-Arts architectural style in France, seen in such gaudy structures at the Exposition as A Laprade's pavilion for Studium Louvre and AC Boileau's pavilion for Au Bon Marché. The style had lost favour with its former patrons, who now preferred the simplicity and functionalism of a more contemporary, machine-related style.

In 1930, a new organization was formed to give identity to the group of designers who took Modernism as their doctrine: this was the Union des Artistes Modernes (UAM). Members included René Herbst, Francis Jourdain, Hélène Henri, Robert Mallet-Stevens, Pierre Chareau, Raymond Templier, Edouard-Joseph Djo-Bourgeois, Eileen Gray, Le Corbusier and Charlotte Perriand. These architects and designers rejected the excessive ornamentation characteristic of the Paris salons of the early 1920s, and gave priority to function over form. They designed furniture in materials such as steel, chrome and painted-metal tubes, in which individual elements were designed for mass production.

LEFT This exotic bronze chair was concocted by Armand-Albert Rateau, one of France's most original – if somewhat eccentric – designers. But for its leopard skin cushion, it is awash with marine motifs – scallop shells at the top and along the back, and tentacle-like legs. Rateau's best-known commission was to fit out the Paris home of Jeanne Lanvin.

Certain designers, such as Pierre Legrain, Jean Dunand and Marcel Coard, adopted a middle ground in which they incorporated only the angular forms of the newly emerging Modernist style while continuing to work almost exclusively in rare and precious materials. Their clientele was limited increasingly after 1925 to patrons such as the influential couturiers Jacques Doucet and Madeleine Vionnet.

Modern interiors and tubular-metal furniture began to be featured in *Art et Décoration* and *Mobilier et Décoration* soon after the 1925 Exposition. By 1927 furniture by such Modernists as Adolf Rading, Hans Ludwig Hildesheimer, Le Corbusier, Pierre Jeanneret, Mart Stam and Marcel Breuer was being featured in arts reviews, providing an increased awareness of the internationalism of the new Modernism.

Final, and complete, acceptance came in the selection of metal rather than wood for salon and dining-room furniture, to be seen and used by guests.

The infiltration of Modernist furniture into the home and office was not restricted to France. It had, in fact, developed more quickly in more progressive countries. Germany is often considered the pioneer nation in the development of the modern movement. The Belgian designer Henry van der Velde founded the Weimar School of Applied Arts in 1906, which was absorbed in 1919 by Walter Gropius who, in turn, founded the Bauhaus. This was an attempt to unify all disciplines within the decorative arts under the general direction of architecture.

F UNCTIONALISM

The Bauhaus instructors and their students advocated rational and functional design, and an increased dependence on the machine for mass-production. One of the most important Bauhaus furniture designers was Marcel Breuer who, with Mart Stam and Ludwig Mies van der Rohe, was the first to develop the cantilevered tubular metal chair. Later, in England, Breuer explored further the use of industrial materials in his design of a laminated-plywood lounge chair, manufactured by the Isokon Furniture Company, London.

The De Stijl group was formed in 1917. Theo van Doesburg, Gerrit Rietveld and Félix Del Marle

ABOVE The Parisian interior decorating firm, the *Compagnie des Arts Français*, founded by Louis Süe and André Mare, created this stunning cabinet in 1927. Veneered in Macassar ebony and featuring a marquetry floral bouquet of mother-of-pearl and abalone, the showpiece was part of the furnishings designed for the Saint-Cloud villa of French actress Jane Renouardt. The wing-like feet and leafy gallery are elements of 18th-century French furniture updated and streamlined by Süe et Mare; in the Louis XV period, however, they would have been gilt-bronze, not carved wood.

designed furniture intended to fill the Utopian interior spaces conceived by the leaders of the movement, Piet Mondrian and van Doesburg. Their furniture was angular and skeletal, of simple construction, employing planar, wooden boards painted either black or in the primary colours used by the De Stijl artists.

By the late 1920s, the functionalism championed by the Bauhaus had begun to assert itself in Scandinavia. This influence was felt most strongly in Sweden, which was more receptive to avant-garde German ideology than its neighbours. Some of the Bauhaus's most fruitful and artistic ideas were evident in furniture shown at the landmark 1930 Stockholm exhibition, held at Nordiska Kompaniet (NK) department store. The exhibition revealed a revolutionary attitude to domestic design, with special emphasis on residential architecture and furnishings. In keeping with modern concerns for practicality, flexibility and hygiene, dwellings at the exhibition had large windows, light walls and a minimum of furnishings. The furniture was geometrical in shape and extremely light, with restrained decoration.

The new furniture forms developed by the Bauhaus architects had a profound impact on international design by the 1930s. Noteworthy were Breuer's bent tubular-steel models, which were imitated, with modifications, throughout Europe. In Scandinavia, however, designers preferred to incorporate Breuer's functionalism with traditional materials, such as wood, in serial production.

Bruno Mathsson is probably the best-known Swedish designer of the period. One of his more notable furniture designs was the *Eva* chair of 1934, produced by the Firma Karl Mathsson in Varnamo.

RIGHT Gerrit Rietveld's *Rood Blauwe Stoel (Red and Blue Chair)* of 1918 has become an icon of modern design, its simple lines and bright colour blocks reflecting the works of the De Stijl painters in Rietveld's native Holland.

Made of bent beech upholstered in woven fabric, the model was sculpturally moulded to fit the human body. Mathsson's experiments in bent and laminated wood, combined with his studies of function and maximum comfort, generated many popular designs which have remained in continuous production since their conception.

At the same time, designers in Denmark moved into new areas of experimentation. Kaare Klint made furniture which combined practicality with economy. His first independent commission was to design exhibition cases and seats for the Thorwaldsen Museum of Decorative Arts in Copenhagen. His *Red Chair*, designed in 1927 for the museum, was widely acclaimed.

Alvar Aalto began to design modern furniture in the 1920s. His *Scroll* or *Paimio* armchair, of around 1929, has become a classic of modern Finnish design. The frame and seat are made of laminated and painted bentwood. The model captures the qualities of functionalism and lightness sought in tubular-metal furniture, adding a pleasing note of grace in its use of natural wood and sinuous curves. Aalto's bent and laminated wood stacking stools of 1930–33, produced by Korhonen in Turku, were also very successful commercially due to their formal simplicity and inexpensiveness. The stools have

BELOW LEFT This suite of living room furniture was designed by Félix Del Marle in 1926 for a certain 'Madame B' in Dresden. The French painter Del Marle was a Futurist converted to Cubism and then to the forms of the Dutch De Stijl movement, the latter of which were applied to this geometric suite of painted wood and metal and frosted glass. Mondrian was an admirer of Del Marle's furniture.

LEFT Viennese-born Paul T Frankl, who emigrated to the United States in 1914, designed the man's cabinet and mirror, c.1938. Red and black lacquered wood comprise the cabinet with half moons of silver- and gold-plated metal enhancing its doors. Silver leaf was applied to the top, gold leaf to the bottom.

remained entirely practical and adaptable to multiple requirements in the variants produced later.

Other Scandinavian designers also experimented with tubular steel. In 1929, Herman Munthe-Kaas of Norway designed an armchair produced by the Christiania Jernsengfabrikk, of Oslo. Although its form is based on Breuer's tubular-steel prototype, the model differs in its incorporation of an unusual metal-strap back and a series of simple string hooks that support the upholstered seat.

Serge Ivan Chermayeff, a Russian émigré who trained initially as an artist in Paris, has been credited with the introduction of the modern movement into Britain. His chromium-plated metal tubular furniture and unit storage systems represented a dramatic departure from the sterile tradition-bound models of his adopted country.

The designer John C Rogers was also instrumental in bringing the modern style to England. In an article in the *DIA Journal* (the publication of the Design and Industrial Association), Rogers had begun as early as 1914 to instil a new spirit of design into British industry. He pleaded for a national conversion to Modernism and for a final rejection of the Arts and Crafts philosophy. In 1931, Rogers visited the Bauhaus in Dessau with Jack Pritchard and Wells Coates, a trip which inspired the furniture he exhibited at Dorland Hall, London, two years later. In 1932, in collaboration with Raymond McGrath and Coates, Rogers redesigned the interior of the BBC; he later emigrated to the United States.

RIGHT The famous Zebra chaise-longue in black lacquer by Pierre Legrain of 1925.

F URNITURE **I** N THE **U** NITED STATES

In the United States, the high Parisian style of the 1925 Exposition was rejected by the public, who viewed it as a Gallic eccentricity too exuberant for traditional local tastes. When Modernism established itself in America in the late 1920s, it was the northern European strain of machine-made, mass-production metal furniture which found acceptance.

Although Paris was across the Atlantic, it was not too far for its influence to be felt in the United States. American designers were well aware of the prevailing Modernist style in Paris through periodicals of the day, and through a succession of exhibitions that travelled across the country in the second half of the 1920s. A loan exhibition of items from the 1925 Exposition opened at the Museum of Fine Arts, Boston, in January 1926, from where it proceeded to The Metropolitan Museum of Art, New York, and six other American cities. More than 36 museum and department store exhibitions of avant-garde European furnishings and decorative arts followed in as many months across the United States.

Correspondingly, attempts were made on occasion to introduce a flamboyant European style of furniture, some noteworthy. The Company of Mastercraftsmen in New York, for example, produced shameless copies of contemporary French models, replete with marquetry panels and ivory trim. Joseph Urban, an Austrian architect better known as a designer of stage and cinema sets, likewise designed somewhat theatrical furniture, such as a table and armchair, around 1920, of classical proportions and adorned with mother-of-pearl inlays, manufactured by the Mallin Furniture Company. Paul Frankl, whose 1930 cry, 'Ornament = crime', was taken up by a good many *moderne* American designers, created distinctive skyscraper bookcases and cabinets, with stepped sections and intricate compartments. Kem Weber and JB Peters, two Los Angeles designers, also adapted the skyscraper style to their tall pieces, and Chicagoan Abel Faidy produced a leather settee with a whimsical design derived from architecture for a private penthouse apartment which could easily have been custombuilt for Radio City or the Chrysler Building or some equally contemporary complex.

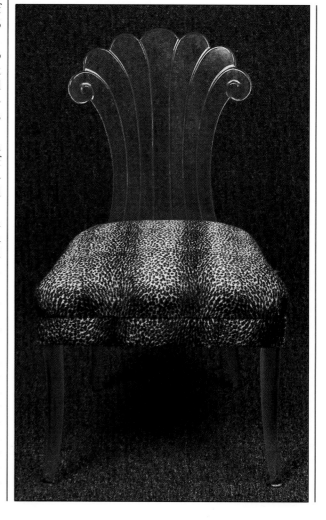

FAR RIGHT Elsie de Wolfe, one of New York's premier interior designers in the 1930s, created this side chair for Hope Hampton, c.1939. Its scallop back is reminiscent of German Biedermeier furniture, but what makes the chair so astonishing is its out-of-the-ordinary use of Lucite – a durable acrylic plastic made by the E. I. du Pont de Nemours firm – for the 'traditional' back and legs.

LEFT Donald Deskey, responsible for the interior decoration of Radio City Music Hall in New York, designed the executive suite for SL Rothafel, furnishing it with desk, chair and lamps of chrome-plated steel and tubular aluminium.

ABOVE Desk and chair (1936–9) by the American genius of architecture Frank Lloyd Wright. This set, called *Cherokee Red*, made from enamelled steel, American walnut and brass-plated metal, was designed for the SC Johnson & Son Administration Building in Racine, Wisconsin. The designs represent the saner, rational and more utilitarian attitudes to modern furniture design. Not necessarily inexpensive, the desks and chairs could at least be mass-produced.

FAR RIGHT American designer Paul T Frankl's Chinese-style chairs are a pair from a set of 14. The lacquered chairs were inspired in part by Frankl's visit to the Orient early in his career.

The German Karl Emanuel Martin (Kem) Weber was trapped in California at the outbreak of World War I. Refused permission to return to his homeland, he settled finally in Los Angeles, where he joined the design studio at Barker Bros as a draughtsman. In 1927 he opened his own design studio in Hollywood, listing himself as an industrial designer. Not only was Weber virtually the only decorative-arts designer to embrace the Modernist creed on the West Coast, but his style was highly distinctive. For the John W Bissinger residence in San Francisco, Weber created a striking suite of green-painted bedroom furniture enhanced with Hollywood-type decorative metal accents.

The metal and wood furniture of Frank Lloyd Wright was not as severe as that of the Bauhaus school. For instance, his renowned 1936–39 desk and chair, called *Cherokee Red* and designed for the SC Johnson & Son building in Racine, Wisconsin, have their steel frames enamelled in a warm russet-brown tone which complements the American walnut of the chair arms and desk top, as well as the chair's brown-toned upholstery. The two pieces are an essay on the circle, oval and line – and undoubtedly far more inviting to an office worker than, for example, the shiny chrome-and-black leather pieces of Breuer *et al.*

Eliel Saarinen, Eugene Schoen, Wolfgang Hoffmann (son of the Viennese Josef Hoffmann and an American emigrant), Gilbert Rohde and Joseph Urban were among the many designers who applied their talents to creating furniture for the American market. On the whole, their pieces were sturdy,

mass-produced and distinctly modernist, some with echoes of French, German and Viennese design, others uniquely American in their form, colour and materials. Aluminium, chromium and other metal furniture was in the ascendancy, but wooden pieces continued to thrive, with veneers of native woods such as holly, birch, burr maple and walnut handsomely covering large surface areas.

One of the finest Modernist furniture designers in the United States was Eliel Saarinen, a native of Finland. For his house at Michigan's Cranbrook Academy, Saarinen designed a dining-room ensemble which drew on the principles of French Modernist design. The chairs have classically fluted backs emphasized by the contrasting colours of the pale fir veneer and intersecting black-painted vertical

stripes. The accompanying table is inlaid with an elegant geometrical pattern which recalls the restrained parquetry designs introduced by Dominique and DIM in Paris some years earlier.

Eugene Schoen, a native of New York, also created furniture in a restrained Modernist style. After visiting the 1925 Exposition, he established his own interior decorating firm in Manhattan. Some of his more notable models, manufactured by Schmied, Hungate & Kotzian, betrayed a strong French influence in their Directoire-style sabre legs and fluted backs.

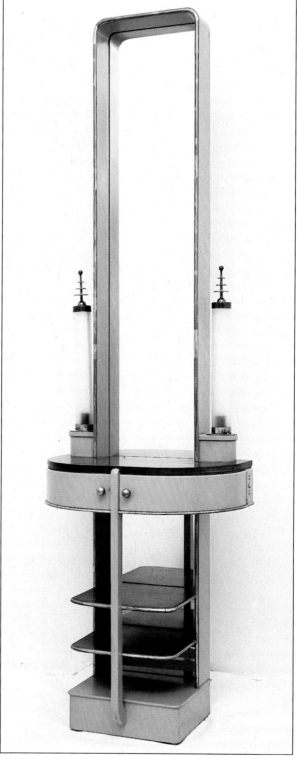

LEFT California-based Kem Weber designed this side table for a San Francisco couple, the Bissingers. Made of burl walnut, glass, silvered and painted wood, chromium-plated metal, maple and cedar, the piece is crisp and architectonic (especially its skyscraper-like sidelights).

FAR LEFT Paul T. Frankl: *Skyscraper* bookcase/cabinet, birch and lacquer, about 1928. The first designer in the United States to embrace the skyscraper as a decorative motif, Frankl quickly denounced it as a 'monument to greed' when the economy began to unravel following the Wall Street crash.

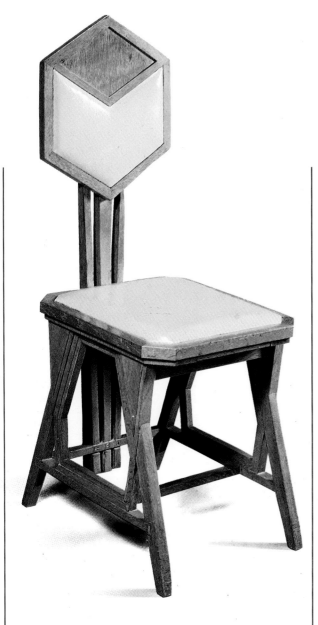

Many other designers in the United States created Modernist wood furniture, much of it manufactured in the industry's principal centre, Grand Rapids, Michigan, by firms such as Berkey & Gay, the Johnson-Handley-Johnson Company and the Imperial Furniture Company. Included were Herman Rosse, Ilonka Karasz, Jules Bouy, Herbert Lippmann, Ely Jacques Kahn, Robert Locher, Winold Reiss, and Norman Bel Geddes. Furniture manufacturers such as the Herman Miller Furniture Co., in Zeeland, Michigan, the Troy Sunshade Co, in Troy, Ohio, and the Ypsilanti Reed Furniture Co, in Ionia, Michigan, retained designers such as these to provide them with models for their lines of mass-produced furniture.

In metal furniture, Donald Deskey emerged as the country's premier designer, combining the luxury of French Modernism with the technology of the Bauhaus. One of the finest examples was his dining table for the Abby Rockefeller Milton apartment, in

1933–34. Although the piece included a Macassar ebony top, it was the inclusion of new materials – polished chrome and glass, and the siting of a bulb beneath the top to provide dramatic lighting effects – that drew the critics' praise. For his interiors for the Radio City Music Hall in 1932, Deskey set convention aside in a display of ostentation intended to buoy the Depression-wracked nation seeking refuge in movies and live entertainment. The private apartment above the Music Hall which Deskey designed for the Music Hall's impresario, Roxy Rothafel, was even more lavish.

Several other designers in the United States created excellent metal furniture in the late 1920s and 1930s, in particular Gilbert Rohde, Wolfgang and Pola Hoffmann, Warren McArthur, Walter Dorwin Teague, and the lighting specialist Walter von Nessen. Walter Kantack, a New York metalware manufacturer, also produced inspired metal pieces of furniture, as did the architect William Lescaze, of Howe & Lescaze.

At the far end of the spectrum was TH Robsjohn-Gibbings, in California, working in a luxurious, fiercely anachronistic neo-classical style which greatly appealed to wealthy clients in the show-business community. Classical motifs such as scrolls, palmettes, lyres, rams' heads and hoof feet adorned his tables, mirrors and chairs, mostly made of parcel-gilt carved wood and gilt-bronze.

By the mid-1930s, it was evident that metal had won the battle with wood for the domestic American furniture market. Whereas wood continued to be preferred in some sectors of the household market, metal continued increasingly to win adherents.

Such synthetic materials as Formica and Lucite were already being used in furniture design, with an armchair by Elsie de Wolfe, its traditional scrolled-back design of moulded Lucite, demonstrating a strange but witty meeting of the old and the new.

I N T E R I O R
D E C O

In 1911 the term *ensemblier* appeared, and with it the suggestion that a new concept in interior decoration had emerged. In opposition to the Art Nouveau credo, following which furniture designers and architects had attempted to design every element of an interior to ensure that it was entirely *en suite*, a tendency

FAR LEFT The great American architect Frank Lloyd Wright designed this oak side chair for the Imperial Hotel in Tokyo. The c.1916–22 chair is an essay in geometry. Like many of his creations, the chair is attractive but not very comfortable.

ABOVE TOP Deskey: adjustable table, aluminium and bakelite, about 1930.

ABOVE Kem Weber: armchair in Macassar ebony, probably for the Kaufmann department store, San Francisco, about 1928.

emerged for decorators to collaborate on certain com-missions. Evidence of this collaboration, which was apparent at the 1913 salons, reached fruition after the war in the interiors of the French embassies in Warsaw and Washington, the Parfumerie D'Orsay, Jean Patou's residence, and luxury ocean lines such as the *Paris* and the *Ile-de-France*. All of these were designed with an unprecedented spirit of co-opera-tion. The Ambassade Française pavilion at the 1925 Exposition drew the combined participation of all of the members of the Société des Artistes Décorateurs.

The first patron of the new Modernist style was the couturier Jacques Doucet, who in 1912 commis-sioned Paul Iribe to design and furnish his new apartment on the Avenue du Bois, Paris.

In 1924, Doucet again sought Modernist designers to decorate the studio which he had com-missioned the architect Paul Ruau to design for him in Neuilly to house his collections of Oceanic and African art. Pierre Legrain, who had worked for Paul

RIGHT The young man's bedroom by M Guillemard, was furnished by Primavera, the atelier connected to the Parisian department store, Au Printemps. Note the built-in bed, the centre table with wrought-iron base and the geometric designs on the carpet, echoed throughout the decidedly masculine room.

ABOVE This dining room which was displayed at the 1925 Paris Exposition, was conceived by R Quibel. The furniture wood is palissander; glass and silver by René Lalique and Jean Puiforcat, respectively, were also part of the entire ensemble.

RIGHT Suite of furniture in bronze, marble, wrought iron, corduroy and silk by Raymond Subes. A detail that is particularly unique is the swag in corduroy cloth over the armrest of the chair, which is purely decorative. Note also the gentle sweeping arch containing the tall mirror behind the table, and its echo in reverse on the table legs.

BELOW The opulent decoration of New York's Chanin Building, on 42nd Street and Lexington Avenue, was not confined to the facade and lobby. This is the tiled Executive Suite bathroom, which was reserved for Irwin S Chanin. Its decoration, like that of the entire building, was supervized by Jacques Delamarre, department head of the massive Chanin Construction Company. The building's architects were Sloan & Robertson; it dates from 1929.

Iribe during Doucet's earlier commission, was joined in Neuilly by a cross-section of Paris's most avant-garde artist-designers.

The elegance and opulence of Parisian Art Deco were best expressed in the stunning interiors of the 1920s and 1930s, often the products of collaboration between furniture and textile designers, sculptors, painters, lacquerworkers and numerous other talented artists and artisans. The *ensemblier* came to the fore, with such names as Emile-Jacques Ruhlmann, Robert Mallet-Stevens, Francis Jourdain, Eileen Gray, and the partnership of Louis Süe and André Mare taking on the rather formidable task of creating a total design, or *ensemble*, for a room.

Art Deco designers often paid homage to the rich heritage of the Louis XV, Louis XVI and Empire periods, as well as creating entirely new forms of their own. They used both innovative and traditional materials, although their techniques were generally subsidiary to the overall aesthetic effect. Colours were often bright and vibrant, but subtle pastel shades and deep, dark greys, browns and blacks were also in evidence.

In the United States, there appears to have been only one major Modernist collector at the time, Templeton Crocker. A member of a prosperous California railway and banking family, Crocker commissioned Jean-Michel Frank in 1927 to decorate his San Francisco duplex penthouse apartment.

TEXTILES AND CARPETS

TEXTILES: FABRICS

As in other disciplines, Parisian textiles, carpets and wall hangings of the 1920s and 1930s were highly innovative and influential. But the designs of England and the United States excelled as well, and there was much interchange between these and other western countries – not to mention the fact that a number of women were making their mark in virtually all of them.

The taste for colour changed more rapidly in the field of textile design than in any other medium. The electric colours that dominated Parisian textile design in the early 1920s were the result, in part, of the deprivation experienced within the city during World War I. In 1920 the impulse to celebrate manifested itself partly in a search for flamboyance. Vivid, sometimes discordant, shades of lavender (Lanvin blue), orange-red (tango) and hot pink, were juxtaposed with lime-greens and chrome yellows to generate a psychedelic palette rivalling that of the 1960s.

Many of the same Parisians who designed carpets also worked on textiles and fabrics. There were, in addition, a number of other extremely talented practitioners, among them Robert Bonfils, Francis Jourdain, Hélène Henri, Paul Poiret and, the most famous of all, Raoul Dufy, who designed charming and colourful tapestry upholstery, screens, wall hangings and the like, which were produced by the renowned manufactories of Gobelins, Aubusson and Beauvais.

Dufy played an extremely important role in textile design. The fashion designer Paul Poiret had set up the Atelier Martine before World War I, and it was Dufy who produced the most inspired designs for the workshop. The diluted character of his post-Fauvist style proved to be well-suited to textile work. Other designers like Emile-Jacques Ruhlmann also found it necessary to work in the medium in order to provide coverings for their furniture.

Hélène Henry's silk and rayon fabrics were notable for their thick, 'natural' textiles, in appropriate earthy tones of yellow, grey and brown. Her motifs were usually geometric, but far subtler than the rather 'loud' arcs and angles of Maurice Dufrêne, Sonia Delaunay and the Burkhalter and Valmier fabric houses.

Designs on fabrics and upholstery were generally more pictorial and painterly than those on carpets. Dufy presented elaborate scenes of well-dressed ladies at horse races (a frequent watercolour subject of his), as well as densely packed panoramas of fishermen, harvesters and dancers. These last were made in cotton by Bianchini-Férier, most often in black and white, but sometimes also in yellow and white or red and white. Léger and Jourdain designed in more abstract and geometric terms, as did Ruhlmann, who created large, bold, circular patterns for furniture covering, which were quite innovative and repeated by many other designers; these often had floral or foliate motifs which echoed those appearing on some of the furniture of the period. Jean Lurçat's tapestry designs could be busily pictorial, but some were restrained and appropriate to upholstery – a sofa covering, for instance, imitating fringed valances.

In England, Marion Dorn, Vanessa Bell, Duncan Grant, the partnership of Phyllis Barron and Dorothy Larcher, Alec Hunter, Nancy Ellis, Enid Marx, Norman Webb, Gregory Brown, Frank Dobson, Minnie McLeish and Charles Rennie Mackintosh among many others, designed fabrics and textiles. Most tended towards distinctive *moderne* patterns which featured stylized flowers, birds and human figures, as well as abstract and rigidly geometric designs.

The delicate artistic style of Vanessa Bell and Duncan Grant translated well into the printed fabrics that they designed for Allan Walton. Although their Omega Workshops, devoted to the promotion of household furnishings painted with post-impression-istic designs, had closed in 1919, Bell and Grant continued their artistic efforts in a style that came to depend less on post-impressionism than on purely decorative appeal. From 1931 until the outbreak of World War II they introduced more than a dozen designs which exuded the 'cosy' character of English 19th-century printed fabrics.

In the 1920s Bell and Grant also designed needlepoint canvases which were successfully worked by Ethel Grant, Duncan Grant's mother, and the painter Mary Hogarth.

As in so many other things, the most outlandish and original designs were produced by Sonia Delaunay. The vivacity of her designs was matched only by the work of some of the best Russian textile designers.

In Russia, Varvara Stepanova and Liubov Popova created brightly hued fabrics and textiles grounded on the circle and the square. Indeed, nowhere more than in tapestries and textiles did the fine arts make so great an impact in the 1920s and 1930s, with painterly patterns translated into cloth and yarn.

In Germany, the Bauhaus weaving workshop produced carpets, woollen wall hangings and fabrics in strong shades, usually in geometric or abstract patterns. Their emphasis was often on texture and they employed an extensive range of fabrics. Gunta Stölzl and Anni Albers, two of their most influential figures, eventually settled respectively in Switzerland and the United States.

Perhaps the most significant contribution of the 1920s and 1930s to textile design was the growing belief in the doctrine of truth to material. Among the

ABOVE The gifted all-round designer, Maurice Dufrêne, created this handsome fabric in around 1925–30. He began his career at the turn of the century, and, interestingly, the Art Deco-era fabric illustrated bears vestiges of the earlier curvilinear and organic style known as Art Nouveau.

Modernists this took the form of a virtual abandonment of printed decoration, which was now seen as an attempt to imitate costlier woven fabrics. Interest centred on the innate qualities of the fibre. Good weaving, it was felt, would help to bring out the beauty of the fabric through its texture, in contrast to the deceptive manipulation of printed or other 'applied' decoration. This attitude was fuelled in part by the principles of the Bauhaus weaving workshop, the full effects of which were felt only after the war in the mass-production of large-scale woven fabrics.

Abstract Modernist art made inroads into the Scandinavian textile industry in the 1920s and 1930s. This was most prominently felt in the traditional form of weaving, the *ryijy*, or *rya* rug. In textiles, however, emphasis was on structure, an inspiration drawn from the work of the Bauhaus weavers.

On the other side of the Atlantic, Americans, like the British, were slow to accept the modern French aesthetic, but once they had done so, proceeded with remarkable ability.

Ruth Reeves, a major figure in American textiles, designed wall hangings, rugs and fabrics which were joyfully *moderne* and undeniably American, with names like *American Scene*, *Manhattan*, and *Homage to Emily Dickinson*. Her colours were often quite subdued – browns, greens, black – allowing the strong patterns to predominate.

Colours and motifs were more equally balanced in the work of the Karasz sisters, Ilonka and Mariska – the former, the designer, the latter, the producer –

who emigrated to the United States from Hungary in 1913. Abstract floral designs in bright colours characterized their hand-worked pieces, with more than a passing nod to their Eastern European heritage. The 'silk murals', as she termed them, of Lydia Bush-Brown were more pictorial, usually incorporating stylized borders, often inspired by oriental or Middle Eastern subjects.

WALLPAPERS

The patterns of many of the French and American designers were also used for wallpaper. Ruth Reeves, Raoul Dufy and Donald Deskey were among those whose creations could be found covering just about every element in a room – wallpaper, rugs, curtains, upholstery. Since the techniques used to reproduce designs on paper were similar to those for cloth, the crossover from one medium to the other was almost effortless for the designers.

Wallpapers were also produced for the Wiener Werkstätte by Salubra Werke and Flammersheim & Steinmann. Peche created a large selection of designs in 1919 and again, a year before his death, in 1922. One of these was selected as the catalogue cover to the Austrian design section of the 1925 Paris Exhibition. His colleague Maria Likarz-Strauss created a portfolio of wallpaper designs in 1925, and examples of Mathilde Flogl's work were included in the workshops' 1929 collection, three years before they were forced to close through bankruptcy.

The popularity of the Wiener Werkstätte's fanciful wallpaper patterns in this period was enormous. Literally thousands of patterns were produced by Josef Hoffmann, Dagobert Pêche, Mathilde Flögl, Franz von Zülow, Ludwig Heinrich Jungnickel, Arnold Nechansky, and the Rix sisters, Kitty and Felicie. Hoffmann's designs in the mid-1920s simplified the enchanting herringbone and dash patterns of his pre-war style. Notwithstanding, the workshops' light-hearted designs in the 1920s reflected a digression from their original crusade for artistic reform.

Interestingly enough, Le Corbusier abhorred the use of patterned wallpaper or any other kind of wall covering, advocating instead white-painted walls (which would indeed become the norm by the 1930s).

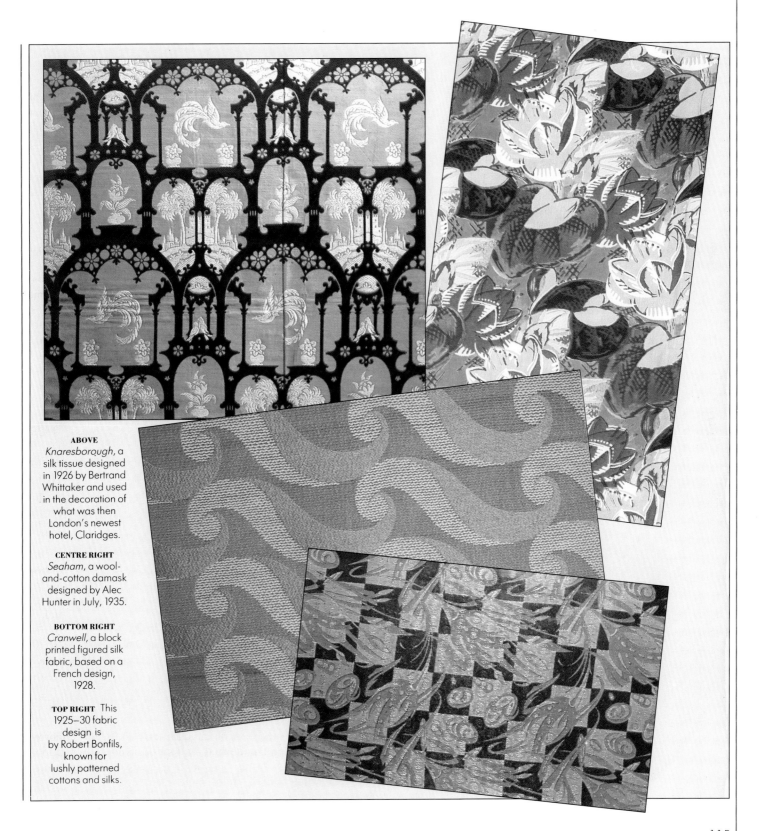

ABOVE
Knaresborough, a silk tissue designed in 1926 by Bertrand Whittaker and used in the decoration of what was then London's newest hotel, Claridges.

CENTRE RIGHT
Seaham, a wool-and-cotton damask designed by Alec Hunter in July, 1935.

BOTTOM RIGHT
Cranwell, a block printed figured silk fabric, based on a French design, 1928.

TOP RIGHT This 1925–30 fabric design is by Robert Bonfils, known for lushly patterned cottons and silks.

CARPETS AND RUGS

The tradition of carpet-making is an old and respected one in France, and the Art Deco period witnessed not only a proliferation of rugs in different shapes and sizes, but also an increase in their significance in terms of overall interior design.

In the 1920s, rugs provided a decorative accent to the lavish interiors of the Paris *ensembliers*. Maurice Dufrêne, Paul Follot, Süe et Mare, Emile-Jacques Ruhlmann, Jules Leleu, René Gabriel, Fernand Nathan, Francis Jourdain and André Groult, among others, designed carpets to complete their decorative schemes. Towards the end of the decade, rugs took on the added importance of providing the only element of warmth and ambience in the austere metal-dominated interiors presented by Pierre Chareau, Djo-Bourgeois and René Herbst at the initial exhibitions of the Union des Artistes Modernes.

Modernist fabric designers and manufacturers turned their hand to rugs and carpets with equal facility, generating the same selection of floral, abstract and geometric patterns. Contemporary literature reveals a host of fresh designs by Aubusson (Edouard Bénédictus, Paul Véra, Henri Rapin, P Deltombe and L Valtat); Myrbor (Louis Marcoussis and Jean Lurçat); La Maîtrise (Maurice Dufrêne, Jacques Adnet, Suzanne Guiguichon and Mlle

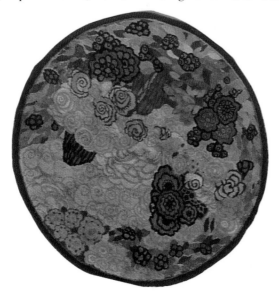

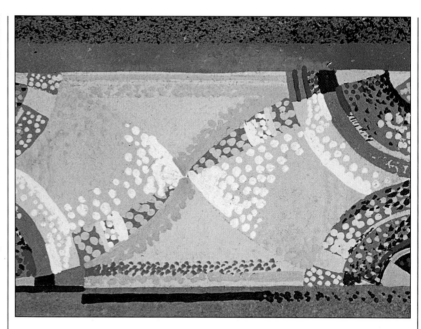

ABOVE Eric Bagge's carpet, *Arc-en-Ciel (Rainbow)*, produced by Lucien-Boux, c.1926. Bagge was a French architect interior decorator.

FAR LEFT Interior decorator Maurice Dufrêne designed this carpet in 1922. Its all-over floral motif is found on many Art Deco floor coverings. From 1921 Dufrêne was in charge of the Galeries Lafayette's workshop, *La Maîtrise*.

Marionnée); the Atelier Martine (Raoul Dufy); Pomone (Paul Follot); DIM (Dresa); Primavera (S Olesiewicz); Süe et Mare (Paul Véra and André Mare); and Pierre Chareau (Jean Lurçat and Jean Burkhalter). Other designers of merit appear to have worked independently: Marcel Coupé, Jacques Klein, Mlle Max Vibert, Élise Djo-Bourgeois, Maurice Matet, Boderman, Raoul Harang, J Bonnet and Mme S Mazoyer.

The greatest French rug designer of them all, however, was Ivan Da Silva Bruhns, whose deeply coloured, geometric creations mirrored much of the fine art of the period, ie Cubist and Constructivist, as indeed did many other rug designs. They also took their inspiration from deep-wool Berber carpets often in red and black, fine examples of which had been seen at exhibitions of Moroccan art in Paris in 1917, 1919 and 1923. Similar carpets were designed by Jean Lurçat, Henri Stéphany, Louis Marcoussis, Sonia Delaunay, Eileen Gray and Evelyn Wyld, the last two British expatriates who lived in Paris. Eileen Gray's rugs were especially innovative and witty; one, her *Blackboard* of 1923, is in production again today.

Other Parisian designers created carpets with Fauve-like colours, which were often round and prettier in concept, with floral designs. Edouard Bénédictus, Paul Follot, André Groult, Süe et Mare, Maurice Dufrêne, and the Ateliers Martine, Pomone and Primavera were some of the exponents of this more decorative school. Marie Laurençin produced a scallop-edged round carpet with mermaids, fish and doves in pastel shades of pink and blue, and many of Bénédictus's huge rugs were awash with bright floral patterns.

The finest carpets were hand-knotted (*à la point noué*). As synthetic fibres made their entry into the medium, experimental pieces in cellulose and vegetable fibres, and new washable linen materials, were shown at the Paris salons.

In England, two carpet designers of note emerged, E McKnight Kauffer and his wife Marion Dorn; both were American-born, and collaborated on Modernist rugs for Wilton Royal, as well as designing on their own. McKnight Kauffer's rugs were quite painterly, comprising stripes and blocks of pure colour, sometimes overlapping, while Marion Dorn's were more sensitive to the medium, often employing cut pile to attain layered effects. Her designs were also less rectilinear than her husband's, featuring interlocking loop patterns, sometimes symmetrical, sometimes free-flowing, as well as tiers of zigzags. And her colours were rather earthy – beiges, browns, greys – as opposed to his more vivid, even off-beat, hues and combinations. The team influenced such other English designers as Ronald Grierson, Ian Henderson and Marian Pepler. Betty Joel, the furniture designer, also created rugs, in effect becoming the English near-equivalent of a Parisian *ensemblier*. The Omega Workshops had also produced rugs earlier including one of about 1913 by Vanessa Bell, with an abstract pattern of intersecting lines which could well have been made 20 years later by Marion Dorn or Marian Pepler.

In other European countries, such as Austria, Sweden and Germany, Modernist designs appeared on many hand-woven and machine-made rugs, but traditional folk-art patterns were employed as well. Bruno Paul and Ernest Boehm were two talented German designers whose products were either geometric or floral, with muted shades and interesting plays of light and dark.

Most Scandinavian weavers created hangings and *ryijy*, or *rya*, rugs in small studios. Motifs were derived from native, particularly Finnish, folk motifs, some of which in the 1920s were Cubist-inspired. Texture continued to play an important part, especially as a heavy pile was required to provide warmth and comfort.

American rugs were influenced largely by the geometric arm of French rug design, with such talents as Donald Deskey, Gilbert Rohde, Eugene Schoen, Ruth Reeves and Loja Saarinen making significant contributions. Deskey's designs, although usually geometric, often approached abstraction. Ruth Reeves was also responsible for a bold and colourful design, her *Electric* rug of 1930, which was decorated with a zigzag pattern in red, green and blue.

The Cranbrook Academy, north of Detroit, played an important role in the dissemination of Scandinavian ideals to a generation of American weavers whose work came to prominence after World War II. Rugs and decorative hangings were seen as an extension of the *Gesamtkunstwerk* concept of the interior as a total environment. Loja Saarinen's weaving studio was established in October 1928 to complete special commissions, and in 1929 a weaving department was founded, staffed with Swedish expatriates, to execute commissions by architects and designers such as Frank Lloyd Wright. Loja Saarinen's style was marked by a restrained palette and an absence of either sharp geometry or purely representational motifs.

Some of the handsomest Art Deco American carpet designs, however, were anonymous; these included a variety of geometric-patterned rugs made by the huge Bigelow Hartford and W. & J. Sloane Manufacturing companies.

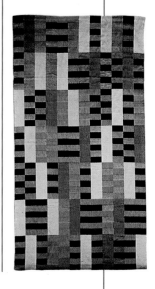

GRAPHICS
AND
FINE ART

PAINTING

There is really no such thing as specifically Art Deco painting. It is possible to talk of Cubism, Surrealism, and Expressionism as coherent styles, but Art Deco painting never really existed in any convincing way. Strictly speaking, Art Deco derived its name from the *Exposition des Art Décoratifs et Industriels,* which did not allow for a painting pavilion. Although the distance between the decorative arts and fine art is not as great as many people think, the best painting of the 1920s and 1930s certainly had little to do with the Art Deco style – if anything, the best painting and sculpture produced in Paris, Germany and Russia was itself an influence. What does still exist are examples of work by particular individuals that describe, or record in some way, the spirit of Art Deco.

Art historians looking back at the art between the wars find examples of the best art in the work of

Picasso, Matisse and the Surrealists. There is really very little question that artists of the stature of Picasso, Mondrian, Kandinsky and others pushed forward the limits of painting, enriching the visual language beyond a stale academicism. Although these artists are now seen as the giants of 20th century art, it would be wrong to disregard the contributions of less well-known artists who communicated their message more readily, and illustrated the taste of the age. Between the two extremes there is no contest on the grounds of quality, but minor art is often a more accurate indicator of public taste than works of geniuses ahead of their time.

The history books almost totally ignore the work of Tamara de Lempicka – surely the most representative of the period's portrait painters – the murals of Jean Dupas, the portraits of Kees van Dongen, or the later works of Raoul Dufy, reproducing instead the abstract innovations of Paul Klee, Pablo Picasso's classic nudes of immediately after the First World War, or the rigidly thought-out and constructed canvases of Piet Mondrian. This actually misrepre-

ABOVE Aldo Severi: untitled, oil on canvas.

ABOVE RIGHT Erica Giovanna Klein: *Tango*, casein on canvas.

sents the prevailing taste of the period. The artists commanding the highest prices at auction in Paris between the wars were Maurice Utrillo and Maurice Vlaminck. In retrospect, we can see that the host of canvases they produced then were just watered-down versions of their early work, but that was what the public wanted. There is no use either in being high-brow or snobbish about the decorative arts of the period – even artists as great as Picasso turned their hand to stage design, pottery and furniture.

What is perhaps curious about the painting that reflected the taste of the period most accurately was that it was almost always figurative, and in particular there are a great number of portraits that, even if dismissed as vulgar and modish, give a clear insight into the character and taste of their sitters. The many

portraits or figure studies in the Art Deco style were really just illustrations of the period. It is in poster design, where there is no question of high or low art, that a style could truly be said to exist. Graphic artists of the calibre of Rockwell Kent and Cassandre could employ all the devices of Deco design, without needing to feel guilty. Their success relied directly upon their ability to reach the largest audience, to produce a popular image. Abstract art, which had taught so many designers the advantage of using clear form, and strong bold design, was not itself streng-thened by Art Deco. It was, rather, watered down and made acceptable in its application to consumer items. Although there was generally little place for abstraction in Art Deco-style painting, there were exceptions to the rule.

LEFT A popular printmaker of the Art Deco period was Louis Icart, whose 1926 drypoint and etching, *Fumée (Smoke)*, appears here. His blatantly erotic females were often surrounded by fur – either in the guise of a sleek canine companion or, as here, a lavish bed covering.

the war he had distilled his art into pure abstraction, where fields of intense colour collided with one another. Developing a style that was called Orphism, Robert Delaunay's work provided inspiration for Art Deco design. The sweeping circular curves and fields of intense colour could be easily adapted to almost any other medium. It was his wife, however, who really developed and used the possibilities of the Simultanist style to the full. Photos of Sonia Delaunay-Terk at the 1925 Exposition show her in Simultanist dresses sitting on a motor car also painted in the house colours. Her designs were all the rage, becoming *the* look for the wealthy, sophisticated and avant-garde culture vulture. Bright and pleasing to the eye, her style brought a refreshing change after the heavy, exotic palette made popular by Bakst and Erté costume designs for the Ballets Russes. The cut was also far more practical, severe, and modern.

Robert Delaunay and his wife Sonia had been deeply involved with the most advanced art in Paris since before the First World War. Quickly adopting the lessons of Cubism from Picasso, Braque, Juan Gris and Fernand Léger, Robert Delaunay produced paintings of Paris, the Eiffel Tower, Saint-Severin church and other motifs of the modern world such as the aeroplane and the motor car. By the outbreak of

Another painter who is still regarded as important, and could be said to reflect Art Deco preoccupations was Fernand Léger. A friend and ally of Le Corbusier and Amédée Ozenfant, his pictures hung in the *Pavillon de l'Esprit Nouveau* at the 1925 Exposition. If Le Corbusier's architectural preferences

RIGHT This oil-on-canvas depicts a couple from French pantomime, *Pierrot et Columbine*. The 1921 painting is by Irene Lagut.

FAR RIGHT
Japanese-born Tsuguharu Foujita lived for a short time in London before settling in Paris, where he painted this picture in 1917. Most of his art combined traditional oriental techniques with Western subjects, although this figure with bird is wholly Eastern in flavour. Foujita also produced etchings and lithographs.

were to provide a house that was a machine for living in, Léger painted large murals and canvases that reflected the age's obsession with machinery. His canvases are peopled with robot-like figures in the brightest of colour combinations. What he aimed to do was personalize the machine and employ it as subject matter, an attitude that ran throughout Art Deco in its more modernist vein.

The painters Henri Matisse and Raoul Dufy also contributed to Art Deco influence. Matisse's interest in exotic subject matter, inspired by his visits to Morocco, reflected the contemporary French obsession with the colonies. Oriental art had been in vogue since the mid-19th century, but Matisse's exquisite sense of decoration reinstilled it with a vigorous modern feel. Dufy, who had failed to win a commission for a large mural for the swimming pool of the *Normandie*, produced painting after painting of the Côte d'Azur and Marseilles and its sailors. The South of France became the playground of the rich.

The many-faceted nature of Jean Dupas' talent was also applied to painting. In Emile-Jacques Ruhlmann's *Hotel d'un Collectionneur* at the 1925 Exposition, Dupas displayed a large mural entitled *Les Perruches* (the parakeets), a theme that was

equally dear to Matisse. His many murals and folding screens for the *Normandie* and other private commissions, although executed in lacquer among other media, were in essence large paintings. Exotic and rich in subject matter, they were fine examples of the decorative tendencies of painting in the Art Deco style.

Tamara de Lempicka, who had been a pupil of André Lhotte, was probably the most typically Art Deco of all the portrait painters. Born Tamara Gorska to a prosperous Polish family near Warsaw, she married a Russian, Thadeus Lempitzski (Lempicki), while in her teens. The couple arrived in Paris towards the end of World War I. Deserted by her husband in the 1920s, de Lempicka decided to support herself and her daughter Kisette by painting. She enrolled at the Académie Ransom, where she studied with Maurice Denis, a disciple of Cézanne, and André Lhote, the theoretician of Cubism.

De Lempicka's portraits of women, in vogue again, are lavish studies in eroticism. The Folies Bergères, Ziegfeld's follies, Josephine Baker dancing in the nude are all highly suggestive and informative portraits of the risqué fast set that Nancy Cunard was part of. Semi-clad nudes provoke with pointed breasts

ABOVE The oil-on-card painting *Flamant Rose (Pink Flamingo)* was painted by Raphael Delorme. He was noted for his bulky female nudes, most of whom he situated in strange architectural settings. The vase-bearing woman here is seen amid a variety of Cubist motifs, with the title subject open-winged behind her.

behind thin layers of diaphanous silk, or thin coverings of black Spanish lace. Like Foujita's sitters or the hermaphrodite little girls in Balthus paintings, de Lempicka's sitters look at the spectator with a coy, langorous look. Between 1924 and 1939 she painted about 100 portraits and nudes; these were dramatically composed works, usually boldly coloured (but sometimes black and white), highly stylized and charged with energy, sensuality and sophistication. Partly angled Cubism, partly fashion illustration, they were positive expressions of the Art Deco style and should have given her a classic reputation accordingly.

RIGHT *La Naissance d'Aphrodite*, or *The Birth of Venus*, was depicted in a Cubist manner by Paul Véra in the 1925 oil-on-canvas. Véra was a versatile painter, wood-engraver, sculptor and fabric designer. The ornate frame, like so many for modern art, seems incongruous.

FAR LEFT This watercolour is by André Edouard Marty, whose illustrations often appeared in *La Gazette du Bon Ton*. Although a design for an interior, the 1939 drawing captures a loving moment between a stylishly gowned *Parisienne* and her child. Marty also enamelled jewellery and other pieces for Camille Fauré's workshop at Limoges.

LEFT Jean Dupas: *Woman in Furs with Borzoi*, oil on panel, 1920s.

FAR RIGHT Besides his many lacquered *objets*, the versatile Jean Dunand produced some lovely mixed-media flat works, such as the *Portrait of Louise Boulanger*, of watercolour, charcoal, pastel, and gold and silver paint. The subject's face shines, even above her shawl.

Other painters of this sort of genre were Otto Dix and Christian Schad, who did for Berlin what de Lempicka had done for Paris, but better.

In sharp contrast to her handsome, somewhat aggressive works were the ethereal paintings of Marie Laurençin, which are often characterized as highly feminine because of their pastel hues, female subjects and innate 'prettiness'. They were strong, distinctive images none the less, and they appeared prominently in contemporary interiors, including those of her brother-in-law André Groult.

Female figures dominated Art Deco canvases, and nowhere more boldly than in the paintings of Bordeaux-trained Raphael Delorme, whose bulky, muscular nudes were often situated in bizarre architectural settings, wearing only incongruous headdress or surrounded by fully dressed maidservants. Indeed, an entire group of Bordeaux artists emerged in the Art Deco period, including not only Delorme but also Jean Dupas, Robert Pougheon, André Lhotte, René Buthaud and Jean Despujols. Although their monumental and allegorical paintings of women tended towards the neo-classical, they were wholly of the period in terms of drawing and colours, as well as in such specific details as stylized flowers, make-up, hairstyle and costume.

Pougheon studied at the Ecole des Beaux-Arts in Bordeaux and that in Paris, where he developed an abstract style in which the subject's anatomy was given a pronounced angular muscularity, often of heroic proportions. Some of his works are quintessentially Art Deco in their extreme stylization, while others portray allegorical figures in naturalistic settings.

Domergue, another student of the Bordeaux Ecole des Beaux-Arts and Prix de Rome recipient, painted portraits of Parisian socialites, theatre celebrities and nudes, in an engaging style in which certain facial features were exaggerated. Buthaud, like Dupas, switched media with great facility. His paintings, often rendered initially as cartoons for his stained-glass windows or *verre églomisé* panels, incorporate all the softness and sensuality of his designs for ceramics.

One of the most popular Art Deco artists, especially in the United States, was the French-born Louis Icart, whose coloured etchings and aquatints perfectly captured the image of the chic, attractive, sometimes slightly risqué woman of the 1930s, part-Hollywood poster girl, part-Parisian fashionplate. She reclined in a gossamer gown; her hair was usually marcelled, her high-arched brows pencil-thin, her eyes heavily shadowed, and her lips a reddened Cupid's bow. She was often smoking and accompanied by a greyhound, poodle or borzoi.

German, Austrian, Scandinavian and American painters also created works that can loosely be termed Art Deco, especially their stylized portraits of chic or

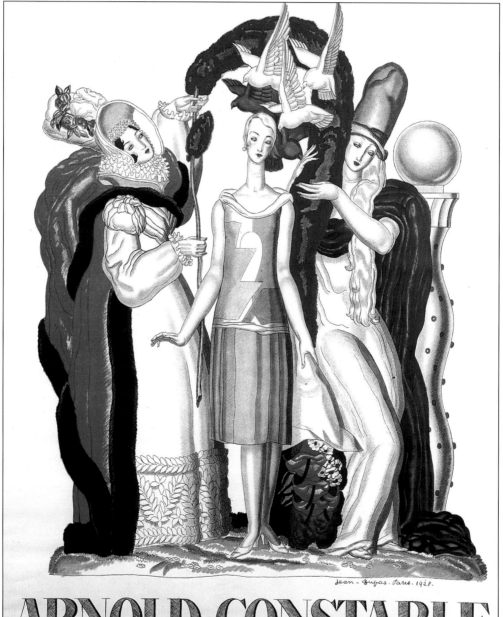

ARNOLD CONSTABLE

COMMEMORATING THE MODE OF YESTERDAY

PRESENTING THE MODE OF TO-DAY

FORECASTING THE MODE OF TO-MORROW

androgynous women. The Paris-based American Romaine Brooks, for instance, depicted Una, Lady Troubridge, in a dapper man's suit and short hair, complete with monocle and a pair of dachshunds, while the Danish-born Gerda Wegener painted sensuous female nudes in erotic poses, but in distinctly modern settings.

Interesting and anecdotal, no Art Deco style painting is ever great art, it is more an example of entertaining camp.

GRAPHICS: **P**OSTERS AND **M**AGAZINES

By the end of the 19th century artists like Steinlen, Henri de Toulouse-Lautrec, Aubrey Beardsley and Edward Penfield produced works that truly understood the limitations and advantages of the poster medium. From them other graphic artists learnt the skills of successful poster design, and its role in 20th-century society. A poster had to be inexpensive to mass-produce, striking in design, and arresting enough to catch the viewer's attention for long enough to tempt him to read the accompanying text. This latter attribute was not even essential, as the poster could work on the same level as a medieval stained glass window, educating and informing an illiterate audience and suggesting to them what they might like to acquire. Although the message was more mundane and down to earth than that of the medieval craftsman, the result in terms of beauty was not

LEFT The eau-de-cologne label is for the scent *Pois de Senteur*. Its English name noted parenthetically, *Sweet Pea*, leads one to believe that this product was intended for the British or American market.

necessarily less. The best posters were equal to if not better than a lot of so-called fine art, and this was especially the case with Art Deco.

The Art Deco poster was the first full-blown example of a sophisticated understanding of the advantages and idiosyncracies of the world of advertising. This was hardly surprising as the growth of the advertising industry and the medium of poster design were inseparable. Art Deco, the style of the consumer age, was applied with great success to the promotion of all the new consumer items; the gramophone (phonograph), radio set, the motor car (automobile), aeroplane, ocean-going liner, cosmetics, household appliances and, of course. the Hollywood movies.

Printing methods, especially colour reproduction processes, had vastly improved in the 19th and early 20th centuries, as had the quality of the finished product, encouraging top-ranking artists and illustrators to accept commissions.

Graphics had become bolder, broader, more geometric, less ornamented and, perhaps most important, highly legible. The first of the century's sans-serif typefaces, *Railway*, had been designed in 1918 by Edward Johnston, for the London Underground system. The Bauhaus typographer Herbert Bayer's *Universal* typeface introduced in 1925 was void not only of serifs and other decorative elements, but indeed even of capital letters! Even the Cyrillic

alphabet took on strongly angular lines in the 1920s, in graphics by, among other, Vladimir Tatlin, El Lissitzky and Natalia Goncharova. In 1920s France, however, decorative touches were added to – rather than subtracted from – typefaces, a logical development, considering the vogue for decoration in every other medium. This was manifested primarily in the juxtaposition of thick and thin elements within a single letter, or in decorative shading that entirely eliminated a part of a letter. MF Benton's *Parisian* (1928) is an example of thick-thin characters, and AM Cassandre's *Bifur* (1929) consisted of letters that were nearly unrecognizable, except for their grey areas.

The motifs of many of the vividly coloured posters and graphics of the period were characterized by sheer energy and exuberance, in part the result of the new obsession with speed and travel that accompanied the fancy motor cars, fast trains and elegant ocean liners which were so much an expression of the 1920s and 1930s.

The one lasting theme and motif that ran throughout the Art Deco poster and illustration was that of the modish, chic, self-possessed and highly energetic woman. She would be the role model that any woman bent on self-improvement would have to emulate. Ever changing, she inspired people to part with their money in order to keep up with her. Unlike all the idealized nudes and nymphs that peopled Art Deco sculptures the women in posters were modern in every sense of the word. The sketches of Ernest Deutsch Dryden are a superb contemporary record. Women in the latest fashions stand with their companions around a Bugatti motor car ready to step in and set off to where? Deauville, Cannes, Long Island, or a weekend party at a country house?

The two greatest Art Deco poster designers were without a doubt Paul Colin and Cassandre.

AM Cassandre (1901–1968), born Adolphe Mouron in Russia, was the outstanding poster artist and typographer of Art Deco Paris. His distinctive graphic style – bright colours combined with subtle shading, bold lettering often juxtaposed with wispy characters, and strong, angular, flat images – won him numerous awards. He is best known for his travel posters, the most famous among them, a streamlined, angled locomotive puffing decoratively for the *Nord Express* (1927) and a fiercely frontal view of the liner *Normandie* (1935). The prow of the ship pushes forward out of the picture, as the majestic giant dwarfs

TOP AND TOP CENTRE
The two couples, above, were drawn in 1920 by George Barbier. The delicate ornament and costume of Asia were of great appeal to Art Deco designers, as was the lush exoticism of Africa.

the small tug beneath it. The stark outlines of the design and the stylized realism of the picture suggest to the viewer qualities that the *Normandie* certainly had, strength and elegance.

Paris's second most important poster designer was Paul Colin, whose often light-hearted illustrative style, although neither as austere nor as classy as Cassandre's, was equally effective. Originally the poster artist and stage designer for the Théâtre des Champs-Elysées, Colin's images include a memorable depiction of a saucy Josephine Baker with two black jazz musicians in a poster advertising *La Revue Nègre*. He depicted Miss Baker in several paintings as well, and also designed stunning posters advertising not only other performers but cigarettes and other products, nearly all of which featured human figures, sometimes highly stylized, sometimes lovingly caricatured in recognizable detail.

Colin also produced posters to advertise the visiting jazz giants at the Folies Bergères and other venues. It is with posters like these that the Art Deco style comes closest to gaining the name the Jazz Style. Deriving loosely from Cubist painting with its disjointed sense of perspective, the colours are jazzed up, as unlikely combinations of electric blue are juxtaposed with red and livid greens. The overall effect was initially jarring but then resolved itself into an energetic and fully comprehensible pictorial logic.

Charles Gesmar, who is best remembered for his posters of the Casino de Paris performer Mistinguett, designed in a more curvilinear and ornate style, *à la 1900*. He usually used stark lettering, but occasionally became rather fanciful, with letters resembling those of Jean-Gabriel Domergue on his poster for the dancers Maarcya & Gunsett.

Three memorable posters were created for the 1925 Paris Exposition – by Charles Loupot, Robert Bonfils and Girard. Loupot's design cleverly juxtaposed industry and decoration, depicting a massive factory with wisps of black smoke cutting across clouds shaped like stylized flowers. Bonfils' image was totally decorative, featuring a stylized Greek maiden carrying a basket of stylized flowers, and accompanied by a dark leaping deer.

Another notable poster designer, René Vincent, forsook his architectural studies at the École des Beaux-Arts, Paris, for a career in the graphic arts and, to a lesser degree, ceramics. An illustrator for *La Vie Parisienne*, *The Saturday Evening Post* and *L'Ilustration*, Vincent also designed posters for the giant Parisian department store Au Bon Marché. His compositions often featured fashionable demoiselles playing golf or bearing parasols done in a crisp, illustrative style heightened with contrasting blocked colours.

Many other French graphic artists provided the world of poster art with intermittent works. Jean Dupas, for example, turned his hand to a series of delightful advertisements for Saks Fifth Avenue, Arnold Constable and others, with a facility that showed his great versatility. Also from Bordeaux, René Buthaud transposed the lithe maidens on his stoneware vessels on to paper, some to herald the annual Paris salons. The identity of the prolific artist Orsi, whose name appears on more than a 1,000 posters, including images of Josephine Baker at the Théâtre de l'Etoile, remains an enigma. From the world of fashion, Georges Lepape and Natalia Goncharova created posters in a predictably colourful and theatrical style which depicted Paris as the pleasure capital of the world.

In Britain, the United States and Germany, most poster designs were pared down and geometric, using the bold rectilinear typefaces that were fast becoming the norm. Edward McKnight Kauffer, the American-born designer who also created rugs (see the section on carpets), worked both in England and in Hollywood, producing striking designs for, among others, the film *Metropolis*, Shell Petroleum and London Transport. While his London Transport posters tended to be quite Cubist and abstract, those of other designers were more colourful and representational, but always with easy-to-read typefaces. The French artist Jean Dupas designed a poster for London Transport, showing a scene of elegantly dressed ladies in Hyde Park.

In Belgium, the Swiss-born Léo Marfurt formed a 50-year association with the tobacco company van der Elst, for which he designed advertising, packaging and posters. In 1927 he formed his own studio, Les Créations Publicitaires, where he produced two masterpieces of travel poster art: *Flying Scotsman* (1928) and *Ostende-Douvres* (around 1928). The former emerged as one of the most recognizable and popular images of the inter-war years. René Magritte, a magazine and advertising illustrator before he turned to Surrealism, also created some vibrant Art Deco poster images in the mid-1920s.

Two other Low-Country artists, Willem Frederik ten Broek and Kees van der Laan, produced posters for Dutch shipping lines.

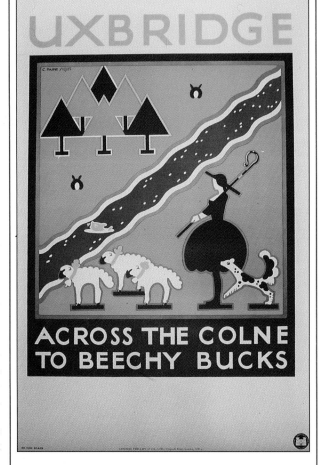

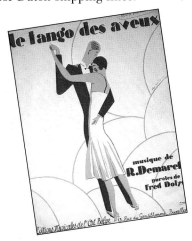

LEFT René Magritte: *Le Tango des Aveux*, sheet-music cover, about 1925.

In Switzerland, Otto Baumberger, Herbert Matter and Otto Morach designed for the fashionable men's clothing store PKZ, as did the German Ludwig Hohlwein. Baumberger, trained as a lithographer and posterist in Munich, London and Paris, worked principally in Zurich, where he helped to establish the Swiss School of Graphic Design. Matter is known principally for his pioneership of the photo-montage technique in travel posters such as *Winterferein* (1934) and *All Roads Lead to Switzerland* (1935).

Ludwig Hohlwein was Germany's most popular and prolific poster artist. His preference for virile masculine images to advertise coffee, cigarettes and beer later won him many commissions for Nazi propaganda posters. Hohlwein's real gift lay in his use of colour in unexpected combinations.

Austrian-born Lucien Bernhard studied at the Munich Academy, from which he emerged as a versatile artist-architect, designing buildings, furnish-

LEFT The strong sans-serif typeface used by London Transport from 1918 can be seen on this colourful poster. The setting may be pastoral, but the illustrative and design elements are decidedly *moderne*. The artist was C Paine.

RIGHT Lithographic poster for the Alliance Graphique. The ocean liner *Atlantique* caught fire 16 months after it was launched and burned and sank off the coast of France.

FAR RIGHT The dramatic and somewhat frightening bow of an unnamed French ship looms overhead in the stunning 1935 poster by AM Cassandre (the same image was used to advertise the *Normandie* liner). The Russian-born Cassandre was France's best-known poster artist, as well as a significant designer of typefaces. Alliance Graphique, the advertising agency which he co-founded with Maurice Moyrand, was extremely successful, with cigarette companies, newspapers, and railroad lines among its clients.

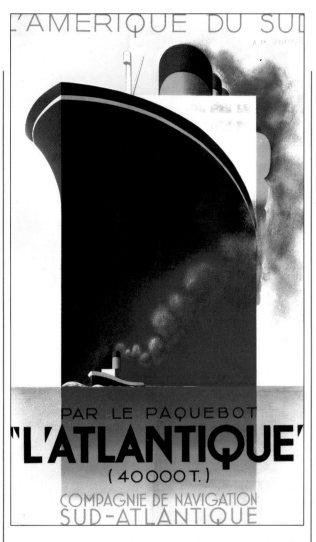

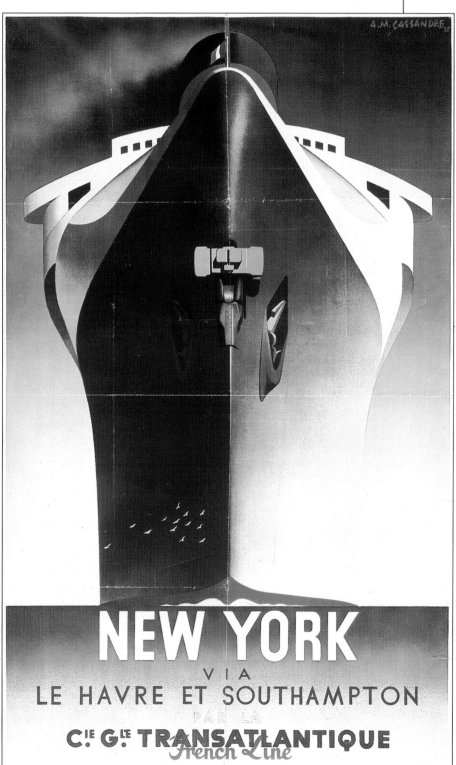

ings, and graphic works. In 1923 he emigrated to the United States, where in 1929 he co-founded the Contempora Group in New York. His poster style appears laboured and undirected, but he was invariably treated with respect by contemporary critics.

Magazines of all sorts proliferated in the West in the 1920s and 1930s, the most influential in terms of graphics being those published in Paris. These included *Gazette du Bon Ton*; *Art, Goût, Beauté*; *Luxe de Paris*; *Vu* and *L'Illustration des Modes* (later *Le Jardin des Modes*). Their fashion and other illustrations, produced by such famous names as Georges Lepape, George Barbier, André Marty, Erté and Bernard Boutet de Monvel, had a great influence on design both in France and abroad.

Leading European and American magazines included the German *Style*, *Harper's Bazaar*, *Femina*, *La Femme Chic*, *Pan*, *The New Yorker* and *Fortune*. *Vogue*, was influential on both sides of the Atlantic.

BOOK **B**INDINGS **A**ND **J**ACKETS

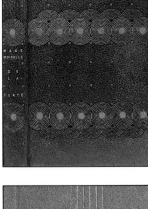

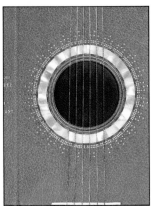

By long tradition, books in France had been published with flimsy paper covers, making them unacceptable to the serious collectors, who employed bookbinders to design and create covers for favourite volumes. This system prevailed right up to the early years of this century. The binding's function was to preserve the text, and it was not considered as a means of artistic expression until the emergence of the Art Deco movement. At that point, however, the principles of artistic excellence together with excellence in craftsmanship caused a radical change.

Credit goes to Pierre Legrain for revolutionizing the art. In 1912, when Jacques Doucet disposed of his renowned collection of antique furniture at auction, he presented his correspondingly important library of eighteenth-century books to the city of Paris, retaining only his collection of works by contemporary authors. The young Legrain, who had been more or less unemployed since his former employer Paul Iribe set sail for the United States in 1914, was retained to design the bindings in a modern style. Without prior experience, and largely self-taught, Legrain undertook the task in the *atelier* of the binder René Kieffer. Doucet was immediately impressed, and commissioned more bindings, and by the early 1920s Legrain's abilities had drawn the attention of other collectors, such as Baron Robert de Rothschild, Henri de Monbrison and Baron Gourgaud, all of whom became regular and valuable clients.

Legrain's ignorance of traditional binding techniques served him well, for it allowed him to make free use of his creativity and to introduce materials not used before. From the start, his designs were avant-garde, in keeping with the revolution in design taking place throughout the decorative arts in Paris. In place of the lightly ornamented floral bindings of the pre-war years, he introduced forceful geometrical patterns in the same precious materials employed at the time by Modernist *ébénistes* such as Émile-Jacques Ruhlmann, Clément Rousseau and Adolphe Chanaux.

Bookbinding became, in many ways, an extension of the Art Deco cabinet-making craft, as exotic veneers and skins were borrowed in search of a means to modernize the age-old craft. Hides such as snakeskin, *galuchat* (sharkskin) and vellum were interchanged with binding's traditional Moroccan leather. Decorative accents were provided in innumerable ways. For instance the binding could be inlaid with a mosaic of coloured leather sections, or with gold, silver, platinum or palladium fillets, or it could be gilt-tooled, blind-stamped or painted.

Beyond Legrain, Paris was home to a host of premier binders who worked in the Modernist idiom. Foremost among these was another Doucet protégée, Rose Adler, with Georges Cretté (the successor to Marius Michel), René Kieffer, Paul Bonet, François-Louis Schmied, Lucien Creuzevault, Georges Canape and Robert Bonfils. Less known were the works of Paul Gruel, André Bruel, Jean Lambert, Alfred Latour, Jeanne Langrand, Yseux, Louise Germain and Germaine Schroeder, whose creations in many instances matched those of their more celebrated colleagues.

The new enthusiasm for bookbinding also drew in graphic artists, for example, Maurice Denis, George Barbier, Georges Lepape and Raphael Drouart. The artist-turned-decorator André Mare incorporated a pair of love birds, in engraved and tinted parchment, for his cover design for *Amour*, commissioned by Baron Robert de Rothschild.

LEFT The opulent leather bookbinding made in Lyon, France, in 1936, covers Maurice Barrès' book, *La Mort de Venise*. It was bound by JK van West. The architectural form extending across the spine of the volume and creating a symmetrical design on the front and back covers was an unusual device begun in France in the 1920s. Before that, most bindings' decoration was limited to the front, with the back left plain. Note the silvery palladium highlighting the black tower, a metal inlay first used by Pierre Legrain, the most influential Art Deco bookbinder.

Many of these binders collaborated on commissions with artist-designers, and even with other binders. Schmied, in particular, was extremely versatile, participating in commissions as a binder, artist or artisan, with Cretté and Canape. Jean Dunand was likewise very active, creating lacquered and *coquille d'oeuf* plaques, and even wooden ones inlaid with detailed marquetry designs, for these and other binders.

The 1920s binder drew mostly on the same repertoire of motifs used in other media. Combinations of lines, dots, overlapping circles and centripetal or radiating bands, were used to create symmetrical or asymmetrical compositions. The influence of the machine and new technology became increasingly felt towards 1930, particularly by Paul Bonet, who emerged as Legrain's successor. The preferred motifs of the Paris salon in the early 1920s – the stylized floral bouquet or gazelle, for example – quickly yielded to a fiercely geometric vocabulary found especially in works such as Creuzevaults's *La Seine de Bercy au Point-du-Jour*, Legrain's *Les Chansons de Bilitis*, Kieffer's *Trois Eglises*, and Bonet's *Les Poilus*.

Some binders incorporated photographic elements in their covers, among them Laure Albin Guillot, who specialized in microphotography, enlarging minute biological specimens – plankton, for instance – to produce unusual, pseudo-abstract designs. Other of her bindings included human images, such as an erotic, back-posed nude on Pierre Loüys's *Les Chansons de Bilitis*.

In other western countries, the finest bookbinders adhered largely to traditional materials, methods and designs. However, mass-produced, printed covers in Germany, Britain, the United States and elsewhere often depicted Art Deco figures and motifs. The stylized lettering which came to be associated with 1920s Paris was also frequently seen. A 1932 English-language edition of Bruno Bürgel's *Oola-Boola's Wonder Book* displays such lettering – bold, in several sizes and decorated in blind stamping with simple vertical and horizontal bands.

In the United States, the Greek-born John Vassos and Ruth Vassos designed and produced bindings of note, often for their own coloured-cloth-on-board books, which included *Contempo* (1928), *Ultimo* (1930) and *Phobia* (1931). These catchy, contemporary titles appeared in thick bold lettering on grounds highlighted by equally bold geometric designs. Vassos was also known for his industrial designs.

Birth and death dates are given wherever possible, but due to the incomplete documentation of this relatively recent art movement some have been omitted.

Abbreviations used: SAD, Société des Artistes Décorateurs; SAF, Société des Artistes Français; UAM, Union des Artistes Modernes.

AALTO, Hugo Hendrik Alvar
1898–1976
Architect and designer

Born in Finland, studied architecture at the Helsinki Polytechnic. He began his professional practice two years later with neo-classical designs. His style then moved towards Modernism and in 1930 he designed simple Modernist rooms for the Helsinki Museum 'Minimum Apartment' Exhibition. In 1933 he moved his office to Helsinki and his furniture was shown for the first time outside Finland, at Fortnum & Mason in London. Along with Maire Gullicsen and his wife, he formed a company named Artek to produce his furniture, as it still does today.

ARGY-ROUSSEAU, Gabriel
1885–1953
Glassmaker, ceramicist

Born in Paris as Joseph-Gabriel Rousseau, entered the National High School for Ceramics at Sèvres in 1902. Adopted his wife's family name after 1913 and became known as Argy-Rousseau. Best known for his work in *pâte-de-verre*, first exhibited in 1914; also developed the technique of *pâte-de-cristal*. Many examples of his work in both techniques displayed at the salons in Paris in the 1920s, including the 1925 Exposition.

BARBIER, George
1882–1932
Graphic and poster artist, theatre designer

Prolific and gifted artist, influenced by the Ballets Russes, developing a similar graphic style for fashion illustrations, theatre set and costume design, posters, advertisements, magazine covers, etc, for which he often used the *pochoir* process. Illustrated many books on dance, eg *Dances de Nijinsky* (1913) and costumes for the Folies Bergères and Casino de Paris. In the late 1920s he worked briefly in Hollywood. He died while at work on Louy's *Aphrodite*.

BASTARD, Georges
1881–1939
Dinandier

Born in Andeville, France, Georges Bastard came from a family of *tabletiers* (makers of chess- and draughts-tables), and began working in his father's *atelier* after studying at the Ecole des Arts Décoratifs. He worked in delicate materials — rare woods, mother-of-pearl, ivory, tortoiseshell, horn, rock crystal, and semi-precious stones — producing small *objets d'art* such as fans boxes and letter openers, often with carvings inspired by naturalistic forms. He collaborated with Ruhlmann and Montagnac on several pieces shown at the 1925 Paris Exposition, as well as showing his own pieces. In 1938 he was made director of the Sèvres porcelain manufactory.

BEL GEDDES, Norman
1893–1958
Architect and industrial designer

Born in Michigan, attended the Cleveland School of Art and the Art Institute of Chicago before joining the Chicago advertising agency, Barnes-Crosby, as a draughtsman. In 1918 he started a successful career in New York as a stage-set designer, and in 1927 he took up industrial design and opened his own firm. His early commissions (1929–32) were for domestic products such as furniture for the Simmons Co (1929), counter scales for the Toledo Scale Co (1929), and a range of gas stoves for the Standard Gas Equipment Corp. (1932). His prototype *House of Tomorrow* (1931) and his skyscraper cocktail shaker (1937) proved his adaptability to many design fields.

BELL, Vanessa
1879–1961
Painter, decorative arts designer

Sister of the writer Virginia Woolf and originally a painter, strongly influenced by the style of the French post-Impressionists. Through her association with the Omega Workshops (1913–19) she joined a group of artists in their attempt to bring a painterly style to the decoration of household furnishings. Her life after the Omega Workshops period was devoted to her residence, Charleston, which she shared with the painter Duncan Grant, and to work in a variety of media.

BENEDICTUS, Edouard
1878–1930
Tapestry and rug designer

Trained as a painter, later undertook decoration and finally turned to tapestry. He executed designs for Tassinari, Chatel, Brunet, Meunier & Co and others as well as various rug designs.

BLONDAT, Max
1879–1926
Sculptor

One of the artists who successfully made the transition between the Art Nouveau and Art Deco styles. He exhibited at the salon of the SAF from 1911–25. He was responsible for many public projects such as fountains, memorials, tombs, portraits and allegoric representations. He was awarded the Légion d'Honneur in 1925. Aside from his public commissions, he also excelled in decorative design, and was represented at the 1925 Exposition by two lunette-shaped reliefs for the dining room of the *Pavillon de l'Ambassade*.

BONET, Paul
b. 1889
Bookbinder

Born in Paris, studied at Ecole Robert-Estienne under Desmules and Giraldon, with extra instruction from gilder Jeanne. First exhibited at *Exposition du Livre* (1925), then Salon d'Automne and Société des Artistes Décorateurs. Collector Carlos R Scherrer, of Buenos Aires, became his most important patron, also Doucet. He developed new photographic and sculptural bindings techniques in the 1930s, and pioneered the use of new materials such as duralumin. Major works included *La Belle Enfant* and *Calligrammes*.

BONFILS, Robert
1886–1971
Designer, poster and graphic artist, bookbinder

Born in Paris, emerged as one of the most versatile French Art Deco designers, producing a wide range of works on canvas and paper and designs for textiles and ceramics. One of three artists commissioned to design the official posters for the 1925 Paris Exposition.

BOUCHERON, Frédéric
Jeweller

Opened his first jewellery store at the Palais Royale in 1858, and soon acquired fame as a fine technician and a creator of beautiful designs. In 1893, he was the first jeweller to set up shop at the Place Vendôme, where he continued to serve the social élite, and where the firm still operates successfully today. Over the years, the Maison Boucheron opened branches worldwide, and the London store, established in 1907, is still flourishing.

BRANDT, Edgar
1880–1960
Wrought-iron worker

Born in Paris. He studied technical and scientific subjects, and designed and made jewellery and wrought-iron work prior to opening his *atelier* in 1919. He produced his own designs, but primarily executed the work of other designers. Brandt was a major contributor to the 1925 Paris Exposition, with his own stand. In 1926 he was commissioned to do the ironwork for the Cheney building in New York City, and shortly after opened Ferrobrandt, his New York branch. Among his other important commissions were the ramp for the Mollien staircase at the Louvre, the gate for the new French Embassy in Brussels and the Eternal Flame for the Tomb of the Unknown Soldier in Paris.

BRANDT, Marianne
1893–1983
Metalworker

Born in Germany, studied at the Bauhaus from 1923–28. In 1924 she worked with Moholy-Nagy in a metal workshop, designing prototypes of everyday objects for industrial production. In 1928–29 she worked with Gropius on the Dammerstock housing project, and from 1929–32 she designed metal objects for Ruppleberg in Gotha. After the war she taught at the High School of Applied Arts in Dresden, and from 1951–54 in Berlin at the Institute of Applied Arts.

BREUER, Marcel
1902–81
Architect and furniture designer

Born in Hungary, spent a brief period in Vienna before moving to the Bauhaus in Weimar in 1920, where he specialized in furniture. From 1925–28 he taught at the Bauhaus in Dessau as head of the furniture workshop. He designed his famous Wassily chair in 1924 and a modular system of storage furniture the following year. In 1928 he set up private practice in Berlin. In 1928 he designed the Cesa chair, his own enormously successful version of the cantilevered chairs pioneered by Stam and Mies van der Rohe. He went to the United States in 1927 and worked as an architect in partnership with Walter Gropius until 1941. He was a professor of architecture at Harvard from 1937 to 1947.

BUTHAUD, René
1886–1986
Ceramist

Originally trained as a painter in the French town of Bordeaux, and was later awarded both the Prix Chenavard and the Prix Roux. He applied his neo-classical style to pottery after 1928, and was exhibited at the Rouard Gallery in Paris from the late 1920s to the end of his artistic career.

CARDER, Frederick
1863–1963
Glass designer, founder Steuben Glass Works

Born in Staffordshire, England,

worked for various local potteries and glass manufactories before becoming a designer for Stevens & Williams of Brierley Hill. Left England in 1903 to found the Steuben Glass Works at Corning, New York. Here he acted as designer and developed intarsia, iridescent, bubbled and metallic glasses which competed with Tiffany's products. When the factory was taken over by Corning Glass in 1918, Carder continued in the post. Held the post of art director from 1932 and retired in 1959.

CASSANDRE (MOURON,
André)
1901–1968
Poster artist, painter, theatre designer, typographer

Born in the Ukraine. Studied at the Académie Julien, Paris. First poster done in 1923, and until 1928 he designed for Hachard. He carried out masterpieces for the French National Railways and ocean liners, and also designed typefaces. In 1930 he formed Alliance Graphique with Maurice Moyrand. He exhibited in the United States in the 1930s, including covers for *Harper's Bazaar*. He committed suicide in 1968.

CHAMBELLAN, René Paul
1893–1955
Architectural sculptor

Born in Hoboken, New Jersey, studied at New York University from 1912–14 and later at the Académie Julien in Paris. After World War I he established himself as one of America's foremost architectural sculptors. His work was sought for important public commissions, and his most important private ones include the façades for the American Radiator Building and the Daily News Building (both in conjunction with the architect Raymond Hood), the Stewart and Co. Building, the New York Life Insurance Building, the Cromwell-Collier Building, the foyer of the Chanin Building and the ceiling of the RKO Center Theater in Rockefeller Center.

CHANIN, Irwin S.
b. 1900
Architect

Son of immigrants from Poltava, the

Ukraine, built a substantial private fortune as an architect and real-estate developer. He worked for his father on building jobs and later for a subway contractor. His major career break came when he developed cost-efficient housing in Brooklyn. He went into partnership with his brother, Henry, forming the Chanin Construction Company in the early 1920s. Several major commissions followed shortly after, including the Fur Center Building, the Forty-sixth Street Theater and the Majestic and Century apartment complexes. The Chanin Building in New York was an edifice to his individual success.

CHERMAYEFF, Serge
b. 1900
Architect and furniture designer

A Russian emigré educated at Harrow in England. He worked as a journalist before 1924, and then became chief designer for the decorating firm E Williams Ltd. In 1928 he was appointed director of the Modern Art Studio set up by the London furniture manufacturers Waring & Gillow. His designs for furniture, carpets and decoration were strongly influenced by the 1925 Paris Exposition. He used black glass, silver cellulose, Macassar ebony and abstract patterns. From 1931–33 he was in private practice as an architect and designed modern interiors for the BBC. From 1933–36 he was in partnership with Eric Mendelsohn, their best-known collaboration being the De La Warr Pavilion at Bexhill, and in 1936 he designed unit furniture for Plant Ltd. In 1939 he emigrated to the United States and taught design and architecture.

CHIPARUS, Demêtre
Sculptor

Born in Rumania but worked in Paris, first exhibiting at the salon of the SAF in 1914 where he was awarded an Honourable Mention. Best known for his figures in bronze and ivory which are carved from fine-quality African ivory, using the grain of the material as part of the design of the figure. His early work, groups of small-scale figures of children at play, developed into

larger and more sophisticated /odels of dancers, personalities, and exotic creatures.

CHRISTOFLE, Charles
1805–63
Silversmith

Founded the firm of Christofle in 1839, investing in it an entire personal fortune. The firm was famous for its superbly crafted silverplate, and won many awards. It is still active today.

CLIFF, Clarice
1899–1972
Ceramicist

Born in Staffordshire, England, and apprenticed as an enameller at Lingard Webster & Co at the age of 13. At 17 she was hired as an engraver at AJ Wilkinson Ltd, and here, from 1918–25, she acquired a talent for pottery techniques. Her first *Bizarre* wares were produced about 1929, and although she continued to design pottery in more conservative styles after World War II, she is best remembered for her more light-hearted, even frivolous, wares.

COATES, Wells
1895–1958
Industrial designer

A leading figure of the British avant-garde. Born in Japan, son of a Canadian missionary, he studied engineering in Vancouver from 1913. He began to work as a designer after 1927 and in 1931 won a competition to design a stand for the Venesta Plywood Company at the Manchester British Empire Trade Exhibition. In the same year he and Pritchard formed the Isokon Company, in 1931 he designed the sound studios for the BBC in Portland Place, London, and in 1933 he helped form the MARS group as an English chapter of the Congrès Internationaux d'Architecture Moderne. His later designs included the *Thermovent Ekco* fire (1937) and *Ekco* television with a lift up top (1946), the *Radio Time* combined wireless and alarm clock (1946) and aircraft interiors for De Havilland and BOAC (1946–47).

COLIN, Paul
1892–1985
Graphic artist, stage and costume designer

Arrived in Paris 1913. He achieved fame with his 1925 poster announcing Josephine Baker's *La Revue Nègre* in Paris, and did numerous music-hall posters, paintings and book illustrations, including Baker and her jazz musicians. He also designed stage sets. In 1926 he opened the Ecole Paul Colin, a school for graphic arts where he taught for nearly 40 years.

COOPER, Susie (**VERA,** Susan)
b. 1902
Ceramicist

Born in Staffordshire, England, and attended classes at the Burslem school of art in 1919. In 1922 she began work for the AE Gray Co Pottery. Her work was exhibited in the 1925 Paris Exposition. She subsequently showed remarkable marketing as well as design talent in her tablewares, which enjoyed considerable success in Britain in the 1930s. She also executed subdued designs in the post-war period, and her firm was eventually bought out by Wedgwood.

COPIER, Andries Dirk
b. 1901
Glassmaker

Born in Holland, studied in Utrecht and Rotterdam from 1917–25. Joined Leerdam Glass as an apprentice in 1917 and started to produce glass with new forms and techniques. Was awarded a silver medal at the Paris Exposition of 1925. Held first exhibition of *Unica* pieces at Stuttgart in 1927. Leerdam Glass gained great recognition in Europe under his artistic direction.

COWAN, Reginald Guy
1884–1957
Ceramicist, founder Cowan Potteries

Born in Ohio to a family of potters and received practical and formal training. He provided the forum for many of America's most gifted ceramists through his Cowan Pottery, which was for 10 years (1921 until late 1930) at the forefront of modern American ceramic design. In the early 1920s the Cowan Pottery Studio began commercial production and distribution of *comports*, figurines, vases and bookends with roughly 1,200 national outlets. Commercial success came from early adoption of the Modernist style. In 1929 financial difficulties developed, and quality fell as the Depression began to affect the volume of sales.

CREUZEVAULT, Lucien
1893–1958
Bookbinder

Succeeded the binder Dodé in 1904. Exhibited at the Musée Galliera in 1927 and 1928, receiving first prize, and at the 1929 salon of the SAD. He designed numerous bindings in a geometric Art Deco style, including *La Bataille, Le Pot au Noir,* and *La Rose de Bakawali.* In the 1920s he was joined by his son, Henri, also a binder.

DA SILVA BRUHNS, Ivan
Rug designer

Began as a painter and interior decorator, and received his first rug commission from cabinetmaker Louis Majorelle. The da Silva Bruhns workshop was located in Aisne, and his rugs were often part of major decorative arts exhibitions in the 1920s and 1930s, such as the Exposition Coloniale of 1931.

DAUM FRERES

Jean-Louis-Auguste and Jean-Antonin Daum came from Lorraine and established their first glass factory in Nancy in 1875. They initially made gold-ornamented glass partly based on Arabian designs and fine cameo glass (about 1890). While under Gallé's influence and later under Maurice Marinot's, the Daum factory had an active role in developing high standards of craftsmanship, and the family won numerous prizes. Until 1920 the Daums were designing exclusively in the Art Nouveau style, but when Paul Daum entered the firm simpler forms began to appear. These were exhibited at the 1925 Paris Exposition. The firm was later directed by Michael Daum, who introduced a sculptural quality to the glass.

DECORATION INTERIOR MODERNE (DIM)

Founded in 1918 by René Joubert and Georges Mouveau with the idea of designing and realizing furniture and interiors. They were joined in 1924 by Philippe Petit, and began successfully manufacturing mass-produced furniture as well as fine and luxurious pieces. Modernist in their design orientation, they sought a pared-down look, and produced light fixtures to complement their interiors before eliminating them completely in favour of recessed lighting.

DECORCHEMENT, François-Emile
1880–1971
Glassmaker

Born in Conches, France. First works were done in a fine opaque glass paste known as *pâte-d'email.* About 1907 he succeeded in creating a true *pâte-de-verre* using powdered glass purchased from the Cristalleries de Saint-Denis. Eventually he made his own glass and introduced metallic oxides for different colour effects. Around 1920 he found a formula for a hard translucent substance composed of crystal, and combined the oxide colours with silica. Pieces made in this way were shown at the 1925 Paris Exposition. From 1933 to the outbreak of World War II he worked on *pâte-de-verre* leaded glass windows churches.

DELAUNAY, Sonia
1885–1979
Textile and fashion designer

Studied in Paris and married painter Robert Delaunay in 1910, adopting his Fauvist style in her textiles. A 1922 design for abstract dresses led to an invitation to work for a Lyons textile firm, and her design programme for clothing and accessories, 'La Boutique Simultanée', was widely acclaimed at the 1925 Paris Exposition.

DELORME, Raphael
1885–1962
Painter

Born in Bordeaux, attended the city's Ecole des Beaux-Arts. Studied under Gustave Lauriol and Pierre-Gustave Artus. A cousin, Mme Metalier, offered him her castle in Valesnes, where he painted in a style which mixed Art Deco and neo-classical images, including *trompe l'oeil* and perspective effects. Claimed to have sold only one painting.

DESKEY, Donald
b. 1894
Designer, all fields of applied arts

Began his career in advertising, and started to work as a designer in the late 1920s. He became well known in 1932 as the designer of furniture and interiors for Radio City Music Hall in New York. His furniture of the early 1930s set the precedent for the modern style; using aluminium, bakelite and other industrial materials he pioneered a style based on a mixture of influences from France and Germany. By the end of the 1930s he had turned his attention to industrial and packaging design, and by 1950 his firm Donald Deskey Associates was one of the leading American industrial design firms. He also invented a high-pressure laminate called Weldtex.

DESPRES, Jean
1889–1980
Jeweller

Born in Souvigny, and worked as a labourer in the aviation industry during World War I. His experience with industrial design and metalwork led to his interest in precious metals and jewellery design. Much of his jewellery was painted and engraved by Etienne Cournault.

DIEDERICH, Wilhelm Hunt
1884–1953
Wrought-iron, ceramic and fabric designer

Born in Hungary, emigrated to the United States at the age of 15. He lived in Boston with his uncle, the artist William Morris Hunt, before beginning his studies at the Pennsylvania Academy of the Fine Arts. He worked in ceramics and fabric design, but is best known for his work in wrought iron.

DJO-BOURGEOIS,
Edouard-Joseph
1898–1937
Furniture designer

Born in Bezons, France. Studied at the Ecole Speciale d'Architecture, and in 1923 joined Le Studium Louvre and made his début at the salons. At the 1925 Paris Exposition he exhibited two ensembles in the Studium Louvre pavilion: a smoking room and office/library. After 1926 he established his own business and developed a group of avant-garde clients. He used modern furniture materials in his designs, replacing his earlier preference for combinations of wood and glass with tubular metal, aluminium, iron and concrete. Frequent collaborators through the years were Paul Brandt and Louis Tétard.

DORN, Marion
1899–1964
Rug and textile designer

Studied graphic art education at Stanford University. Moved to Paris in 1923 and began a lifelong relationship with the graphic designer Edward McKnight Kauffer, whom she married in 1950. She first made textile hangings in the 1920s and turned to collaboration on rugs in 1927.

DUFRENE, Maurice
1876–1955
Interior designer

Born in Paris, studied at the Ecole des Arts Décoratifs. In 1899 he started to work as a designer for Julius Meier-Graefe's La Maison Moderne. In 1904 he became a founding member of the SAD, through which he exhibited for 30 years. In 1921 he was appointed artistic director of La Maîtrise. He edited three volumes of *Ensembles Mobiliers*, devoted to the interior design shown at the Paris 1925 Exposition, and also published an album of plates of interiors at the 1926 salon of the SAD. He did a similar album for the Paris Exposition of 1937.

DUFY, Raoul
1877–1953
Painter, graphic artist, textile designer

Best known as a painter, but also noted for his illustrations to Guillaume Apollinaire's *Bestiare* (1908). In 1911, he met and was employed by Paul Poiret to design fabrics for the Atelier Martine; the following year he moved to the firm of Bianchini-Feriér, where he designed clothing and furnishing fabrics until 1930. For the next three years he designed printed silks for Onondaga of New York.

DUNAND, Jean
1887–1942
Dinandier and lacquerer

Born in Switzerland, went to Paris in 1896 after studying in Geneva. He intended to become a sculptor, but turned to *dinanderie* around 1902, working in copper, steel and pewter. His first works were Art Nouveau in feeling, but gradually his forms and decorations evolved to more simple, geometric stylizations, and he increased his repertoire of objects. He began learning the technique of lacquer in 1912, and this became his most important means of artistic expression. He worked in close collaboration with Legrain, Printz, Ruhlmann and Goulden, and among his important works were lacquer panels for the ocean liners *Ile de France, l'Atlantique* and *Normandie*.

DUPAS, Jean
1882–1964
Painter and poster artist

Attended the Ecole des Beaux-Arts, Bordeaux, with advanced studies in Paris. He won the Prix de Rome in 1910. In the early 1920s he painted two important works, *Jugement de Paris* and *Les Antilopes*. He carried out posters and catalogue covers for the SAD, and porcelain decoration for Sèvres, and a mural on the subject of history of navigation in the grand salon of the ocean-liner *Normandie*.

FOLLOT, Paul
1877–1941
Interior designer

Born in Paris, the son of a successful wallpaper manufacturer, studied design under Eugène Grasset. His furniture in the prewar years is today classified as 'pure' Art Deco, and the Musée des Arts Décoratifs anticipated the importance of his work by purchasing several pieces directly from the 1912 Salon. In 1923 he accepted the directorship of the design studio Pomone, opened by Au Bon Marché. With assistance he designed all the rooms in the Pomone pavilion at the 1925 Exposition and he remained with Pomone until 1928, when he joined Chermayeff at the newly established Paris branch of Waring & Gillow. When the firm disbanded its Paris office in 1931, he reverted to his role as an independent decorator.

FOUQUET, Georges
1862–1957
Jeweller

Born in France, took charge of La Maison Fouquet in 1895 and redirected it towards new designs in collaboration with two independent designers, Desrosiers and Mucha. He was initially inspired by natural forms, but later moved towards modern designs, emphasizing geometric shapes and variety of colour. He played a leading part in the 1925 Paris Exposition and later international expositions, contributing outstanding creations in collaboration with leading designers. La Maison Fouquet closed its doors in 1936, but Georges continued to work for his regular clients.

GESMAR, Charles
1900–1928
Poster artist, theatre designer

His first poster dates from 1916, shortly before he became a constant companion of Mistinguett, ageing Parisian music-hall sensation. He designed costumes, stage sets, programme covers and posters for her performances at the Casino de Paris and Moulin Rouge.

GOULDEN, Jean
1878–1947
Enameller, silver designer

Born in Alsace into a wealthy farming family, studied medicine in Paris, and was a brilliant student. After World War I he learned enamelling from Dunand, and became involved in the decorative arts movement in Paris, producing clocks, *coupés* and boxes in a distinctive Cubist style. He also designed for Dunand.

GOUPY, Marcel
b. 1886
Designer, all fields of the decorative arts

Born in Paris, studied architecture, sculpture and interior design at the Ecole des Arts Décoratifs. In 1909 met Georges Rouard and joined La Maison Georges Rouard as artistic dirctor, a position he kept until 1954. He was a prolific designer of utilitarian glass, much of it enamelled, as well as matching porcelain and ceramics, most of it made by Théodore Haviland at Limoges, and he also designed silver. At the 1925 Paris Exposition he displayed a wide range of his work in various pavilions and was the vice-president of the Glass Jury.

GRANT, Duncan
1885–1978
Painter, decorative arts designer

British painter and co-director of the Omega Workshops with Vanessa Bell (1913–19). He contributed to the work of the Omega, and after its closure to a variety of special commissions as well as carrying out schemes for Charleston, his joint residence with Vanessa Bell. Vivid colour, an elaborately calligraphic style and a remarkable freshness and originality characterize his decorative work.

GRAY, Eileen
1878–1976
Furniture and textile designer

Irish born, with a wealthy and artistic background. She studied at the Slade School in London, and soon developed an interest in Japanese lacquer. In 1902 she went to Paris, where she retained a flat for the rest of her life. She apprenticed under lacquer-craftsman Sougawara, and in 1913 her exhibit at the SAD salon came to the attention of Jacques Doucet, who subsequently commissioned three important pieces, the celebrated *Le Destin* screen and two tables. In 1922 she opened the Jean Désert gallery, displaying unique pieces, and from 1925 she began to introduce chromed tubular steel and aluminium into her furniture.

GREGORY, Waylande DeSantis
1905–1971
Ceramicist, sculptor

Studied at the Art Institute of Kansas City and then at the Art Institute of Chicago, starting as a sculptor in bronze and gradually turning to ceramic work. He worked at the Cowan Pottery from 1929–32. He then moved from Ohio to the Cranbrook Academy of Art, where he became an artist-in-residence with his own studio and kiln. In this decade he was given two important commissions for the 1939 New York World's Fair: *The Fountain of the Atom* and *American Imports and Exports*, the latter for General Motors.

GROPIUS, Walter
1883–1969
Architect and designer

Born in Berlin, studied architecture in Munich and Berlin from 1903–7. He started an independent architectural practice in 1910, and designed buildings for the 1914 Deutscher Werkbund exhibition in Cologne. After World War I he was appointed director of the Weimar school of art, which he reorganized as the Bauhaus. In 1928 he resigned to set up office in Berlin. In 1934 he moved to England, where he entered into partnership with E Maxwell Frey. He became controller of design for the Isokon Furniture Company in 1936. In 1937 he went to the United States where he taught architecture until 1952. From 1938–41 he was in partnership with Marcel Breuer.

GROULT, André
1884–1967
Furniture designer, decorator

Born in Paris and made his debut at the salons around 1910 as a decorator. His furniture designs were executed by a small group of craftsmen at his *atelier* in Paris, and were notable for their sumptuous materials, especially shagreen and horn. Groult was prominent at the Paris 1925 Exposition, for which he designed the ladies' bedroom in the Ambassade Française. He also designed textiles and wallpapers.

HERBST, René
1891–?
Furniture designer

Born in Paris, trained as an architect. He made his début as a furniture designer at the 1921 Salon d'Automne, displaying furnishings for a rest area in the Musée de Crillon. In 1926 he began to replace the earlier wood components in his furniture with metal, glass and mirror. He was co-founder of the UAM in 1929, and in the 1930s he won the commission to decorate the palace of the Maharajah of Indore in India.

HOFFMANN, Wolfgang
b.1900
Interior designer

The son of Josef Hoffmann, the leading spirit of the new decorative arts movement which emerged in Vienna at the turn of the century. Wolfgang studied architecture and the decorative arts and emigrated to the United States in 1925. He opened his own studio about 1927, designing a wide range of interiors – wood and metal furnishings, rugs, linens, etc in collaboration with his Polish-born wife, Pola. Their marriage and business partnership were both dissolved in the 1930s. Hoffmann was in the vanguard of the New York Modernist movement, and participated in all the New York exhibitions in the late 1920s.

HOOD, Raymond
1881–1934
Architect

Born in Pawtucket, Rhode Island, Hood attended Brown University

before transferring to the Massachusetts Institute of Technology to prepare for a career in architecture. After graduating in 1903 he joined a New York architectural firm, Bertram Goodhue, working as a draughtsman for six months before studying at the Ecole des Beaux-Arts in Paris. In 1922, he won the Chicago Tribune Competition with John Mead Howells with a Gothic-inspired design for the Chicago Tribune Tower. Major commissions in New York included the American Radiator Building (1924), the Daily News Building (1930) and the McGraw-Hill Building (1932), all of which bore distinct Modernist ornamentation.

ICART, Louis
1880–1950
Printmaker, painter, book illustrator

Self-taught as a printmaker, arrived Paris in 1907 and worked for a lithographic postcard company. The following year he opened his own studio, printing magazines and fashion brochures. In World War I he contributed cartoons to the satirical reviews *Le Rire, Fantasia* and *La Baïonette*. From 1918 he concentrated on etchings, creating a large number of lithographs in a romantic and sensual style.

IRIBE, Paul
1883–1935
Designer, all branches of applied arts

Born Paul Iribarnegaray, in Angoulême, trained as a commercial artist and became famous as a caricaturist for a range of Parisian journals including *L'Assiette au Beurre* and *Le Rire*. His creativity was confined largely to four years, from 1910–14. In the early 1900s he developed a skill as interior decorator, probably encouraged by Paul Poiret, for whom he designed a range of jewellery, fabrics, wallpapers and furniture. In 1912 Jacques Doucet commissioned him to furnish his new Paris apartment, which sealed Iribe's fame as a furniture designer. With his young assistant Pierre Legrain, Iribe designed a range of modern furniture, three pieces of which were subsequently donated to the Musée des Arts Décoratifs.

JENSEN, Georg
1866–1935
Silversmith, jeweller

Born in Raadvad, Denmark, into a working-class family. His father was a grinder in a steel plant manuacturing knife-blades, and Jensen began his apprenticeship in a brazier's workshop. When he was 14 the family moved to Copenhagen, and he was apprenticed to a goldsmith, achieving journeyman status after only four years. He wanted to be a sculptor, and worked as a goldsmith while studying drawing, engraving and modelling, but he did not meet with great success in this field. In 1904 he opened his first small shop in Copenhagen.

JOEL, Betty
b.1896
Furniture and textile designer

Born in China, the daughter of an English administrator there. She started a furniture workshop on Hayling Island in 1921 with her husband David, after which a factory was opened in Portsmouth and a shop in London. Joel's early furniture was primarily in the Arts and Crafts idiom, but in the 1930s she developed a more Modernist approach. She also designed carpets, which were made in China, and fabrics, woven in France.

KAHN, Ely-Jacques
1884–1972
Architect

Son of an Austrian-born importer of glass and mirrors. Kahn established himself in the late 1920s both as a brilliant architect and as America's leading exponent of Modernist architectural design. He attended Columbia University and the Ecole des Beaux-Arts in Paris before joining a New York architectural firm, previously Buchman and Fox, in 1915. Within 10 years he had become a partner and was designing commercial buildings throughout the city, over 30 of which were erected from 1935–31.

KARASZ, Ilonka
1896–1981
Textile, ceramics and silver designer

Hungarian-born, emigrated to the United States in 1913 with her sister Mariska. Produced hand-dyed and embroidered textiles showing a successful integration of folk motifs in a modern context, as well as ceramics, silver and other crafts. Her work was carried by a large number of textile mills and retailers, including Rockledge, Schwartenbach & Huber, and Ginzkey & Maffersforf Inc. The textiles were usually executed by Mariska to Ilonka's designs.

KELETY, Alexandre
Sculptor

Born in Hungary, studied in Toulouse and Paris. Modelled small-scale figures of dancers, ladies of fashion, mythological characters etc, and animals, generally mounted on marble bases. Some were utilitarian objects such as *luminaires*, some were bronze and ivory statuettes, and some were decorated in damascene and niello with flowers and geometric patterns. All were elegant, sophisticated and out of the ordinary.

KIEFFER, René
1876–?
Bookbinder

Educated at the Ecole Robert-Estienne before spending 10 years in the *atelier* of the binder Chambolle. First exhibited at the Salon des Artistes Français in 1903. Co-founder of the SAD in 1910. Between 1917–1923 executed most of Legrain's bookbinding designs for Doucet, adjusting successfully to the Art Deco style.

KISS (KIS), Paul
Wrought-iron designer

Born in Rumania, but became a naturalized Frenchman. He collaborated with Edgar Brandt, and then opened his own *atelier*, where he designed and executed a full range of wrought-iron furnishings and lighting as well as larger items of furniture. He had his own stand at the 1925 Paris Exposition. He worked for Paul Poiret, and also designed and executed a monumental grille for the palace of the King of Siam (Thailand).

KLINT, Kaare
1888–1954
Furniture designer, architect

Born in Denmark, studied architecture under his father and then with Carl Petersen. In 1914 he collaborated with Petersen on the design of neo-classical furniture for the art gallery at Faalborg. In 1924 Klint became a lecturer in furniture design at the Copenhagen Academy, and became a professor of architecture at the Academy in 1944. He was given many official commissions, including furniture for the Thorwaldsen Museum (1922–25), and his designs were shown at many exhibitions.

KOSTA GLASSBRUK AB

Founded in 1742, the oldest Swedish glassworks still in production. Its early makers created a variety of objects including *Kosta* chandelier with 12 arms dating from about 1760, now hanging in a church at Herråkra. From the turn of the 20th century the firm began an association with well-known designers including Lindberg, Morales-Schildt and Wärff. The Kosta factory now includes the sister factories of Boda and Åfors.

LACHAISE, Gaston
1882–1935
Sculptor

French by birth, emigrated to the United States in 1906 after training in Paris. In 1917 he married his former mistress and model Isabel Dutaud Nagle, who was the inspiration for the voluptuous but geometrical female forms which became his trademark. He was commissioned to design reliefs for the RCA and International buildings at Rockefeller Centre in 1929. He is now considered to have been one of the major figures in the development of a modern idiom in American art, although it was only towards the end of his career that he began to receive critical recognition.

LALIQUE, René
1860–1945
Jewellery and glass designer

One of the foremost exponents of the Art Nouveau style in his early years, Lalique's greatest triumph as a jeweller was at the Paris Exposition of 1900, which made him world famous. Around 1905 he began to produce mirrors, textiles paper-knives and other small items, using engraved glass, and from 1906 he was commissioned to produce glass perfume bottles for François Coty. After this, glass became his main interest, and at the 1925 Paris Exposition he not only had his own pavilion but also designed and manufactured a glass table, wine-glasses and candlesticks for the Sèvres porcelain pavilion. In 1932 he supplied glass panels and chandeliers for the liner *Normandie*.

LALIQUE, Suzanne
b.1899
Painter, textile designer and ceramist

Daughter of the famous jeweller and glass designer, trained as a painter and studied briefly under Eugène Morand. She produced delicate designs for textiles, as well as porcelain for the Sèvres Manufactory, and Haviland & Co, Limoges.

LAMBERT-RUCKI, Jean
1888–1967
Sculptor, painter

Born in Poland, moved to Paris in 1911 after attending the Cracow School of Fine Arts. Exhibited at the Salon des Indépendants (from 1920), with the Section d'Or (1922–24), at the Léonce Rosenberg gallery (1924), and the Salon des Tuileries (from 1933). He was given a retrospective at the Claude Robert Gallery in Paris in 1971. He was influenced by Cubist principles and by African art, and used a wide variety of materials in his work, such as painted plaster, metal, wood and mosaic, both singly and in combination.

LEACH, Bernard
1887–1979
Ceramicist

England's most prolific and prominent studio potter, who integrated Japanese philosophies of art and craft into his work, and influenced several generations of potters. He established the St Ives pottery in Cornwall in 1920, and another studio in Devon in 1936, and continued working until 1972.

LE FAGUAYS, Pierre
1892–?
Sculptor

One of the most diverse and prolific of the Art Deco sculptors in France. His subjects were mythological characters, ideal figures, allegorical representations, etc, modelled in bronze, silvered bronze, bronze and ivory, and with a damascened pattern similar to that used by Kéléty and Bouraine. His style developed over the course of his career from the fairly realistic to the hyper-stylized.

LEGRAIN, Pierre
1887–1929
Bookbinder, furniture designer, interior decorator

Educated at the Collège Sainte-Croix in Neuilly and the Ecole des Arts Appliqués Germain Pilon. In 1908 drew cartoons for Iribe's *Le Témoin*, *L'Assiette au Beurre* and *La Baïonette*. With Iribe, he decorated Doucet's apartment at 46 Avenue du Bois, Paris. In 1917 he designed the first of nearly 400 bindings for Doucet, which revolutionized the medium. In 1923 he established his own bindery and furniture studio. Clients included Doucet, Tachard, Meyer, Viscount de Noailles, Suzanne Talbot.

DE LEMPICKA, Tamara
1900–1980
Painter

Born Tamara Gorska outside Warsaw. In her teens married Thadeus Lempitzski, a Russian. She arrived in Paris c.1918, and when her husband abandoned her in the 1920s, enrolled at the Académie Ransom.

Her highly distinctive style can be seen in roughly 100 portraits done between 1925 and 1939. She and her second husband moved to the United States in the late 1930s and eventually settled in Texas.

LENOIR, Pierre-Charles
b.1879
Sculptor

Born in Paris, son and pupil of Charles-Joseph Lenoir. Also studied with Chaplain and Mercie. Exhibited at the salon of the SAF, winning second-class medals in 1905 and 1907 and a travelling scholarship in 1911. Lenoir designed many monuments and memorials, and his small-scale work retains a monumental quality.

LEPAPE, Georges
1887–1971
Painter, poster and fashion artist, illustrator

Studied at the Ecole des Arts Décoratifs, Paris and the *ateliers* of Humbert and Cormon. In 1911 illustrated *Les Choses de Paul Poiret* and the following year programmes for the Ballets Russe. Innumerable magazine covers and fashion plates for *La Gazette du Bon Ton* and *Vogue*.

LINDSTRAND, Vicke
1904–83
Glassmaker

Born in Gothenburg, Sweden. Began as a newspaper editor and cartoonist, only becoming interested in glass at the age of 24, in 1928. He then started as a designer with Orrefors and in the following years exhibited his work in many national and international exhibitions. In 1940 he left Orrefors to work with the Uppsala-Ekeby ceramic firm, and in 1950 he joined Kosta as a designer and director of design. His designs for this firm are spontaneous and filled with movement.

LINOSSIER, Claudius
1893–1955
Dinandier

Born in Lyons to a working-class family and at the age of 13 appren-ticed to a metalworker in a work-shop manufacturing religious articles. After mastering all the metal-work techniques, he went to Paris, and shortly after World War I he re-turned to Lyons and opened a small *atelier*. He took the art of metal in-crustation to new heights, develop-ing his own alloys, as he wanted to provide a richer range of tones and colours than those of silver and copper.

LUCE, Jean
1895–1964
Glass and ceramic designer

Born in Paris, worked first in his father's ceramic *atelier*, and in 1923 established his own. His early glass used clear enamel for decoration, but in 1924 he turned to sandblast-ing for his designs, which consisted of abstract patterns and stylized flowers. He designed porcelain and glass for the ocean-liner *Normandie*.

LURÇAT, Jean
1892–1966
Painter, tapestry designer, ceramist

Studied under Victor Prouvé, an exponent of the Art Nouveau style, and was a painter from 1919–36. He was largely responsible for the revival of tapestry in the modern style in the late 1930s. After World War II he worked in pottery.

MALLET-STEVENS, Robert
1886–1945
Architect, interior designer

Born in Paris, took the surnames of his father, Maurice Mallet, and his Belgian maternal grandfather, Arthur Stevens. He attended the Ecole Speciale d'Architecture, to which he returned in 1924 as a pro-fessor. In the 1925 Exposition he had a resounding success, partici-pating in five different projects, which included a studio for La Société des Auteurs de Film and a hall in the Ambassade Française. In 1930 he was appointed president of the newly formed UAM.

MANSHIP, Paul Howard
1885–1966
Sculptor

Born in the American Midwest, moved to New York in 1905. From 1909–12 he lived in Rome and trav-elled throughout the Mediterranean, and Greek and Greco-Roman anti-quities considerably influenced his style. Through the architects Charles Platt and Welles Bosworth he was given several commissions for garden sculpture, and at the same time he was working on small-scale bronze models based on classical subjects. In 1915–16 he held two successful exhibitions which gave rise to a series of commissions.

MARE, André
1887–1932
Painter, furniture and textile designer

Born in Argentan, France, studied painting in Paris. By 1910 his interest in the decorative arts had increased and ·he began designing book-bindings, furniture and ensembles. From 1911–13 he collaborated with several leading artists, exhibiting his controversial 'Maison Cubiste' in 1912. He formed his association with Louis Süe immediately before the war, though it was not formalized until the establishment of La Com-pagnie des Arts Français in 1919. During the war his wife Charlotte executed his furniture, carpet and fabric designs. Süe et Mare furniture designs were very distinctive and profoundly French.

MARINOT, Maurice
1882–1960
Glassmaker, painter

Born at Troyes, and went to Paris in 1901, where he trained as a painter and exhibited with the Fauves while studying. He discovered glass-making at the Viard works at Bar-sur-Seine and quickly turned his attention to it, exhibiting his work at the Salon des Indépendants in 1911. He developed a unique style of glass which is considered primarily sculptural. His early work consisted of clear glass decorated with col-oured enamels, followed by a phase of free-form molten glass characterized by their internal bub-bles. Later came sculptures in glass etched in acid or shaped by the wheel, and after 1927 he was pro-ducing moulded glass. He continued to make glass and exhibit until 1937 when he returned to painting after the closing of Viard.

MARTEL, Jan and Joel
both 1896–1966
Sculptors, designers

Twin brothers who turned their hand to a variety of media in order to re-alize their designs. They embody the spirit of French Art Deco both in terms of their novel use of these media, the sophistication and clean-ness of their design and their con-stant implementation of new ideas. The 1925 Exposition included a variety of contributions from the Martel brothers, and Sévres pro-duced terracotta and porcelain figures designed by them. These figures were sometimes also pro-duced in bronze.

MATHSSON, Bruno
b.1907
Architect, furniture designer

Born in Sweden, trained in his father's cabinet-making workshop in Varnamo, where he worked from 1923–31. He is best known for his *Eva* chair (1934) with a curvilinear, laminated wood frame and web-bing in the upholstery. It was pro-duced from 1935 with and without arms. From 1945–57 he was primar-ily working as an architect, but then returned to furniture design with Piet Hein.

MIES VAN DE ROHE, Ludwig
1886–1969
Architect, furniture designer

Born in Aachen, worked as a draughtsman of stucco ornaments before moving to Berlin in 1905 to study under Bruno Paul. From 1908–11 he worked in the office of Peter Behrens; in 1926 he became vice-president of the Deutscher Werk-bund, and in 1927 he organized the Stuttgart Exhibition. For the Barce-lona 1929 Exhibition he designed a German pavilion furnished with X-framed chairs constructed of chrome-plated steel strips. The *Barcelona* chairs have been produced by Knoll since 1947. In 1930 he became the last director of the Bauhaus, which he moved from Dessau to Berlin. In 1938 he went to the United States to teach at the Illinois Institute of Technology.

MÜLLER-MUNK, Peter
1904–67
Silversmith

Born in Germany, studied in Berlin. He exhibited at the 1925 Paris Exposition, and went to the United States a year later, working for Tiffany and Co before opening his own studio in 1927. His work is characterized by simple lines and refined, neoclassical designs. He stressed the importance of hand-work. In the mid-1930s he became an Associate Professor at the Carnegie Institute in Pittsburgh, Pa, and he also founded an industrial design firm which still bears his name.

NASH, Paul
1889–1946
Painter, designer

Trained as a painter and designer at the Slade School of Art in London. He was a war artist during World War II. He designed ceramic tableware and textiles in the 1930s, and was one of the founders of Unit One, an avant-garde group of architects and artists.

NICS FRERES

Hungarian brothers, Jules and Michel, who settled in Paris. In the 1920s, they went into partnership and produced the usual range of decorative wrought-iron furniture and lighting. Their work is characterized by a pronounced *martelé* effect. They designed and executed wrought-iron work for a hairdressing salon designed by Ruhlmann.

PECHE, Dagobert
1887–1923
Designer in all fields of the decorative arts

Born near Salzburg, studied architecture at the Vienna Polytechnic from 1906–8 and at the Vienna Academy until 1911. One of the most brilliant decorative artists of the early 20th century, in spite of a tragically short life. Entering the Wiener Werkstätte in 1915, he produced almost 3,000 designs, developing his own decorative vocabulary full of fantasy and based on the precedents of the Austrian Baroque and Rococo styles. He designed furniture, silver, ceramics, glass, bookbindings, textiles and paper.

PFLUEGER, Timothy L.
1892–1946
Architect

Affiliated with the San Francisco architectural firm of JR Miller & Timothy Pflueger. He designed several important commissions including the Medical & Dental Building (1930) and the Luncheon Club in the San Francisco Stock Exchange, but his most celebrated architectural achievement was the theatre he designed for the Paramount-Publix chain, in Oakland, California (1931).

POERTZEL, Otto
b.1876
Sculptor

Known as 'Professor Poertzel', one of the most prominent German sculptors at the turn of the century, best known for his chryselephantine statuettes of theatrical subjects, cabaret and burlesque performers and circus stars as well as for more sedate figures of women and dogs.

POIRET, Paul
1879–1944
Couturier, painter, ensemblier

Born in Paris, the son of a draper. From an early age he showed a strong aptitude for drawing and designing clothing and costumes, and at age 19 was invited by Jacques Doucet to join his establishment. Designed clothes for Rejane and Sarah Bernhardt, and in 1903, after a brief association with Gaston Worth, decided to set up his own business and opened La Maison Poiret. In 1912 he established Atelier Martine, largely to market the designs of his pupils at the Ecole Martine, a school of interior decoration for young women. The students specialized in 'naive' colourful fabrics, wallpapers and murals, and furniture with veneers and brightly painted wood. They decorated Poiret's three houseboats at the 1925 Paris Exposition.

POMPON, François
1855–1933
Animalier sculptor

The son of a French cabinetmaker, learned the basics of carving at an early age, and apprenticed to a marble cutter in Dijon before studying architecture, etching and sculpture. In 1875, he moved to Paris, and worked as an assistant to Mercie and later Falguière, Saint-Marceaux and finally Rodin. Encouraged by Rodin, he began to model his own figures – some portraits but mostly animals. These animals had an impressionistic quality similar to that of Rembrandt Bugatti's bronzes, but later he developed the smooth, sleek style which is regarded as the quintessential Art Deco *animalier* style.

PONTI, Gio
1892–1979
Architect, designer

Italy's most prominent figure in the decorative arts, designing ceramics, furniture and lighting fixtures. He trained as an architect, and established the review *Domus* in 1928, which he edited until his death. From 1936 he taught at the Milan Polytechnic, and in 1957 he published *Amate l'Architettura*.

POOR, Henry Varnum
1888–1971
Painter, ceramicist

Studied at Stanford University, then in London and Paris, returning to the United States in 1912 to teach in San Francisco. He concentrated on ceramics from 1923–33. His work was deeply rooted in French Modernist painting, many subjects showing a Fauvist influence, and his ceramics and painting styles did not vary greatly, although he did introduce some abstract motifs into his pottery. Poor accepted several commissions including a mural entitled *Sports* for the Hotel Shelton in New York City and an eight-panelled tile mural, *Tennis Players and Bathers*, for the financier Edgar A Levy.

POUGHEON, Robert-Eugène
1886–1955
Painter

Born in Paris, studied under Charles Lameire and Jean-Paul Laurens. Worked also in Bordeaux. His early neo-classical style evolved into a Modernist one in which the human figure was sharply elongated. Today considered one of the most successful Art Deco artists.

POWOLNY, Michael
1871–1954
Ceramicist

A seminal figure in the development of 20th-century ceramics. He founded the Wiener Keramik in 1906, which merged with the Gmündener Keramik in 1913. Powolny's long tenure at the Kunstgewerbeschule in Vienna (1909–36) permitted him to influence a generation of ceramic artists studing abroad.

PREISS, Johann Philippe Ferdinand
1882–1943
Sculptor

Leading sculptor whose company Preiss-Kassler (PK) controlled the production of bronze and ivory sculpture in Germany. He began his career in Milan, then moved to Berlin in 1906 and opened the workshop with his friend Arthur Kassler. In 1910 they were joined by two ivory carvers, and the production of multimedia sculptures began in earnest. Preiss designed most of the models himself, and his very personal style became almost a national one. The figures are small in scale but exquisitely finished and detailed. There was a strong international market for the figures, especially in England where, due to the anti-German feeling after World War I, Preiss was advertised as an Austrian sculptor.

PUIFORCAT, Jean
1897–1945
Silversmith

Born in Paris, studied silversmithing in his father's *atelier* and sculpture with Louis Lejeune. He first began exhibiting his designs in 1923, and was renowned for his pure forms in silver, often incorporating semi-precious materials a rare woods. He was chairman of both the 1925 and 1937 International Expositions, on the board of the Salon d'Automne, a founding member of the UAM, and a member of both the SAD and 'Les Cinq'.

RATEAU, ArmandAlbert
1882–1938
Furniture designer, decorator

Born in Paris, studied drawing and woodcarving in Paris. In 1905 he took over the directorship of the Ateliers de Décoration de la Maison Alavoine, where he oversaw the commission to furnish the New York town house of George and Florence Blumenthal. In 1919 he became an independent decorator, opening the Atelier Levallois in Neuilly. In the 1920s he was commissioned to decorate Jeanne Lanvin's apartment. His style was distinctive, its inspiration the Orient and antiquity, and he usually limited his furniture production to editions of three.

RAVILIOUS, Eric
1903–42
Painter, engraver, ceramics designer

One of the most prominent artists of the interwar period. He studied at the Royal College of Art in London and later worked in mural, watercolour, wood engraving, and lithograph techniques. He was commissioned to produce pottery for Wedgwood as well as furniture Gallery.

REEVES, Ruth
1892–1966
Textile designer

Studied at the Pratt Institute, New York, and with Léger during her years in Paris (1920–27). In the late 1920s printed textiles were her speciality, in a style distinctly influenced by Cubism. Her one-person textile show at the New York department store W & J Sloane showed her enthusiasm for experimentation. She had the ability to bring a colourful blend of Modernism to any subject, whether classical, primitive, figural or abstract.

ROHDE, Gilbert
1894–1944
Furniture designer

Born in New York to Prussian-immigrant parents, and showed an early interest in woodworking and mechanics. He was employed by Abraham and Strauss as a furniture illustrator, and became aware of the Modernist movement while in Europe in 1927. By the 1930s he was doing less custom work and more design intended for mass-production. He designed for the Heywood-Wakefield Company, Koehler Manufacturing Co. and the Herman Miller Furniture Co. He exhibited at the 'Design for Living' house at the 1933 Century of Progress fair in Chicago, and played a major role in the design for the Administration Center at the 1936 Texas Centennial Exhibition.

RIETVELD, Gerrit
1888–1964
Architect, furniture designer

Born in Utrecht, started his own cabinet-making business in 1911, continually experimenting with designs. He produced his famous red-blue chair about 1918. In 1919 he joined the De Stijl group and remained a member until 1931. In 1927 he began to experiment with chairs of moulded fibre and later with plywood. After World War II his architectural career flourished, but he maintained an interest in furniture design.

RUHLMANN, EmileJacques
1879–1933
Furniture designer

Born in Paris, the best known of all the French Art Deco furniture designers, After World War I he organized a large furniture workshop, Etablissements Ruhlmann et Laurent, as well as designing silks, carpets, textiles and lighting. By 1920 his reputation was established, and at the Paris 1925 Exposition his Hôtel du Collectionneur was the centre of attention. This incorporated the work of the best designers of the period including Puiforcat, Brandt, Legrain and Dunand. In the late 1920s and early 1930s his luxury furniture, made of the rarest mater-

ial, was based on French neo-classical styles but later, changing tastes and the influence of the UAM forced him to use slightly more modern materials and forms.

SAARINEN, Louise 'Loja'
Gesellius
1879–1968
Textile designer

Studied in her native Helsinki and at the Académie Colarossi in Paris. In 1904 she married Eliel Saarinen and emigrated to Michigan in 1923, establishing the studio, Loja Saarinen, at the Cranbrook Academy in 1928. She was responsible for all textile designs for the complex itself and for dozens of commercial commissions, and participated in numerous museum and international exhibitions.

SALTØ, Axel
1889–1961
Ceramicist

Trained as a painter at the Copenhagen Academy of Art and later as a draughtsman and ceramicist. His initial work was for Bing & Grøndahl, then for Nathalie Krebs, and subsequently for the Royal Copenhagen porcelain manufactory.

SANDOZ, Edouard Marcel
1881–1971
Animalier sculptor

Born in Switzerland, studied with Injalbert, then with Marius Jean Antonin Mercie and at the Ecole des Beaux-Arts in Paris. Classically trained, he modelled many memorials, public monuments and portraits, but is best remembered for his animal sculpture – large figures of birds of prey, groups of dancing frogs, foxes, monkeys, etc.

SANDOZ, Gérard
b.1902
Jeweller

Born into a family of jewellers from the Jura, and exhibited an early aptitude for painting and design. At the age of 18, while in the family firm, he started designing jewellery characterized by rigorous geometric lines, and his pieces shown in the 1925 and 1937 Paris Expositions

epitomized his belief in simple, clean design lines.

SERRE, Georges
1859–1956
Ceramicist

Began as a colourist for Sèvres and travelled to Saigon where he became an art teacher in 1916. Returning in 1922, he opened his own studio and from 1940–50 directed the ceramic work of the Ecole des Arts Appliqués.

SOUDBININE, Séraphin
1870–1944
Ceramicist

Born in Russia, but moved to Paris, where he became a protégé of Rodin. After seeing Near Eastern ceramics in New York, he began to produce sculptural ceramics in stoneware and porcelain.

STAM, Mart
b.1899
Furniture designer

Born in Holland, studied drawing in Amsterdam, and worked as an architectural draughtsman in Rotterdam, until 1922. He is best known for the cantilevered tubular-metal chair, constructed of gas pipes, which he designed in 1926. In 1926 he was invited by Mies van der Rohe to design three houses at the Deutscher Werkbund's Stuttgart Exhibition.

STORRS, John Henry Bradley
1885–1956
Sculptor

Born in Chicago, but lived and worked in France. He worked in a variety of new materials and experimented with the Art Deco, Cubist and International Styles. He studied in Paris with Rodin and as the sculptor's favourite student was chosen to oversee the installation of Rodin's works at the Panama-Pacific Exposition in San Francisco in 1917, to draw his death portrait. He returned to the United States frequently, exhibited in New York and received major architectural commissions in Chicago, including the aluminium figure of Ceres for the top of the Chicago Board of Trade Building (1930).

SUBES, Raymond
1893–1970
Wrought-iron designer

Born and studied in Paris, was made artistic director of Borderel et Robert in 1919, and became one of the most important wrought-iron designers and producers of his time. His early work was ornate and naturalistic, but later became geometric and linear. His most important work was in architecture, and his grilles and doors can be seen all over Paris.

SÜE, Louis
1875–1968
Architect and designer

Born in Bordeaux, moved to Paris in 1895 to train as a painter. In 1912 he organized his interior decorating business, the Atelier Français, designing textiles, furniture and ceramics. In 1919 he and André Mare founded the Compagnie des Arts Français. At the Paris 1925 Exposition the firm received acclaim for its designs, and in the same year they designed a Paris shop for Parfums d'Orsay. In 1928 the designer Jacques Adnet took over the direction of the company from Süe, who continued to be active as an architect and designer. At the 1937 Paris Exposition he designed much of the interior decoration of the pavilion of the SAD, becoming president in 1929.

TEAGUE, Walter Dorwin
1883–1960
Industrial designer

Born in Decatur, Indiana, he moved to New York in 1903, attending night

classes while working for an advertising agency. Opened his own office in 1911, specializing in book and advertising designs, and in the mid-1920s established himself as an

industrial designer, after creating designs for packaging and piano cases. First major client (1928) was Eastman Kodak, and his best-known designs include the Marmon

car (1930), the plastic Baby Brownie camera (1933), the Scripto pen (1952), coaches for the New Haven Railroad, and Texaco gas stations. For the 1939 New York World's Fair he designed the Ford exhibition, including chairs of aluminium and Lucite.

TEMPLIER, Raymond
1891–1968
Jeweller

Born in Paris, one of a family of Parisian jewellers. In 1919 he joined the Maison Templier, founded by his grandfather 70 years earlier, and he collaborated for nearly 30 years with designer Michel Percheron in rigorously geometric jewellery designs, almost entirely without decoration. He was a founding member of the the UAM.

VAN ALEN, William
1883–1954
Architect

Although he designed several buildings in the modern idiom, van Alen is most remembered for the Chrysler building, which he designed in 1930 for Walter P Chrysler, the purchaser of the building, whose goal was to build the world's greatest monument. The building provides a characteristic example of late 1920s commercial architecture, and with its Modernist ornamentation it has become a classic.

VAN CLEEF & ARPELS

French firm of jewellers begun by Julien, Louis and Charles Arpels and Alfred van Cleef in 1904. They took over a small shop in the Place Vendôme, Paris, and quickly earned the reputation of master jewellers. Branches opened in Cannes, Deauville and Monte Carlo. At the 1925 Paris Exposition they won a Grand Prix for jewellery designs, and a decade later they revolutionized the art of jewellery design by introducing the *serti mystérieux* (invisible setting).

VENINI, Paulo
1895–1959
Glass designer

Born in Italy, first studied law at Milan

university, but turned to glassmaking, and in 1921 became a partner with Cappellin in Murano. Two years later he took over sole control. He is considered one of the finest glass designers of the 20th century, in addition to employing the foremost designers of the period, including Tyra Lundgren, Napoleone Martinuzzi and Gio Ponti.

WALTER, Alméric
1859–1942
Ceramicist and glassmaker

Born in France, worked for the Daum brothers in Nancy but established his own glass workshops in 1919. Some of his work in *pâte-de-verre* was done in collaboration with the painter Henri Bergé.

WEBER, 'Kem' (Karl Emanuel Martin)
1889–1963
Industrial designer

German-born, apprenticed to Eduard Schultz, Potsdam's Royal Cabinetmaker, and studied under Bruno Paul from 1908–10. Went to San Francisco in 1914 to assist in the architectural work on the German pavilion at the Panama-Pacific Exposition, and was trapped by the outbreak of war. He failed to earn a living as an interior designer, and settled finally in Los Angeles, where he joined the design studio at Barker Bros. In 1927 he opened a studio in Hollywood, listing himself as an industrial designer, and within a year was fully launched. His style was extremely distinctive, and he was the only designer on the West Coast to embrace Modernism.

WIESELTHIER, Valerie 'Vally'
1895–1945
Ceramicist

Born in Vienna. Her colourful and carefree style, nurtured under Josef Hoffmann at the Viennese Kunstgewerbeschule and then at the Wiener Werkstätte, came to fruition at the 1925 Paris Exposition. She moved to the United States in 1929, joined the Contempora group and later designed for the Sebring Pottery in Ohio. She created a wide selection of ceramic figures, masks, tableware items, mannequins and busts,

examples of which were shown by both Contempora and AUDAC as well as in national ceramic exhibitions.

WRIGHT, Russel
1904–76
Ceramics, furniture and pewter designer

Born in the United States, entered Princeton in 1923 but left the following year to pursue a growing interest in theatre design. He began selling modelled caricatures to shops in 1930 and designed his first spun-pewter accessories in 1931. Best known for his design of *American Modern* crockery (1939), he also designed furniture and decorative accessories for a short-lived programme called 'American Way', and developed an experimental programme for national park activities in America called 'Summer in the Parks'.

ZORACH, William
1887–1966
Sculptor and painter

Russian by birth, but moved to the United States in 1894. He began his art training at the age of nine, working as an errand boy and later as an apprentice lithographer while attending the Cleveland School of Art at night. In 1907 he moved to New York, and from 1910–11 he lived in France. He exhibited paintings in Paris, Cleveland and New York until 1916. In 1917 he carved the first sculptural work he had done since boyhood, and by 1922 he had given up painting altogether in favour of sculpture. He became one of the leaders in the revival in the United States of direct carving in both various woods and stone, and also cast his models in bronze.

INDEX

143

144

Acknowledgements

l=left; r=right; c=centre; t=top; b=bottom

Arcaid: 12, 14t, 19c; *P. Bayer:* 9tr, 39t, 41t, 73b, 75bl, 81, 89tl; *Bettman Archive/BBC Hulton Picture Library:* 88; *Bridgeman Art Library:* 48t, 129r; *Jean Loup Charmet:* 15, 110, 120br, 122bl, 126, 127t; *Chizami, Antiquaris:* 90r, 92r; *Christies:* 13b, 24, 25, 26r, 27, 28r, 29r, 30l, 31r, 32, 33l&br, 34, 35bl, br&c, 36tr&l, 37b, 38-9, 40, 47t, 53b, 54b, 59b, 62l, 66r, 70, 71tc, 72l, 73tr&bl, 74l, 75t, 76, 77r, 79b, 80, 82b, 84l&r, 85, 93-5, 97r, 98l, 99, 101l, 102, 106t, 107b, 109l, 111t, 117t, 119l, 120bl, 121r, 122t, 123-4, 130lt&b, 131; *Corning Museum of Glass:* 53r, 60r, 61, 63b; *Warren Cresswell and George Matheson Gerst:* 96r; *Design Council:* 9tl&b, 10, 48l, 116t, 117b, 127b; *DeLorenzo, NY:* 65r; *Alastair Duncan:* 11tr, 21, 42b, 44, 45t, 48t, 50, 60l, 62t, 71br, 105l, 106b, 108r; *E.T. Archive:* 125t; *Martin Eidelberg:* 45tr&b; *Allen Eyles:* 22, 22-3t, 23b; *Fifty-50 Gallery:* 109br; *French & Co:* 96l; *Audrey Friedman & Haim Manishevitz:* 64l; *Barry Friedman Inc:* 109tr, 119r, 121l, 122c, 129l, 128l; *Galerie Moderne:* 29l, 30r, 35t, 42t, 53tr, 55, 56, 57, 58, 59t; *Steven Greenberg:* 97l; *Historical Design Collection Inc:* 108l; *Angelo Hornak:* 6, 16, 20, 31l, 33r, 36b, 43t, 46, 47t, 63t, 65tl&r, 66l, 67, 68t, 73t, 79t, 82t, 86t, 87t, 89tr, 90l, 92r, 104t, 107t, 111b, 112b; *John Jesse and Irina Laski:* 16-7, 89b, 91; *Randy Juster:* 12t; *Lewis Kaplan & Assoc:* 78, 86b 17br; *Miles J. Lourie:* 52r, 75br; *Musée Des Art Décoratifs:* 14b, 18b, 39b, 41b, 43b, 49b, 54t, 72l, 76, 77l, 105r, 112tr, 114, 115tr, 116b; *Robert Opie:* 8, 52l, 112l, 125r, 130t; *CNAC G Pompidou:* 26l, 37cl&r; *Primavera Gallery:* 64r, 87r; *Seen Galleries:* 120t; *Sothebys:* 51b, 71l; *Ed Teitelman:* 17t; *Western Americana:* 11tl; *William Doyle Galleries:* 38l, 51t&c; *V&A Museum:* 7; *Virginia Museum:* 28l, 68b, 98tr&c, 100t, 104b; *Robert Zehil:* 69